India and the Rebalancing of Asia

C. Raja Mohan

'This book provides a compelling account of India's emergence as a strategic balancer in the Indo-Pacific. With historical precision and geopolitical insight, Mohan unpacks India's evolving posture – from ambivalence to assertiveness – as it navigates China's rise and deepens ties with the United States. Essential reading for understanding how India seeks to shape a multipolar Asia while preserving autonomy in a complex strategic environment.'

Ken Jimbo, Professor of International Relations, Keio University; Managing Director of Programs at the International House of Japan (IHJ/I-House); former Special Advisor to the Ministry of Defense and the National Security Secretariat (Japan)

India and the Rebalancing of Asia

C. Raja Mohan

IISS The International Institute for Strategic Studies

The International Institute for Strategic Studies
Arundel House | 6 Temple Place | London | WC2R 2PG | UK

First published September 2025 by **Routledge**
4 Park Square, Milton Park, Abingdon, Oxon, OX14 4RN

for **The International Institute for Strategic Studies**
Arundel House, 6 Temple Place, London, WC2R 2PG, UK
www.iiss.org

Simultaneously published in the USA and Canada by **Routledge**
52 Vanderbilt Avenue, New York, NY 10017

Routledge is an imprint of Taylor & Francis, an Informa Business

© 2025 The International Institute for Strategic Studies

DIRECTOR-GENERAL AND CHIEF EXECUTIVE Dr Bastian Giegerich
SERIES EDITOR Dr Benjamin Rhode
ASSOCIATE EDITOR Gráinne Lucey-Tremblay
COPY EDITOR Dr Liat Radcliffe Ross
EDITORIAL Alice Aveson, Lauren Beer, Christopher Harder, Jill Lally, Gráinne Lucey-Tremblay, Lauren Whelan
PRODUCTION Alessandra Beluffi, Ravi Gopar, Tahir Iqbal, Jade Panganiban, James Parker, Jillian Williams, Kelly Verity-Cailes
COVER ARTWORK 'Asiae Nova Descriptio'. From Theatrum Orbis Terrarum, 1572. Private Collection. Creator: Ortelius, Abraham (1527–1598). (Photo by Fine Art Images/Heritage Images via Getty Images)

The International Institute for Strategic Studies is an independent centre for research, information and debate on the problems of conflict, however caused, that have, or potentially have, an important military content. The Council and Staff of the Institute are international and its membership is drawn from almost 100 countries. The Institute is independent and it alone decides what activities to conduct. It owes no allegiance to any government, any group of governments or any political or other organisation. The IISS stresses rigorous research with a forward-looking policy orientation and places particular emphasis on bringing new perspectives to the strategic debate. Inclusion of a territory, country or state – or terminology or boundaries used in graphics or mapping – in this publication does not imply legal recognition or indicate support for any government or administration.

The Institute's publications are designed to meet the needs of a wider audience than its own membership and are available on subscription, by mail order and in good bookshops. Further details at www.iiss.org.

All rights reserved. No part of this book may be reprinted or reproduced or utilised in any form or by any electronic, mechanical or other means, now known or hereafter invented, including photocopying and recording, or in any information storage or retrieval system, without permission in writing from the publishers.

British Library Cataloguing in Publication Data
A catalogue record for this book is available from the British Library

Library of Congress Cataloging in Publication Data

ADELPHI series
ISSN 1944-5571

ADELPHI AP517-519
ISBN 978-1-041-19225-1 / eB 978-1-003-71067-7

Contents

	Author	6
	Acknowledgements	7
	Map of India and the Indo-Pacific region	8
	Introduction	11
Chapter One	**Great transitions**	23
	Introduction 23	
	India at the centre 24	
	The centre does not hold 33	
	Restoring the India centre 39	
Chapter Two	**The China challenge**	45
	Introduction 45	
	Structural divergence 46	
	Border dispute 50	
	South Asia 59	
	Indian Ocean 65	
	Multilateral arena 69	
Chapter Three	**The US partnership**	73
	Introduction 73	
	Defence cooperation 74	
	Pakistan 81	
	The Indo-Pacific 86	
	The Quad 89	
	Trump 2.0 95	
Chapter Four	**Regional dynamics**	101
	Introduction 101	
	Australia and Japan 101	
	Russia 105	
	The United Kingdom and Europe 110	
	South Asia 113	
	Southeast Asia 117	
	Asian reset 121	
Chapter Five	**India as the balancer**	127
	Introduction 127	
	Ideological balance 129	
	Economic rebalance 136	
	Technological rebalance 142	
	Military rebalance 148	
	Conclusion: In Asia and of Asia	163
	Introduction 163	
	Assertive China, disruptive America 165	
	The great triangle 169	
	Alliances, autonomy and burden-sharing 172	
	India's Asian challenges 174	
	Appendix	181
	Notes	183
	Index	213

AUTHOR

C. Raja Mohan is a Distinguished Professor at the Motwani Jadeja Institute for American Studies, O.P. Jindal Global University, Delhi. He is also a Visiting Research Professor at the Institute of South Asian Studies (ISAS) at the National University of Singapore and was previously the Director of ISAS. Mohan is a Distinguished Fellow at the Council for Strategic and Defense Research in New Delhi. Mohan was the founding director of Carnegie India, the sixth international centre of the Carnegie Endowment for International Peace. He also set up the Asia Society Policy Institute branch in New Delhi. He was associated with several Indian think tanks, including the Institute of Defence Studies and Analyses, the Observer Research Foundation and the Centre for Policy Research. Mohan was a Professor of South Asian Studies at Jawaharlal Nehru University in New Delhi and the S. Rajaratnam School of International Studies in Singapore. He served on India's National Security Advisory Board. Mohan was the Henry A. Kissinger Chair in Foreign Policy and International Relations at the John W. Kluge Center at the US Library of Congress in 2009–10. He convened the India chapter of the Pugwash Conferences on Science and World Affairs from 1995 to 2005. Mohan has published widely on India's foreign and security policies, Asian geopolitics and the global governance of advanced technologies. He is the co-author of the IISS *Adelphi* book *Asia's New Geopolitics: Military Power and Regional Order*, published in 2021. He is a columnist for *Foreign Policy* and the *Indian Express*.

ACKNOWLEDGEMENTS

I would like to thank James Crabtree, then director of IISS–Asia, for persuading me to take up this project when I was the Director of the Institute of South Asian Studies (ISAS) at the National University of Singapore in 2021. Without Crabtree's infectious enthusiasm and his help in refining this book proposal, I would not have undertaken this venture. As I developed this project, continuing support from the ISAS, with which I have had an association since 2007, has been very rewarding. I also thank my colleagues in New York and New Delhi at the Asia Society Policy Institute (ASPI), whom I have been associated with since 2022, for offering unstinting encouragement for this book project. Rahul Jaybhay, a research analyst at ASPI, lent me immensely valuable support in drafting and revising this manuscript in 2023. Rishi Gupta has provided much-needed burden-sharing in my official work to let me devote most of my time to completing this manuscript. Special thanks to the reviewers of the manuscript and Benjamin Rhode, Editor of the *Adelphi* Series at the IISS, for his many constructive suggestions in revising the original book proposal and offering sharp editorial advice on restructuring and improving the first draft. I am especially grateful to Liat Radcliffe Ross for her copy-editing, which helped make the arguments of this volume come through clearly and read easily. I am so pleased that my decades-long association with the IISS in London has culminated with the publication of this book.

Map: **India and the Indo-Pacific region**

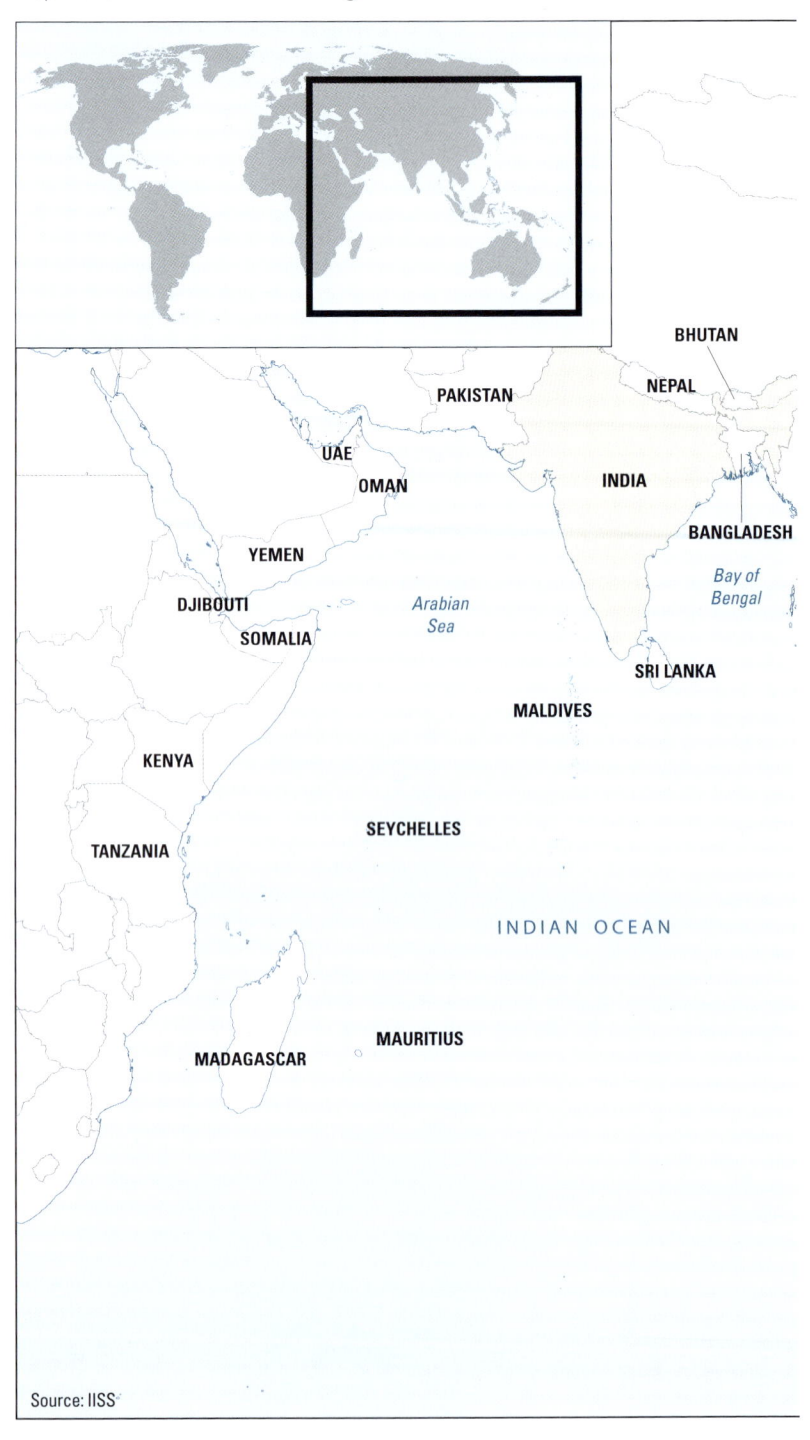

Source: IISS

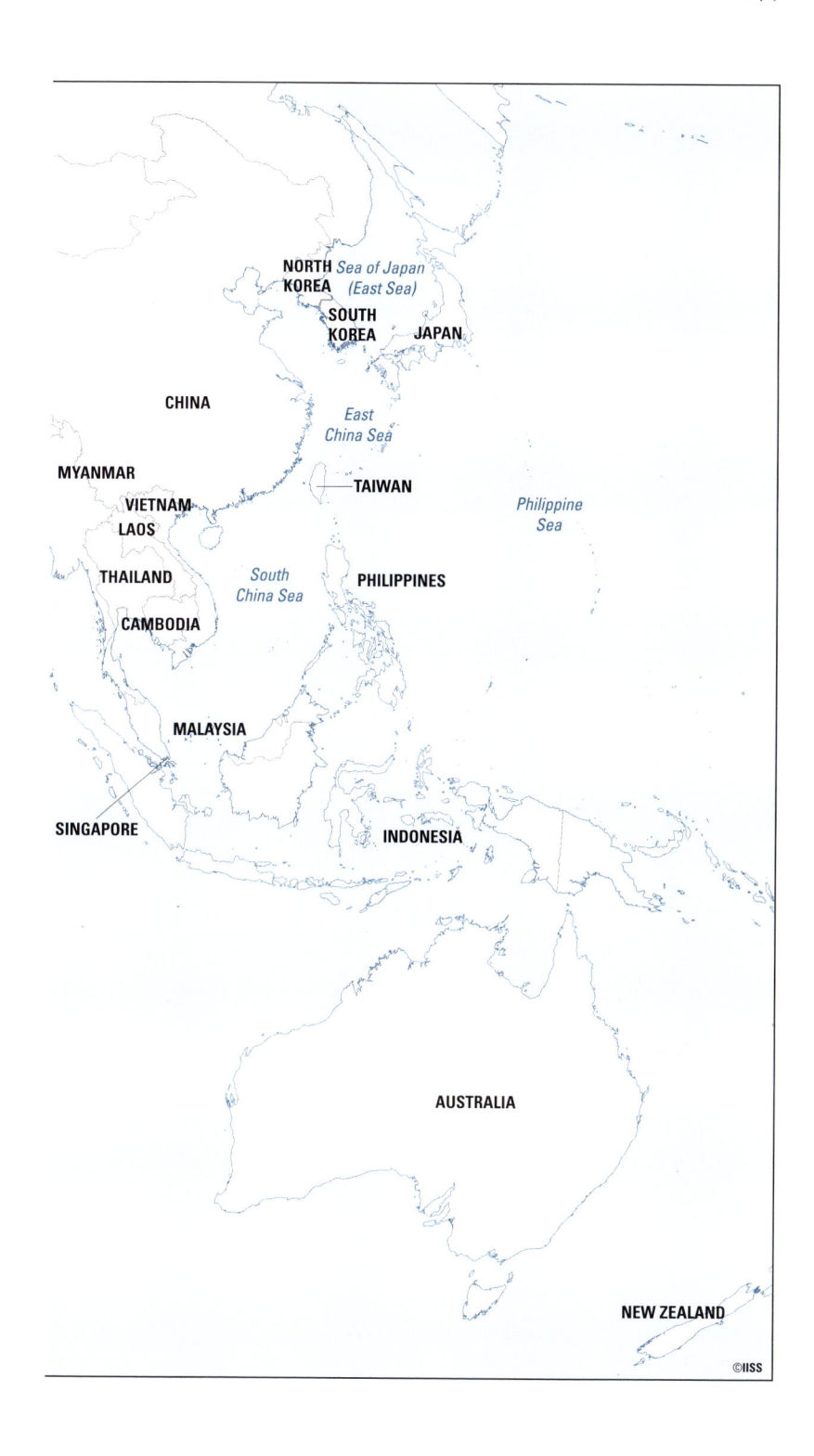

INTRODUCTION

Few regions have transformed as consequentially as Asia in the twenty-first century. The rapid rise of Asia – marked by the dramatic expansion of the continent's economic, military and technological capabilities – now has a great bearing on international security and the global order. Much like Europe in the Cold War, Asia has emerged as the principal strategic theatre today. This is true despite the war in Ukraine, because China has become the main challenger to the Western dominance of the world. With the second-largest economy and with military expenditure second only to that of the United States, China's influence worldwide and within international institutions has grown significantly in the twenty-first century.

The Western expectation at the turn of this century that China would become a 'responsible stakeholder' in the US-led global order began to evaporate in the 2010s, as Beijing made it clear it wanted to set its own rules or at least rearrange the international and Asian regional systems in its favour. Beijing's geopolitical assertiveness and economic policies that exploited the open nature of the international economic order rattled key sections of the US establishment. China's growing technological capabilities compounded the problem by pointing to the possibility that Beijing could end Americans' traditional lead in advanced technologies.

Slowly but surely, the US began to respond to this challenge. Several initiatives since the 2010s have sought to balance against China in Asia. These initiatives, foreshadowed by earlier outreaches to India during George W. Bush's administration, included the 'Pivot to Asia' of Barack Obama's administration; the adoption of the 'Indo-Pacific' construct and the revival of the Quadrilateral Security Dialogue (Quad) with Australia, India and Japan during Donald Trump's first administration; and the elevation of the Quad to the summit level, the construction of the AUKUS security partnership (with Australia and the United Kingdom) and the push towards turning the United States' bilateral alliances with Japan and South Korea into a trilateral forum during Joe Biden's administration. These efforts were reinforced by the expansion of bilateral alliances and the building of new strategic partnerships in Asia. The objective was to strengthen deterrence against China in a new Asian security order. A series of economic measures reinforced these strategic moves. These included imposing higher tariffs on Chinese imports, reducing reliance on critical supplies from China, reinventing industrial policy to shore up manufacturing and advanced-technology production in the US, creating new economic coalitions with trusted economic partners and expanding technology denials against China. Together, these strategic and economic policies have profoundly altered US engagement with Asia.

The rise of an assertive China and its consequences are often presented in terms of 'Asia versus the US' or 'East versus West'. China, in particular, finds it convenient to mobilise the sentiment 'Asia for Asians', which has deep roots in the anti-colonial struggles in Asia and resonates with the enduring anti-Western resentments in the region. The deep divisions within Asia, however, present a more complex reality. Asia's collective rise is real, thanks to the widespread economic development in the region. Yet China has risen faster than its neighbours and today outranks two of its large Asian neighbours – Japan and India – on economic and defence indices by huge margins. China's assertiveness on territorial claims has rubbed up against nationalism in several Asian countries, including India, Indonesia, Japan, the Philippines and Vietnam. Intra-Asian conflicts have created a new basis for strategic engagement between the US and China's Asian neighbours.

Beijing, confident of its own capacity to manage the complex relationship with Washington and prevent the emergence of a regional coalition against it, initially dismissed the US initiatives as transient 'sea foam'.[1] Many Asian states, too, were wary at first of Washington's new initiatives and deeply worried about the breakdown of the cooperative economic order in the region and the potential consequences of a new cold war in Asia. However, as US efforts to rebalance the Asian order began to gain ground in the late 2010s, Beijing began to question them. Many Asian states also adjusted to the new competitive dynamic between Washington and Beijing. The post-1971 regional order, which saw Asia adapt and benefit from the Sino-US rapprochement, was now breaking down amid the simultaneous deepening of tensions between Washington and Beijing and between an assertive China and its Asian neighbours.

The new US interest in balancing against China has been the most consequential for India, because the contradictions between India and China are sharper than those between Beijing and its other Asian neighbours. Heightened concern about China's rise has found the sharpest public and policy expression in India, which has seen a series of military crises on its border with China in 2013, 2014, 2017 and 2020. As China disregarded a series of bilateral agreements that have been in place since the early 1990s to maintain peace and tranquillity on the disputed frontier, India had no choice but to match China's military moves on the border and freeze bilateral political engagement. With the Chinese challenge apparent on a variety of fronts, New Delhi has finally shed its ambivalence about China's rising power and determined upon the need to balance against Beijing – through its own means as well as in collaboration with the United States. If Beijing pushed New Delhi to rethink its China policy, Asian strategy and great-power relations, Washington pulled India closer by turning tentative engagement in the post-Cold War years into a strategic partnership.

In framing the Indo-Pacific as a strategic geography and defining the Quad as a critical new element of regional architecture, the US and its Asian allies have sought to involve India in the rebalancing of Asia to counter China's rise and assertiveness. Put simply, the US Indo-Pacific strategy sought to put the 'Indo' into the 'Pacific'. It tore apart two post-war mental maps about the East. One was the notion that 'South' and 'East' Asia had little to do with each other, and the other was the view that the Indian and Pacific oceans were separate maritime realms. Japan, which initiated the new discourse on the Indo-Pacific, was conscious of the deep interconnections between the two regions. After all, Imperial Japan had marched towards India in the interwar period, and it took a massive coalition of forces – including those of British India, Nationalist China and the Anglo-American powers – to roll back Japanese forces from Burma and Southeast Asia and from the waters of the eastern Indian Ocean. Tokyo had not forgotten the British Indian Army that deployed nearly a million soldiers to fight the Imperial Japanese Army in Burma and Southeast Asia.

Although there is a lot of resistance in East Asia and around the world (including in the IISS) to replacing 'Asia-Pacific' with 'Indo-Pacific', the sheer discursive power of the United States has made 'Indo-Pacific' part of the regional and global lexicon. There is also a great deal of reluctance to see India as part of the East Asian balance of power. However, the range of US regional initiatives, the growing acknowledgement of India's increasing national power and significant changes in New Delhi's foreign-policy ideology have facilitated the (re)integration of India into the regional geopolitical calculus. The Indo-Pacific could eventually look similar to the British sphere of influence in the Indian and Pacific oceans from the nineteenth to the mid-twentieth century. India was then at the centre of the sphere; it could re-emerge as a critical player in this region during the twenty-first century.

Although the Indo-Pacific construct and the Quad partnership have gained a lot of traction in recent years, there are continuing questions about the constraints on India's political will and material capability to balance against China in Asia. While some see India as essential for any stable balance-of-power system in Asia and the Indo-Pacific, others insist that India is the weakest link in the Quad. India's traditional image as a state that is intractably non-aligned also gets in the way of Indians and external observers seeing a definitive role for New Delhi in Asian security.

Such scepticism, however, must acknowledge that successive administrations in Washington have invested in India's prospective role in the Asian balance of power. All US presidents in the twenty-first century – George W. Bush, Barack Obama, Donald Trump and Joe Biden – expanded their political and strategic investments in India with a barely hidden objective of balancing against China. What began as an idea under George W. Bush became an explicit strategy under the first Trump and

Biden administrations, as US–China relations became deeply conflictual from the mid-2010s. The US has also encouraged its Western allies to deepen their strategic engagement with India and strengthen New Delhi in relation to Beijing.

The Indo-Pacific concept is based on a recognition that Asia can no longer be secure in an 'East Asian' or 'Asia-Pacific' framework. Washington, therefore, has attempted to expand the regional map and sought partners outside its traditional alliances to build a larger counterweight to balance against China. From first principles, at least, the sheer mass of India and its expansive economic and military potential make it a natural element in any strategy to rebalance Asia. India may not be the only or the most critical element in a new security architecture, but it is a vital one. It is this Indian potential that the US has been willing to bet on in constructing a new equilibrium in Asia and the Indo-Pacific.

This is not the first time, though, that India has been seen as a natural balancer against China. The US had sought to draw a democratic India into its strategy to contain communism in Asia during the 1950s. India's first prime minister, Jawaharlal Nehru, however, was not interested in the project of containing communism. He preferred to befriend China and build a post-colonial and post-Western order in Asia. On the economic front, he emulated the Soviet model, curbing the role of India's large pre-existing banking and industrial sectors and dramatically enhancing the state's role in accelerating Indian development. In the realm of security, Nehru withdrew India from its colonial role as a key pillar of regional defence in the Indian Ocean and opposed Anglo-American Cold War alliances in Asia in the name of promoting peace through non-alignment.

These economic and foreign policies were steadily chipped away in the decades following the end of the Cold War, as India introduced market-oriented reforms at home, put greater stress on export promotion, and expanded political, economic and security engagement with the West. India, however, did not give up on its long-standing partnership with Russia and opened a new phase in stabilising the China relationship. Yet India's growing power disparity with a rapidly rising and assertive China has made it harder for New Delhi to deal with long-simmering territorial disputes with Beijing, preserve its traditional dominance in South Asia and sustain its considerable salience in the Indian Ocean. India has also found China a major obstacle in realising its aspirations for a permanent seat at the high table, especially at the United Nations Security Council. If coping with China's power will be a multigenerational challenge for India, New Delhi has recognised that any serious response will necessarily involve deepening strategic cooperation with the United States and its allies.

Although the convergence of their strategic interests in balancing against a rising China is real, Washington and Delhi will have to overcome at least four obstacles. One is the seeming incongruity between Washington's well-established tradition of operating through alliances and New Delhi's discomfort with acting within security coalitions. The second is the tension between India's continental and maritime imperatives. The continental imperative points to the management of the large and disputed frontier with China, which demands accommodation with Beijing. The maritime imperative underlines the new possibilities for security cooperation with the US, which is frowned upon by China. The third obstacle is the potential fragility of an India–US relationship aimed solely at balancing against China. Finally, the potential divergence in political values between the US and India could undermine US and Western support for the partnership.

Yet events since the mid-2010s have shown that none of these factors is a deal-breaker for the expanding India–US strategic partnership. Firstly, India and the US are developing institutional formats like the Quad that are short of a formal military alliance but deliver significant political and security cooperation. Secondly, the presumed tension between India's continental and maritime imperatives is more apparent than real. China's challenges to India on both the continental and maritime fronts are real and growing. Washington was helpful to New Delhi in addressing India's military needs during the 2020 military confrontation with the People's Liberation Army in the Great Himalayas. The US stepped in to provide much-needed equipment for use in high altitudes by the Indian armed forces and real-time intelligence on Chinese military activity across the contested frontier. New Delhi has long been anxious about drawing too close to Washington and provoking Beijing into a more aggressive posture on the disputed Himalayan frontier. However, India's reluctance to engage with the US in the security domain has not encouraged China to adopt a relaxed posture on the border. The real problem is that China appears confident that the shifting military balance of power in its favour in the Himalayas has created favourable conditions for redeeming its long-standing territorial claims against India. The answer to that problem can only lie in enhancing India's military capacity to deter China in the Himalayas and to consolidate its maritime advantages in the Indo-Pacific through a strategic partnership with the United States.

Thirdly, the centrality of China in the discourse on India–US cooperation in structuring a new Asian order inevitably raises the question of whether this shared objective is too transitory to survive potential changes in their attitudes towards Beijing. To be sure, many in Washington worry that New Delhi will not be interested in a deeper partnership with the US if Beijing reduces its pressure on the Himalayan border and in Asian waters. There are also some in New Delhi who are concerned that the US – either out of exhaustion, pressures of isolationism or enduring economic interests – will be tempted to reach a strategic accommodation with China. Both India and the United States have significant reasons to pursue a stable and productive relationship with China, which is today an economic and military power to be reckoned with. Neither wants to provoke Beijing into an avoidable war. Yet neither is prepared to simply cede a hegemonic role to China in Asia.

Finally, there are growing apprehensions about India's democratic backsliding in Washington, which is seen as getting in the way of a long-term strategic partnership with India aimed at balancing against China. Although democratic values constitute an important dimension of US engagement with the world, its foreign-policy record in the non-Western world has seen the privileging of security and commercial interests over shared political values. On these first two fronts, India's salience in the US calculus has risen in recent decades.

Given the extraordinary scale of the problems that an assertive Beijing presents to New Delhi and Washington, there is no question that India and the US need each other to secure their positions in a changing Asian order. This structural convergence is unlikely to change amid the tactical moves by Beijing to improve relations with either New Delhi or Washington, or with both. Irrespective of the state of New Delhi's bilateral relations with Beijing at any moment, promoting a multipolar Asia will remain a core Indian objective. Preventing the dominance of the region by any one local power has likewise long been at the heart of Washington's Asia strategy. The expansion of India–US strategic cooperation in the last few years, amid the rise and assertiveness of China, promises to be an enduring trend in global security politics for the foreseeable future.

Even as India becomes an important partner for the US in Asia, New Delhi will continue to build its own independent role in the region as its relative power continues to rise. As a large state with its own great-power aspirations, India will not be a mere appendage of the US in Asia; it will be an important part of a multipolar Asia with many large players, including the Association of Southeast Asian Nations, China, Japan and the United States, shaping its evolution. If India's 'non-alignment' was tilted in favour of the Soviet Union during the Cold War, its 'strategic autonomy' in the twenty-first century will have a strong American hue. What matters, though, is not the terminology to describe India's geopolitical orientation but its emerging regional role as a major security provider in Asia and Asian waters in partnership with the United States. The US, for its part, needs capable and willing partners, not merely those that depend on American military power. This has become especially important at a time when the burden of alliances is coming under greater scrutiny in US domestic politics. Unlike in the past, India has a strong motivation today to balance against China. New Delhi is also willing to compete with China in its quest to become a consequential power in Asia and the world. India and the United States could not agree on how to build a post-colonial Asian architecture in the twentieth century, but their interests align today. For the foreseeable future, that convergence is likely to survive the perturbations within India, the US and the region.

This *Adelphi* book delineates the prospects for an Indian role in structuring a new Asian geopolitical order. Asia and the Indo-Pacific, used quite interchangeably here, refer to a region that includes India and East Asia, as well as the waters off this landmass in the Pacific and Indian oceans. Other regions north and west of India – Central Asia, the Middle East and Africa – are not part of this discussion.

This volume is organised in five chapters. The first reviews the widely neglected evolution of modern Indian foreign and security policies from the colonial era to the twenty-first century. The branding of Indian foreign policy – both at home and abroad – as non-alignment creates barriers to understanding the inner dynamics of Indian grand strategy and its change over time and space. It also prevents sensible assessments of its contemporary responses to the changing geopolitical dynamics around it. The chapter parses the four great transitions unfolding in Indian foreign policy since the end of the Cold War: a) ending the erosion of India's regional primacy in the subcontinent, which had been fuelled in part by the growing salience of China in South Asia; b) moving away from the pursuit of Asian solidarity to the current quest for a balance of power in the Indo-Pacific, in partnership with the US and its allies; c) reducing the importance of Russia in New Delhi's regional outlook; and d) shifting away from Asian and Third World solidarity in opposition to the West to the development of ad hoc coalitions and 'minilateral' institutions with like-minded partners, including Western states.

Chapter Two examines the structural changes in India's China policy in the twenty-first century, including the rise of military tensions on the disputed boundary, growing regional friction with China's increased presence in South Asia and the Indian Ocean – New Delhi's presumed spheres of influence – and Beijing's resistance to India's aspirations for a larger international role. The intensification of tensions along all these axes has compelled India to discard its traditional ambivalence about Chinese power and counter it by strengthening its national power and developing partnerships with other states.

The third chapter delineates the emergence of the US as New Delhi's principal partner in the acceleration of India's economic growth and military capabilities, as well as in balancing against China in Asia. It reviews the growing defence and security cooperation between India and the US and the factors facilitating and constraining it.

Chapter Four examines India's evolving engagement with broader Asian geopolitics. As India's relations with China and the US undergo a major transformation, India's engagement with Asia, too, has begun to change. Embracing the US and challenging China has inevitably complicated some of New Delhi's traditional regional ties, but it has also facilitated stronger engagement with others. Notwithstanding the widespread surprise at India's drift away from non-alignment to closer ties with the US, the prospect of a strong and capable India has encouraged many countries in the region to seek an expansion of relations with New Delhi.

Chapter Five assesses India's concrete role in shaping the Asian balance of power. Although India is well behind the US and China in all power metrics, its capacity to contribute to the regional order is growing in a range of dimensions – ideological, geopolitical, economic, technological and military. The book concludes by assessing India's likely contributions to a new Asian security, political and economic order in the light of both New Delhi's enduring regional interests and the policy changes envisioned by the second Trump administration.

CHAPTER ONE

Great transitions

Introduction

To understand India's changing role in Asian security, it is important to take a longer view of the evolution of its international relations in the modern era. Both academic and popular discourse on India's security politics focus on a specific period in the evolution of modern India – the Cold War era that began with Indian independence from British colonial rule. They assume that the dominant policies of that era are enduring elements of India's worldview. However, it is far more productive to view the policies of that era, such as non-alignment, as a specific response to a particular set of circumstances rather than immutable positions. The tendency to view non-alignment as the foundational principle of India's international engagement misses out on the nuanced application of this policy during the Cold War and the rich alternative traditions that were more prominent before and after the Cold War. By highlighting those traditions, this chapter will point to the four great transitions that now define New Delhi's security politics and have a great bearing on the Asian balance of power.

The next section of the chapter looks at the evolution of India's security politics under the British Raj, before independence.

The subsequent section notes the efforts by India's first prime minister, Jawaharlal Nehru, to dissociate India from colonial foreign policies and the consequences for India. The third section looks at four major transitions away from the Nehruvian framework for India's international relations and security politics in the twenty-first century.

India at the centre

Most analysts of Indian foreign policy implicitly assume that the legacies of the colonial era have no implications for India's post-independence approaches to international security, and that India's international relations began when it became independent. But contemporary Indian foreign policy has deep roots in India's colonial experience.[1] The British East India Company, established at the dawn of the seventeenth century, became a territorial entity in the late eighteenth century and acquired the characteristics of a sovereign state – raising taxes, controlling and expanding its borders, strengthening its armed forces, and engaging in diplomacy with the sovereign princes in and around the Indian subcontinent. The weight and reach of the company-state – taken over by the Crown in 1857 after the Great Sepoy Revolt – steadily expanded and made British India one of the more powerful entities outside Europe. Not only was the Raj reconstituting an expansive empire of the kind the Mughals had built, it was also building it along modern European lines. The Raj brought European ideas of territory, borders and military organisation to India, even as it adapted and improvised on the pre-existing structures. Colonial India, as a notably expansive territorial entity, inevitably became a weighty force in the subcontinent, the Indian Ocean and its abutting areas.

One of the lesser-known features of colonial India was its significant autonomy in conducting regional affairs and its considerable agency in shaping the geopolitics of the

Figure 1: **Adaptation of a 1909 official map depicting the Raj within the larger British Empire**

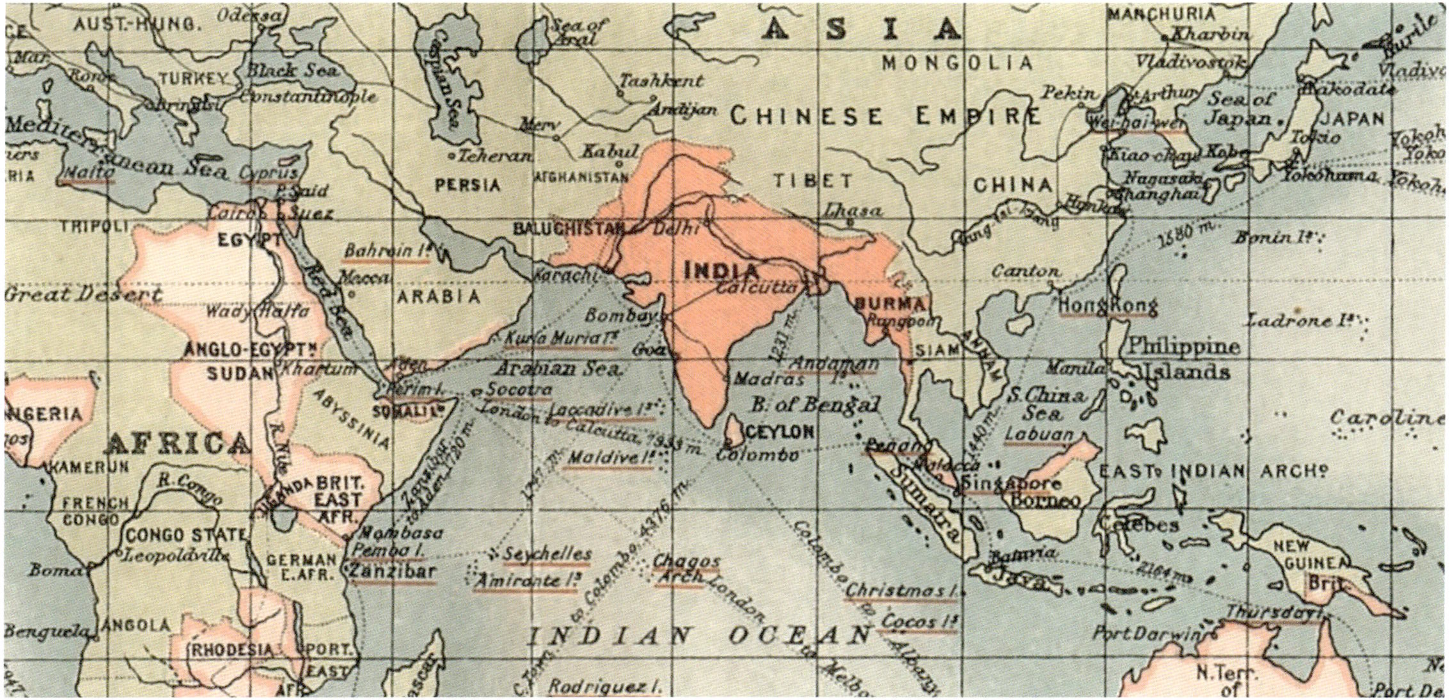

The Empire was composed of territories under direct British control, as well as those under informal control (including protectorates or de facto protectorates). British influence also extended into many additional territories, including Afghanistan, Arabia, Persia, Siam, Tibet and Xinjiang (Antiqua Print Gallery/Alamy Stock Photo)

subcontinent and the neighbourhood. This fact might seem counter-intuitive given the contemporary imagination of colonialism as governing far-flung regions from the metropole. That India was governed by British personnel – civilian as well as military – who had acquired dominance over its polity might also suggest the impossibility of autonomy. However, several contemporaneous imperatives, such as distance, resources and local geopolitical realities, allowed the Raj to acquire considerable autonomy in the early years of British rule in India. Historian Robert Blyth has explored in great detail the relative autonomy of the Raj in developing and implementing foreign and security policies in the western Indian Ocean. Writing about the 'empire of the Raj' in the region, stretching from Persia to the east coast of Africa, Blyth argues:

> In theory, initiative in external policy rested with officials in London rather than the men on the spot or their political masters in Bombay and Calcutta. However, in the days of the East India Company, and for some time beyond, this represented an unrealistic and impractical ideal.

The tyranny of distance, difficulty of communication and need for flexibility on the ground meant 'it was the Indian government, not the remote offices of Whitehall, which handled the minutiae of treaty negotiations, the promotion and protection of commercial activities, and small-scale naval and military operations'. Blyth goes on to assert that there were indeed clear limits to British India's 'independence' in foreign affairs. India could not conduct a foreign policy in opposition to London's interests but had the latitude to pursue policies based on a better appreciation of the regional perspective. By the turn of the twentieth century, Blyth points out, London sought to exercise greater control over the policies of the Raj; yet financial considerations demanded giving a measure of autonomy to the colonial government. After all, 'the Indian sphere, almost wholly financed by the Calcutta exchequer, certainly represented an inherently lucrative deal for the Imperial government'.[2] While 'the men on the spot' and the Raj's political and military leadership were largely British, the Raj could not have functioned without the cooperation of local Indian potentates or the vast reserves of Indian military manpower. Moreover, many of the Raj's key foreign-policy assumptions were derived from that polity's geopolitical location and role within Asia, and were shared by indigenous elites.

The construction of a modern territorial state also entailed clarity about borders and sovereignty, a policy to secure it through military force, a foreign policy of engaging with the entities beyond the spaces controlled by the Raj, and a grand strategy of preventing European rivals from encroaching upon British India. That involved the creation of a complex territorial system that secured India with a cordon sanitaire around it and an expansive sphere of influence across the vast region that we now call the Indo-Pacific – from Aden to Malacca.[3] India became the very centre of organising security in this vast region from the turn of the nineteenth century to the middle of the twentieth.

As it consolidated its early footholds in India and began to expand its territorial control of the subcontinent through the eighteenth century, the British East India Company had to constantly prevent European forces from poaching its newly acquired possessions. British fears of a French invasion of India in the early nineteenth century, followed by concerns about the Russian threat to the subcontinent through the nineteenth century and about German advances towards the subcontinent in the early twentieth century, defined the so-called Great Game on the fringes of India. While there were different schools of thought in the Raj on how best to defend India, they all agreed on the need to secure India as far away from its subcontinental frontiers as possible. Some saw it best done in Afghanistan and Central Asia, while others focused on the Gulf and the Middle East. In practice, this meant cultivating special political relationships and developing military influence in all the regions abutting India, leading to a massive sphere of influence for the British Raj that was far more extensive than the territories it directly controlled. The creation of the Raj's protective cordon sanitaire entailed establishing spheres of influence from Siam (modern Thailand) in the east, to Tibet, Xinjiang, Afghanistan, Persia, Arabia and the Horn of Africa in the west. Through several treaties, the Raj sought to get local chieftains to collaborate in the pacification of the region and the exclusion of foreign influence that would threaten British Indian interests.[4]

The massive sphere of influence was accompanied by the creation of a complex territorial structure for British India. The British were not satisfied with drawing a single line that separated the sovereignty of the Raj from the surrounding regions. Instead, the Raj created a threefold frontier. As Ainslee T. Embree has argued,

> One frontier was the administrative boundary up to which the Government of India exercised full authority enforcing its own legal and political systems as standards for society. Beyond this was a zone claimed as Indian Territory, but in which the Government made no attempt to impose its laws or territorial jurisdiction. Beyond this zone was the third area, the protectorate, the independent kingdom, but tied by special treaties of friendship and obligation to the Government of India.[5]

The maintenance of this ring fence was a dynamic process requiring the constant expansion of political, diplomatic and military influence to maintain the integrity of the glacis [defensive structure]. As Lord Curzon, the viceroy of India at the turn of the twentieth century, put it, 'Spheres of Interest [the lowest form of buffer] tend to become Spheres of Influence; temporary Leases to become perpetual; Spheres of Influence tend to become Protectorates; Protectorates to be the forerunners of complete incorporation'.[6]

At the heart of the system was the imperative of ensuring that the regimes around the subcontinent were friendly to the Raj and kept away from rival European powers.[7] The essence of the arrangement involved the protectorates ceding power over foreign relations to the Raj while maintaining the freedom to govern at home. The need for this cordon sanitaire around India, however, was driven not merely by considerations of external threats from European imperial powers, but by internal challenges as well. As Embree notes,

> Almost always, border policies and foreign policies in general had as a very important component a concern for internal security, as well as for defence from external enemies. Peace on the frontier was related to internal peace. The fear of Russia was not primarily fear of a Russian invasion of India; what was taken seriously in Calcutta all through the nineteenth century was the fear of internal uprisings that might be triggered by unrest on the frontier.[8]

The effectiveness of the Raj depended to a great degree on the Indian Army. The Indian Army's history dates to the turn of the seventeenth century, and its military engagement with the rest of the world to the late eighteenth century.[9] To understand where

India's role as a security provider might be headed, it is important to recall its inherited military and diplomatic traditions, especially the expansive expeditionary role of the Indian Army. Under the British East India Company and the British Crown, the Indian Army served three broad functions. The first was to protect the ever-expanding frontiers of the Raj; the second was to serve as the domestic constabulary. But it is the third function of the Indian Army – as the imperial arm of the Raj beyond the subcontinent – that is of special interest to us. The Indian Army was deployed in an expeditionary mode from the eastern Mediterranean to the South China Sea starting from the late eighteenth century. The first expeditionary operation was mounted in 1762 from Madras in southern India to the Philippines. Through the nineteenth century, Indian troops saw action in theatres ranging from Egypt to Japan, from southern Africa to southern China.[10] Military historians assess that British primacy in the Indian Ocean was rooted in the Royal Navy's command of the seas *and* the role of the Indian Army in acquiring and stabilising the empire:

> The Indian Army was a unique establishment, an Oriental expeditionary force that the British Governor-General in Calcutta, acting on his own authority, could hurl across the seas to intervene in Africa, Arabia, the East Indies, the Mediterranean, or South-east Asia …. No rival power came close to creating and mastering such an institution and, coupled with British sea power, the Indian Army gave Britain the military edge that took it to the top of the imperial tree and enabled it to withstand even the sternest challenge to its mastery of east of Suez. With the power of the Indian Army at its command, the Government of India was always quick to respond to regional threats to India's security, usually leading to imperial gains.[11]

Besides the conquest of new territories and gunboat diplomacy, Indian manpower was indispensable for the British in promoting local security in parts of the empire that were outside India. The Raj developed the tradition of recruiting soldiers in India for service in special local forces in colonies and protectorates both in Asia and in Africa. Sikh contingents, for example, saw service in the African protectorates, and the Malay States Guides regiment was largely recruited in India.[12] Britain's heavy global footprint in the nineteenth century, secured by the Indian Army and tribal levies, generated enormous military activity across a diverse terrain – from mountains to deserts and jungles. This experience provided the basis for the emergence of British special forces in the Second World War, adept at irregular warfare.[13]

The Indian expeditionary operations took on a dramatically larger role during the two world wars, as London turned to its imperial military reserve in India. During the First World War, nearly 1.2 million Indians were recruited for service in the Indian Army. When the war ended, about 950,000 Indian troops were serving overseas. According to the official count, between 62,000 and 65,000 Indian soldiers were killed in that war. India provided a critical contingent of trained troops at a vital moment for Britian in 1914 and played a key role, especially in the Middle East, throughout the war.[14] In the Second World War, the Indian Army saw action on fronts ranging from Italy and North Africa to East Africa, the Middle East and the Far East. In Southeast Asia alone, 700,000 Indian troops joined the effort to oust the Japanese army from Burma, Malaya and Indochina. By the time the war ended, the Indian Army numbered a massive 2.5m men, the largest all-volunteer force the world had ever seen. Throughout the war, the Indian Army continued to maintain its traditional duties of providing territorial defence on the northwestern frontier of the subcontinent and aiding the civil powers.[15]

The creation of a large empire saw the historical transformation of one of the world's oldest and continuous civilisational spaces into a territorial entity on European lines, albeit with unique characteristics of its own. The Raj was not simply an external imposition of rule by force but involved the co-option and accommodation of many indigenous forces to manage the vast empire in the subcontinent.[16] The civilian and military structures of this large state could not be staffed by the British alone. Even as London gained direct control over governing India in the later decades of colonial rule, it had to perforce 'Indianise' the leadership of India's bureaucracy and military. These Indian elements provided significant continuity and stability when transitioning from colonial rule to independence.

Equally importantly, colonial India had to take into account the geopolitical interests of India as an entity even as it pursued London's larger objectives in the region. J.N. Dixit, one of the more distinguished foreign secretaries of India since independence, once declared that the Viceroy Lord Curzon was the 'first Indian nationalist'. This formulation sounds extreme, especially since a large section of Indian nationalists reviled Curzon. India's foreign- and security-policy planners, however, embraced Curzon's expansive definition of British India's security interests and its natural primacy in the Indian Ocean and the abutting regions. A. Wess Mitchell argues that the grand strategy suggested by Curzon – a colonial ruler – does not make it any 'less Indian' because the 'substrate of his reflections was not nationality or ideology, but geography and the permanent interests that it produces for any power looking at the gameboard from India's position'.[17] While this vision was very much part of British imperial defence centred on India, it also suited the ambitions of new nationalists who viewed independent India's dominance as natural and inevitable. But hopes for India inheriting the mantle of the British Raj as the dominant power in the Indian Ocean were undermined by several factors, discussed in the next section.

The centre does not hold

India's expansive importance in the organisation of the British empire in the east and its security is described by Peter John Brobst as the 'India Centre'.[18] Yet sustaining this Indian centrality in post-colonial Asia became impossible as India embarked on a vastly different geopolitical trajectory. Four factors decisively shaped independent India's security politics. One was the great Partition, which broke up the strategic unity of the subcontinent crafted so patiently under British rule and terribly undermined New Delhi's hand. A second factor was the strategy of Jawaharlal Nehru – who as prime minister had a big hand in shaping India's new geopolitics – to dissociate from any possible Anglo-American security connection. More broadly, the nature of independent India's internationalism that Nehru developed reinforced India's alienation from the West. Nehru's worldview was rooted in his imagined post-colonial architecture for regional security based on Asian solidarity and political distance from the West. The effort to build an Asian order led by Asians morphed into an international coalition of developing countries – the so-called Non-Aligned Movement (NAM). Acquiring a radical anti-Western tone under Nehru's successors as prime minister in the later decades of the Cold War, non-alignment continues to colour the Indian elite's worldview in the twenty-first century.[19] Thirdly, in response to the Cold War dynamics in the region, India developed close ties with the Soviet Union, which became its most important partner.[20]

The fourth factor was New Delhi's consistent underestimation of Beijing's power and the nature of the threat from China.[21] Let us briefly review how these four interconnected trends in Asia played out in the second half of the twentieth century.

The Partition profoundly altered the structure of the subcontinent's geopolitics. The division of its two largest provinces – Punjab and Bengal – on religious lines and contentions over other provinces like Kashmir laid the basis for enduring conflicts between the successor states – India and Pakistan. Among the range of new conflicts were territorial disputes, the delineation of new boundaries, the division of river waters of the great Indus and Ganges systems, and the protection of new minorities that emerged in the partitioned subcontinent. The inability to quickly sort out these issues entrenched the India–Pakistan conflict and led to its militarisation and eventual nuclearisation. The vivisection of Pakistan in 1971 (into Pakistan and Bangladesh), however, did not end the persistent tension between New Delhi and Islamabad and only strengthened the revanchist sentiment in the Pakistan Army.

The military consequence of persistent internal conflict in South Asia was the dramatic turn inward of the Indian Army. Compelled by the imperative to defend the new borders of the Indian state, the inward orientation of the Indian Army was reinforced by Nehru's active effort to shed the imperial legacy of the Raj as a regional security provider. Nehru's opposition to such a role was rooted in the unease felt within the Indian nationalist movement about Indian armed forces being used by Britain for imperial purposes. Moreover, fellow nationalist movements in Asia complained about the participation of the Indian armed forces in the defence of European interests after the Second World War. Thus, the nationalism of both domestic and foreign actors reinforced Nehru's active dissociation from an imperial and expeditionary regional role.[22]

A second major factor that shaped independent India's security politics was Nehru's emphasis on non-alignment – although framed in abstract terms, in effect it meant severing the Indian Army's connection to the British. Although India bought arms from the United Kingdom, it wanted to have little to do with the post-Cold War regional alliances being built by Britain and the United States to secure Asia against the spread of communism.[23] Despite facing a relatively minor communist challenge at home, Nehru did not view international communism in the same light as London and Washington did. He saw India as a potential major power and was eager to build a new post-war Asian security architecture on India's own terms. Under Nehru, India signed security treaties with Bhutan, Nepal and Sikkim when they turned to India after the Chinese occupation of Tibet. Nehru also signed security-cooperation agreements with a number of countries, including Indonesia and Burma, as part of an effort to expand India's independent security role in Asia. Nehru also put India's vast military manpower to work for the international public good. By taking the lead in peacekeeping operations – only those sanctioned by the United Nations – Nehru and his successors contributed to international peace and security.[24] Nehru saw Anglo-American alliances like the Central Treaty Organisation (CENTO) and Southeast Asia Treaty Organisation (SEATO) as undermining India's own ambitions in the region and his plans to build a new Asian security order. He actively opposed the emergence of US alliances in the region. As Francine Frankel puts it, 'the US strategy of lining up allies in collective security treaties to stem communist influence in these areas appeared to Nehru as a threat to India's interests and his own leadership'.[25]

The nature of Cold War geopolitics was a third critical factor that shaped India's security outlook. If Nehru's opposition to the United States' regional role became entrenched in Indian foreign policy under his successors, US security cooperation with Pakistan in the Cold War laid the foundation for enduring suspicion in New Delhi about Washington's policy in the region.[26] US president John F. Kennedy's attempt to surmount regional rivalries and bring India into the Western camp – by brokering a settlement on the Kashmir dispute between India and Pakistan and creating a united front against China in the wake of the 1962 conflict between New Delhi and Beijing – only made matters worse. The peace efforts collapsed, Kennedy's attempt to build a new security partnership with India did not go far, and the US, meanwhile, moved towards engagement with China.[27]

The Sino-Soviet rift played out differently for the US and India in the region. The US saw a historic opportunity to exploit the divide between the two communist giants. That Washington was caught in the quagmire of Vietnam also provided urgency to reverse its refusal since 1949 to engage with the People's Republic of China. US president Richard Nixon and his national security advisor, Henry Kissinger, built on earlier contacts with China to move towards the normalisation of bilateral relations that would dramatically alter the geopolitical landscape in Asia. Moscow, which had struggled to cope with the conflict between a fellow communist power and an emerging friend during the Sino-Indian conflict of 1962, now moved closer to New Delhi. For New Delhi, the Sino-Soviet rift and US–China entente laid the foundation for a solid strategic partnership with Moscow.[28]

For India, the Sino-US normalisation was a shock, and it actively sought a partnership with the Soviet Union to restore the regional balance. The crisis in East Pakistan and the 'Nixon tilt' towards Islamabad provided India with an urgent impetus to sign a security treaty with the Soviet Union in August 1971. And Moscow's diplomatic, political and military support for India during the war for Bangladesh's independence elevated the Soviet Union's salience for the Indian political class sky high — a bias that persisted even after its collapse in 1991.[29] Moscow was not only a leading military partner for New Delhi at the end of the Cold War but also its top trading partner in 1990.

The fourth major factor in India's outlook on international security was its view of China. If Nehru's political empathy for the Soviet Union – so visible in early Indian foreign policy – translated into a deep partnership in the latter half of the Cold War, the first prime minister's sense of solidarity with China turned out to be a major misreading of Beijing's regional ambitions and created the basis for persistent conflict with China. Building a friendship with China was central to Nehru's Asia strategy. Despite warnings from colleagues and signs of trouble, Nehru persisted with the premise that the West was the problem and solidarity with China was the answer. The shock of the 1962 Sino-Indian conflict compelled India to revise its threat perceptions, modernise its military and gear up to meet the challenges presented by Beijing. As Beijing turned inwards and was consumed by the Cultural Revolution, it seemed that India was well placed to cope with the China challenge. This optimistic view was bolstered by the renewed focus in New Delhi on befriending the successors to Chairman Mao Zedong following his death in 1976.

The apparent quest for a peaceful periphery by Deng Xiaoping (China's leader from the late 1970s) had, by the late 1980s, produced renewed engagement between India and China. India dropped its precondition of resolving the boundary dispute before normalising bilateral relations and accepted the Chinese offer of a simultaneous effort to resolve the boundary dispute and expand bilateral cooperation. New Delhi also bet that there was room for extensive international and multilateral cooperation with Beijing despite the bilateral disputes.[30] For example, the notion of a shared agenda to limit the dangers of the unipolar moment of the post-Cold War period encouraged India to join hands with China and Russia to form the Russia–India–China (RIC) and Brazil–Russia–India–China–South Africa (BRICS) forums.

By the second decade of the twenty-first century, India began to feel the full heat of a rising China. While trade volumes between the two sides have rapidly risen in the last decade, the border dispute has become more contentious. Indeed, India's trade deficit with China has continued to widen, undermining the premise that economic cooperation would create the conditions for an amicable resolution of the boundary dispute. Besides China's growing assertiveness on the border – marked by military crises in 2013, 2014, 2017 and 2020 – increasing Chinese power began to envelop India in the subcontinent and the Indian Ocean. As China became the world's second-largest economy, Beijing's influence in India's neighbourhood began to grow at a rapid pace. Beijing also intensified its military and security ties with the states of South Asia and the Indian Ocean. As a permanent member of the UN Security Council with growing international clout, Beijing began to offer valuable political support on key issues of concern for regional elites. As far as India was concerned, China became the principal obstacle to India's aspirations to join the Nuclear Suppliers Group and become a permanent member of the UN Security Council. Capping all this was the deepening gap between the comprehensive national power of China and India. Although their economies were similar in size during the 1980s, China's GDP in 2024 at US$18.3 trillion was nearly five times larger than that of India at US$3.9trn.[31] For an India that was driven by the notion of solidarity with China in the middle of the twentieth century, the shift in the balance of power in favour of China has turned out to be the greatest challenge for its national-security policy in the twenty-first century.

Restoring the India centre

The deepening tensions with China have profoundly altered the orientation of India's foreign policy in the twenty-first century. Four great transitions can be identified. Firstly, the growing influence of China in the subcontinent – through trade, investment and security cooperation – spurred India to re-evaluate its neighbourhood in order to regain its traditional primacy. India's high economic growth rates and Pakistan's economic slowdown since the early 1990s saw the gap between the two countries widen in favour of the former – in 2024, India's GDP (US$3.9trn) was ten times larger than that of Pakistan at US$375 billion.[32] Although this economic strength does not translate into dominance over Pakistan, New Delhi under Prime Minister Narendra Modi has moved away from the defensiveness that characterised India's approach to Pakistan in the 1990s and has sought to alter the terms of engagement on the Kashmir question.

While the negative legacies of Partition endure on India's western frontier with Pakistan, New Delhi has tried to overcome the burden in the eastern subcontinent with Bangladesh. New Delhi's successful effort to normalise ties with Dhaka saw the settlement of the boundary disputes – land and maritime — and the expansion of road and rail connectivity, trade and political cooperation. But the ouster of Bangladeshi prime minister Sheikh Hasina in August 2024 saw the rapid deterioration of New Delhi's ties with Dhaka.[33] The quick turn to anti-India hostility in Dhaka reminded India of the entrenched structural tensions introduced by Partition and New Delhi's entanglement in the domestic politics of Bangladesh. With the smaller countries of the subcontinent, India is stepping up its efforts to compete with China and building on the natural geographic advantages that favour New Delhi. This is likely to remain a work in progress for a long time to come.

Secondly, the persistent pursuit of a post-Western order in Asia in partnership with China in the early years of independence has now morphed into a strategy of balancing against Beijing, in partnership with the US. Indian foreign-policy elites, who in the twentieth century tended to dismiss the notion of balance of power, now actively seek to limit Chinese power. India's current foreign minister, Subrahmanyam Jaishankar, has pointed to a 'rising but divided Asia'. Underlining the difficulties with the concept of 'Asia for Asians', often promoted by the Chinese today, Jaishankar said that this slogan 'presumes a stronger convergence within the continent than reality indicates'. He further argued:

> Asia for Asians is also a sentiment that was encouraged in the past, even in our own country, by political romanticism. The Bandung spirit, however, got its reality check within its first decade.[34] Indeed, the experience of the past affirms that Asians are second to none when it comes to realpolitik.[35]

If keeping the US out of Asia was a preoccupation for Nehru, Modi's government recognises the importance of the US in shaping the regional balance. As Jaishankar put it, 'narrow Asian chauvinism is actually against the continent's own interest … There are resident powers in Asia like the United States or the proximate ones like Australia who have legitimate interests.'[36] The US, the distant power, is no longer seen as a threat to India; rather, it is neighbouring China that is viewed as undermining India's core national-security interests. India's decision to reactivate the Quadrilateral Security Dialogue (Quad) in 2017 is directly related to the deepening problems on the China frontier.[37]

If Indian and Western interests in the subcontinent clashed in the second half of the twentieth century, they are beginning to come into synergy in the twenty-first. Washington is ending its hyphenation between India and Pakistan (that is, the notion that its relations with each country cannot be separated) and is joining hands with New Delhi in trying to limit China's influence in South Asia. The decisive US shift towards the Indo-Pacific under the first Trump administration, and the Biden administration's decision to double down on it, provided a solid foundation on which to build a new relationship between New Delhi and Washington. The Indo-Pacific concept, it might be argued, really takes us back to the strategic geography in which Britain and colonial India worked together for nearly two centuries. The partnership between India and the US – although based on very different terms – could reconstitute the India centre in the Indian Ocean and its abutting regions.

The third great transition is a response to the China challenge and India's growing engagement with the US and the West: the slow but certain reduction in Russia's strategic salience in India's geopolitical calculus.[38] The Modi government's refusal to criticise the Russian invasion of Ukraine and its reluctance to support Western sanctions on Moscow have underlined India's long-standing connection with Russia. The Modi government has continued to invest in the Russian relationship. But Moscow's salience in New Delhi's regional outlook has steadily eroded in the twenty-first century. For one, India's rapid economic growth since the 1990s saw it develop a larger economy than Russia's – in 2024, India's GDP at US$3.9trn was nearly double Russia's at US$2.1trn.[39] This gap between the two sides will continue to grow in the coming years.

In terms of trade, Russia has become steadily more marginal to India. In 1991, India's annual trade with the United States stood at US$4.9bn and that with the Soviet Union was US$5.2bn. Three decades later, in 2021, the figures for trade with the US and the Russian Federation were US$113bn and

US$12bn, respectively. After the Russian invasion of Ukraine and the tightening of the oil market in 2022, India's petroleum imports from Russia surged, making it Russia's biggest oil customer. It also took bilateral trade to the unprecedented level of US$65.7bn in 2023–24.[40] It remains to be seen if the expanded oil imports from Russia are a transient phenomenon or an enduring one.

What has endured in the Indo-Russian relationship is New Delhi's dependence on Russian weapons.[41] India has diversified its weapons imports in the twenty-first century by acquiring more arms from France, Israel and the US. Yet Russia remains India's main supplier, although its share of Indian arms imports has shrunk from 76% in 2009–13 to 58% in 2014–18 and then to 36% in 2019–23.[42] In terms of the accumulated stock, Russia still accounts for nearly 65% of India's total military inventory.[43] New Delhi's dependence on Moscow for spares and other equipment remains deep and has acquired a sharp edge amidst India's conflict with China on its long and contested border. It is this dependence that has, among other factors, compelled India to maintain silence over the Russian aggression in Europe. India's continuing strategic attachment to Russia is based on the fact that Moscow helped New Delhi balance Beijing in the past. The ability to sustain that into the future is complicated by Russia's deepening ties with China and its ongoing confrontation with the US and Europe.

Finally, there has been a shift from India's pursuit of Third World leadership, which peaked in the Cold War, to building coalitions of like-minded partners in the twenty-first century. As the idea of Asian solidarity took a back seat after 1962, India's enthusiasm for building a global Non-Aligned Movement gained much ground in the 1960s and acquired considerable traction in the 1970s, as Indian foreign policy acquired a radical tone. After the Cold War, India's focus moved away from the

NAM to emphasise regional cooperation in its immediate and extended neighbourhoods, increased economic cooperation with the major economies, and its great-power relations.[44] India shifted to groupings with major powers, like BRICS, the G4 (Brazil, Germany, India and Japan seeking UN Security Council reform), and the Quad (Australia, India, Japan and the United States). India also devoted much energy to engaging multilateral institutions like the G20 and the G7, and regional institutions like the Association of Southeast Asian Nations and the Gulf Cooperation Council.

In Prime Minister Modi's second term (2019–24), India revived its interest in engaging the so-called Global South. This engagement, however, did not use the old ideological template of mobilising the South against the West. External Affairs Minister Jaishankar has articulated the idea of India as a 'South Western power' which acts as a bridge between the West and the South. The recent emphasis on the Global South can also be viewed as part of India's competition with China for regional and global influence. Having built considerable goodwill in the developing world during the Cold War, New Delhi does not want to simply abandon it. In conversation with the US, India is pitching the proposition that its leadership of the Global South will prevent the non-Western world from drifting into China's orbit.[45] These elements of change in Indian foreign policy point to sophisticated diplomacy that has earned praise from proponents of realpolitik like Henry Kissinger.[46] The sophistication is, of course, anchored in India's growing material power and political self-assurance in the Modi era.[47]

India's transitions unfolding in the twenty-first century make it a critical actor in shaping the security of Asia and its waters. While there remain many limitations to and hesitations in India's trajectory, the growing weight of the Indian economy, its continuing rise in the hierarchies of regional and global power, its sharpening perception of the imperative to balance against China, and its deepening partnerships with the US and its Asian allies provide the basis for New Delhi's role in shaping regional security politics in the twenty-first century. Although it is a very different regional context from the era of the British Raj – structured by collaboration between Indian elites and Britain – the new era is likely to see deeper security cooperation between New Delhi and Washington. As the US looks for capable partners to undertake larger regional responsibilities, India is looking to raise its regional profile. The convergence of these two trends will likely make for a very productive partnership in Asia.

CHAPTER TWO

The China challenge

Introduction

Few countries have loomed larger than China for independent India's international relations. Yet few capitals have more profoundly misjudged Beijing than New Delhi. To be sure, India is not the only country to have got post-war China wrong. Europe, Japan, Russia and the United States have all made assumptions about China that were terribly incorrect. New Delhi has the unique distinction, though, of having repeatedly misjudged Beijing's intentions. For nearly a century, India has sought to befriend China, with very little to show for it. It was only when the series of military crises in 2013, 2014, 2017 and 2020 shook India's China policy that New Delhi moved towards a determined and sustained effort to balance against Beijing. This chapter begins with a review of India's elusive quest for partnership with China over the last century and the sources of New Delhi's reluctance to come to terms with the nature of the Chinese challenge. It then looks at the evolution of the boundary dispute in recent years. The third and fourth sections of the chapter look at China's rising influence in the subcontinent and the Indian Ocean, and India's efforts to counter it. The final section looks at the growing tensions between New Delhi and Beijing in the multilateral arena.

Structural divergence

Although India and China are two old civilisations and neighbours, they had limited contact for a long time. After the spread of Buddhism over the Himalayas and across the Indian Ocean from India to China, contacts between the two sides steadily diminished from the turn of the first millennium. It was only with the arrival of European colonialists that there was renewed contact between India and China in the early nineteenth century. The British trade in opium, cultivated in India and sold in China, saw the linking of the Indian and Chinese markets. The British used the Indian Army to put down the opposition in China to the opium trade. The Indian Army was also part of the international force that crushed the Boxer Rebellion in 1900. While the history of Indian armed interventions in China is not familiar to contemporary Indian audiences, they have not been forgotten in Beijing. Unlike their earlier contacts through the propagation of Buddhism and trade, the colonial impact on the relationship between India and China was viewed as negative in Beijing. The image of India as a tool of the imperialist powers was easily invoked by Chinese leader Mao Zedong when relations deteriorated at the turn of the 1960s. That sentiment resonates today in Beijing as it castigates New Delhi for its deepening partnership with Washington.

A very different set of sentiments – shared Asian identity and anti-colonial solidarity – emerged from the encounter between the nationalist movements of the two countries in the colonial era. The Indian poet Rabindranath Tagore's travels to China in the 1920s exemplified the effort to connect the two nationalist movements but also underlined the difficulty of aligning their broader worldviews. Tagore's talk of a shared 'spiritual civilisation' invited derision from some Chinese nationalists and communists, who bet that a defeated India under the colonial yoke had little to offer China in its quest for social, political and economic modernisation. They wanted material transformation and Westernisation, not Asian spiritualism.[1]

The first formal engagement between the two nationalist movements took place in 1927, at a conference in Brussels that formed the League Against Imperialism, amid surging anti-colonial sentiment in Asia. After the Indian delegation, led by Jawaharlal Nehru, met with the Chinese delegation, the two sides issued a joint statement that laid out the framework for engagement in the twentieth century. They declared their shared interest in overthrowing colonial rule in Asia and building a new post-colonial order in the region. In the 1930s, Indian nationalists expressed strong support for Chinese nationalists fighting against the Japanese occupation. The Indian National Congress held regular public rallies in support of China, and a medical mission from India went to China to treat the war wounded. Nehru also made a trip to Chongqing in 1939 to meet the nationalist leaders of China and prepare the ground for post-war collaboration between the two nations.[2]

But cooperation against the colonial powers turned out to be rather hard in the Second World War, since the Indian and Chinese nationalists were fighting different imperialists. For China, the liberation war was directed at Japanese occupiers; for the mainstream Indian nationalist movement, represented by the Indian National Congress, the focus was on immediate independence from the United Kingdom. China's nationalist leader, Chiang Kai-shek, travelled to India to try to convince Indian nationalist leaders of the need to prioritise the fight against Japan, offering support for the Indian struggle against Britain once the war was over, but he did not succeed. The most critical moment in the twentieth century in Asia – the anti-imperial wars for national liberation – then, did not produce unity between Indian and Chinese leaders.[3]

The end of the Second World War saw India embark on a fresh effort to build unity with China.[4] The defeat of the nationalists and the communist takeover of China did not alter Nehru's focus on building friendly ties with Beijing. That China became India's neighbour – through its occupation and control of Tibet – did not produce the much-needed hard thinking about the consequences. To be sure, there was strong questioning of Nehru's approach to communist China.[5] At home, Nehru's home minister, Vallabhbhai Patel, argued that 'even though we regard ourselves as friends of China, the Chinese do not regard us as their friends'. Patel asserted that China posed a bigger threat than Western imperialism: 'Chinese irredentism and communist imperialism are different from the expansionism or imperialism of the Western powers. The former has a cloak of ideology, which makes it ten times more dangerous. In the guise of ideological expansion lie concealed racial, national or historical claims.'[6] Nehru, however, chose to actively oppose Western efforts to isolate China and to serenade the Chinese leadership, among the many sceptical Asian governments, in the name of building Asian unity. This effort ended in disaster with India's defeat in the 1962 Sino-Indian war.

Yet the 1962 war did not end India's unrequited romance with China.[7] In the 1990s, India was apprehensive about the national-security consequences of the unipolar moment – when the US sought to impose its ideas about peace and security on the rest of the world. Of special concern for New Delhi was US pressure on India to resolve the Kashmir dispute with Pakistan and roll back India's nuclear-weapons programme. To hedge against these US policies, New Delhi joined Moscow's initiative to build a strategic coalition with Beijing to promote a multipolar world. The Russia–India–China (RIC) forum created in the 1990s eventually became BRICS with the inclusion of Brazil and South Africa in the 2000s. Although both forums remain active in the 2020s, their centrality in New Delhi's worldview has declined as the multidimensional challenge from China has mounted in the twenty-first century. The idea that India can work with China in the multilateral domain has taken a knocking with Beijing's reluctance to support India's candidature for permanent membership on the United Nations Security Council.[8]

As the sense that China and India were rising at the same time gained ground at the dawn of the twenty-first century, realists began to argue about an inevitable conflict between the two.[9] But New Delhi continued to insist that Asia and the world were large enough to accommodate the simultaneous rise of China and India. Nevertheless, that illusion has steadily evaporated over the last decade. That India's repeated efforts to build a friendly and cooperative relationship with China have faltered is not in doubt. That brings us to the question, why did India persist with a policy that seemed a Sisyphean exercise? The answer may lie in the anti-colonialist and anti-Western sentiments held by the Indian political class. Equally important was India's underestimation of Chinese nationalism and its lack of sensitivity to Beijing's predictable great-power ambitions. New Delhi also found it hard to accept that Beijing did not reciprocate India's ideological sentimentalism on bilateral relations.[10]

Although the Indian political class was very much a product of Western education as well as sensibility, it was deeply influenced by a range of new ideas (originating in the West) that challenged Western political orthodoxy, including anti-imperialism, socialism, communism, pacifism and cosmopolitan humanism. Indian nationalists came of age in the interwar period amidst a deep schism in Western political thought.[11] Most Indian nationalists aligned themselves with the left in the West, which was sympathetic to the ideas of liberation from colonial rule. Socialist ideas of different kinds, including Soviet communism, which promised accelerated development without the brutalities of capitalism, had a powerful impact on the ideas of nation-building in India and Asia. Pacifist and liberal-internationalist ideals in the interwar period strengthened the Indian nationalist criticism of the balance-of-power politics that brought the 'great war' to Europe and, by extension, much of the world. Meanwhile, as the anti-colonial movements gained ground in the interwar period, new identities began to emerge across the colonial regions; these included transnational identities, such as pan-Asian, pan-Arab and pan-Islamic, and the idea of supranational solidarity among the oppressed peoples of the world.

In the twentieth century, India refused to see China and its policies in power-political terms. That reluctance could be explained by two factors: the roughly equal size and power of the two countries for much of the second half of the twentieth century and, as argued by India's External Affairs Minister, Subrahmanyam Jaishankar, in 2024, a romantic and ideological view of China.[12] As the power gap with China widened, New Delhi began to see the consequences of Beijing's growing military and economic capabilities for India's interests in sustaining peace and stability on their mutual border, retaining its regional primacy in South Asia, playing a lead role in the Indian Ocean and elevating its position in multilateral institutions. The next sections in this chapter look at the changes in India's China policy unfolding in these four areas.

Border dispute

Undefined borders, expansive territorial nationalism in Beijing and New Delhi, and contested trans-Himalayan linkages – in short, China's claim to a role in South Asia and India's claims to a special relationship with Tibet, and their relations with third parties, especially Pakistan, Russia and the United States – triggered persistent tensions, which poisoned relations between India and China. As the overland expansion of the empires of the British Raj and the Qing dynasty converged in the trans-Himalayan region in the late nineteenth and early twentieth centuries, territorial friction between the two large entities was inevitable.[13] Attempts to resolve this tension in the early decades of the twentieth century were unsuccessful. Independent India and the post-imperial republics in China (nationalist and communist) – which were deeply attached to territorial claims inherited from the past – found it hard to come to a settlement on the boundary dispute despite their declared commitment to build peaceful and friendly relations. As China gained control over Tibet and ended the region's semi-independent status, the Indo-Tibetan border became a contested India–China frontier.

The territorial question was further complicated by the special cultural and spiritual relationship between India and Tibet and the political and military ties that had developed between New Delhi and Lhasa under the British Raj. Nehru's government, echoing the position taken by the Raj, argued that it recognised China's 'suzerainty' but not 'sovereignty' over Tibet.[14] Beijing, in turn, was sharply critical of Nehru's approach to Tibet. The attempts to finesse the issue broke down in 1959 amid the Chinese crackdown on Tibetan protests against Chinese Communist Party rule and the escape to India of the young fourteenth Dalai Lama – the spiritual and temporal head of the Tibetan people. As political tensions over the Dalai Lama soared, so did the military skirmishes, which were sparked by China's construction of roads in regions claimed by India. A full-fledged military conflict unfolded in 1962, ending a phase of attempted friendship between the two Asian giants.

After a prolonged freeze in bilateral relations, in the late 1980s, the two sides began to re-engage and constructed a new framework for resolving the territorial dispute while normalising ties. This involved negotiating on the settlement of the border, as well as developing a range of confidence-building measures to maintain peace and tranquillity on the frontier. Agreements penned in 1993 and 1996 were followed by a major effort in 2005 to resolve the boundary dispute.[15] An agreement on the principles and parameters of a boundary settlement outlined a framework to resolve the dispute. But no sooner was the agreement signed than differences emerged on interpreting the terms of the agreement.

This attempt by New Delhi and Beijing to build a stable and peaceful border was reasonably successful and had a positive effect on bilateral relations for nearly a quarter of a century. But the complexities of the border dispute and deep differences on how to address them would trump efforts to stabilise the boundary.[16] The size of the challenge is reflected in the large swathes of territory in dispute. India claims about 38,000 square kilometres of territory in eastern Ladakh, which is now under Chinese control. And Beijing claims 90,000 km^2 of territory in the eastern Himalayas – a region India calls Arunachal Pradesh and China calls South Tibet. The scale of the dispute is amplified by the lack of agreement on extended tracts of the nearly 3,600 km border on the exact nature of the current disposition or the 'line of actual control' (LAC). The areas of overlapping claims on different parts of this border have become zones of continuous military friction.

Once a contested but neglected frontier in the twentieth century, it has now become a tension-prone border, as infrastructure development in the border regions and the capacities of the two militaries to operate close to the border have risen. The more active patrolling of the contested zones has increased the chances of conflict. In the 2013 and 2014 crises in eastern Ladakh, the construction of new infrastructure in zones of overlapping claims triggered military stand-offs that were resolved through high-level negotiations. The site of the third confrontation in 2017 was the Doklam plateau at the trijunction of India, Bhutan and China in the eastern Himalayas. The crisis unfolded in June, when Indian troops intervened to stop the construction of a Chinese road on the Doklam plateau, which is claimed by both Beijing and Thimphu. The area is close to the narrow Siliguri Corridor, the vulnerable 'chicken's neck' that connects the Indian mainland to the northeastern states. The stand-off was resolved ten weeks later with an agreement between New Delhi and Beijing to disengage their troops. Although the escalation was contained, China remains in occupation of the plateau and has continued its construction activity there.

The 2020 crisis in eastern Ladakh was far more serious and proved to be more difficult to resolve. A series of incremental steps, culminating in the October 2024 agreement on restoring patrolling rights in some of the disputed areas, helped defuse the conflict and created conditions for a calibrated bilateral engagement towards normalising the relationship.[17] In April–May 2020, India was surprised by the large-scale mobilisation of Chinese troops on the disputed frontier in violation of the long-standing agreements calling for prior notification of major troop movements and avoiding their concentration close to the border. Unlike the previous crises, the 2020 action by China seemed to be a deliberate political move to gain territory and came in the middle of India's struggle to cope with the unfolding COVID-19 pandemic. New Delhi mobilised more than 50,000 troops and deployed them against the People's Liberation Army (PLA) forces ranged on the border. Even as talks to deal with the crisis began, a violent clash between the two forces in the Galwan valley in June 2020 saw the first deaths on the disputed frontier since the 1967 clashes in Sikkim.

The crisis raised questions about the credibility and sustainability of the old framework for maintaining peace and tranquillity on the border.

From the Indian perspective at least, China's attitude to border management seemed to become more assertive. A seasoned China hand in India attributed the change to the shifting balance of power between the two states:

> Whenever there is no balance of power, the Chinese tend to take India more seriously because they need to have enough other countries with them to ensure a balance in the world. That is why, to my understanding, we saw a number of positive developments between India and China take place between 1990 and 2010. By 2010, the situation had begun to change, and the world had returned to a more balanced state. By this point, the threats had also reduced for China. It had normalized relations with the West, and it had outstripped India economically, diplomatically and militarily. As a result of this, China did not feel compelled to either clarify the LAC or resolve the boundary.[18]

This argument has not been common in the Indian discourse on China. While Indian diplomats instinctively understood the impact of the widening power gap with Beijing at the turn of the twenty-first century, New Delhi's official discourse downplayed the gathering China challenge on the border until the 2010s. On the face of it, China's muscular posture on the border was not exceptional. China was demonstrating assertiveness in the East and South China seas as well. The growing gap between the power of China and that of its neighbours seemed to give Beijing the confidence to redeem its historical territorial claims. It took a while before New Delhi fully grasped the significance of this turn in China's approach – and not until the 2017 and 2020 crises. The 2013 crisis in eastern Ladakh did not make a material difference to the policy of the United Progressive Alliance (UPA) government under Manmohan Singh, which focused on deeper engagement with China and bet on the prospect of a boundary settlement. It also seemed to give credence to the tendentious argument that it was India's growing warmth with the US, marked by the historic civilian-nuclear deal of 2005, that turned Beijing against New Delhi. Whether it believed the argument or not, the UPA government in its second term certainly began to slow down its security engagement with Washington; it also endorsed the idea of 'non-alignment 2.0', which cautioned against drawing too close the US.[19]

Although the National Democratic Alliance (NDA) government that took charge in 2014 did not have the ideological baggage of non-alignment held by the Congress Party, the UPA's predominant coalition partner, the NDA's leader, Narendra Modi, was confident of the possibility of deepening ties with China. During his period as chief minister of Gujarat (2001–14), Modi made frequent visits to China and was impressed by its massive economic growth and pragmatic policies.[20] Yet it was not long before Prime Minister Modi was confronted with his first border crisis with China at Chumar in eastern Ladakh.[21] It burst into public view just as Modi was laying out the red carpet for Xi Jinping's first visit to India as president of China in September 2014. Modi had made special arrangements to receive Xi in his home state of Gujarat. Intense conversations between the two leaders apparently led to a quick resolution of the military crisis after Xi returned home. But Modi had been notified of the new dynamic between New Delhi and Beijing stemming from the shift in the balance of power between the two.

The 2017 stand-off persuaded New Delhi to take a fresh look at the India–China relationship even as it sought high-level engagement with Beijing to find remedial measures. Modi's two summits with Xi in 2018 and 2019 did not produce any progress. The 2020 crisis was the last straw and convinced New Delhi to take concrete actions against China's expansionism. Given that Modi had presented himself to the Indian electorate as strong on security, the pressure on the nationalist government to respond vigorously was real. New Delhi unveiled a series of measures to cope with the breakdown of the old framework of engaging with Beijing. One was to speed up the modernisation of Indian infrastructure on the border to match the transformation on the other side, which had enhanced the PLA's operational capabilities at the border and provided the basis for its assertiveness. Although the importance of closing the infrastructure gap on the frontier was recognised in the UPA years, the NDA government lent urgency to the task.[22] Secondly, New Delhi dropped its relaxed approach to force deployment on the China frontier. During the Kargil conflict with Pakistan in the summer of 1999, New Delhi moved troops from the border with China to the boundary with Pakistan. In the last few years, New Delhi has moved them back to the China border, even as it raises new divisions to cope with the mounting Chinese challenge there.[23]

Thirdly, in the wake of the 2020 crisis, New Delhi sought to raise the costs of conflict for China by scrutinising and curtailing Chinese investments in India, banning Chinese apps and keeping Huawei out of the fifth-generation telecommunications technology (5G) roll-out process.[24] Although India's trade volumes with China have continued to mount, New Delhi has taken a strategic decision to limit India's economic exposure to China. This has included walking out of the Regional Comprehensive Economic Partnership (RCEP) – the free-trade arrangement among the members of the Association of Southeast Asian Nations and five other leading Asian economies.[25] One of the main reasons for New Delhi's withdrawal was its concern that cheap Chinese manufactured goods were hollowing out India's manufacturing capability.

Fourthly, India significantly reduced its political engagement with China. While Indian leaders continued to sit with their Chinese counterparts in Shanghai Cooperation Organisation (SCO), RIC and BRICS forum meetings, New Delhi was unwilling to resume a bilateral dialogue with China without the restoration of the status quo ante on the border, which had been disturbed by the developments in Galwan. In response to continuous calls from China to set the border question aside and normalise the relationship, New Delhi repeatedly insisted that the 'state of the border reflects the state of the relationship'.[26] India has stated that it cannot simply accept China's unilateral attempt to change the territorial status quo on the disputed border and has kept up patient engagement with China on the military-diplomatic level on restoring the status quo ante in the border regions. By the end of 2024, 21 rounds of dialogue at the level of senior commander had helped generate some disengagement at four of the six friction points.[27] Under these arrangements, both sides will step back from the points of direct confrontation and not patrol an agreed no man's land. The friction on patrolling rights in Depsang and Demchok in eastern Ladakh was sorted out at a meeting in October 2024. The military disengagement in Ladakh had opened the door for renewed political dialogue; but the structural tensions on the Sino-Indian border are nowhere near resolution. The military crisis of 2020 and the difficulty of resolving it has raised more basic questions about India's defensive military strategy on the border.[28] Should India continue to uphold the agreements that China has violated?

Should India persist in the policies that have been far too reactive and defensive in their orientation? Should India respond with assertive and proactive policies of its own?

Fifthly, at the broader political level, New Delhi has recognised the need to balance against China by building stronger bilateral defence ties with the US and developing stronger regional mechanisms in partnership with Washington. Following the 2017 crisis, New Delhi acceded to the US request to revive the Quadrilateral Security Dialogue, or the Quad.[29] After 2020, India expanded the annual *Malabar* naval exercises with the United States to include Australia, widened the Quad's agenda and elevated the Quad dialogue first to the ministerial level during the first Trump administration and eventually to the summit level in the Biden era.[30] New Delhi's approach to the Quad is clearly correlated to the shifting dynamic on the Sino-Indian border.

Sixthly, as relations with China worsened after the Galwan crisis, New Delhi began to nuance its long-standing One China policy, which it had so strictly adhered to in the past.[31] Internally, the government of India became far more open in flaunting its connection with the Dalai Lama and Tibet.[32] New Delhi also publicised the use of the Special Frontier Force – composed mainly of Tibetan refugees in India and raised and nurtured by the Indian Army over the decades – in the 2020 border conflict with the Chinese.[33] The 2020 crisis also led to more active Indian engagement with Taiwan, though New Delhi's ties with the island remain well below the level at which other countries in Asia maintain their relations with Taipei.[34]

Although the border dispute is one of the most difficult challenges confronting India and China, it is not the only one bedevilling the bilateral relationship. Even if the border is returned to peace and tranquillity and a new framework is found to resolve the boundary dispute, there are other issues that flow out of the shifting balance of power between India and China. This shift casts a dark shadow over India's near and extended neighbourhood. The next two sections of the chapter discuss the new regional dynamics in the subcontinent and the Indian Ocean.

South Asia

Beijing's growing influence in the subcontinent is one of the factors that creates tension in Sino-Indian relations. While India saw itself as the legatee of the British Raj, which exercised paramountcy in the subcontinent, China refused to accept India's claims to an exclusive sphere of influence in South Asia. Beijing found it easy to develop a strong profile in the subcontinent by exploiting the divisions within partitioned South Asia. If the Indian subcontinent was divided in 1947, China was united under communist rule in 1949. This geopolitical asymmetry continues to give Beijing a major advantage in South Asia's international relations. As China's power rose relative to that of India, Beijing's capacity to undermine New Delhi's dominance of the region became steadily stronger. South Asia's internal squabbles provided a thick rope for China to tie India down within the subcontinent.[35]

Although India sought to sustain its regional primacy after independence, its inward economic orientation and lack of interest in regional trade and connectivity with its neighbours, the rise of anti-India nationalism in the smaller countries of the region, and New Delhi's occasional political and military interventions in the neighbourhood created conditions under which Beijing could – with little effort – find ways to constrain Indian power in the region. Even as India talked about its special relationship with its neighbours, China offered sovereign equality as the basis for engagement. While New Delhi insisted that other powers should keep out of the subcontinent's quarrels, much in the manner of the Raj, its neighbours turned to non-South Asian actors, including China, to balance against India and enhance their strategic autonomy in relation to New Delhi.[36]

China was quick to seize on the long-standing confrontation between India and Pakistan and reached out to Islamabad, offering it substantive and sustained diplomatic, political, economic and military assistance over the decades.[37] That Pakistan was part of the anti-communist alliances in Asia and a close security partner of the United States did not seem to make any difference to China's strategic engagement with Pakistan.[38] China also moved to settle, on an interim basis, its boundary with Pakistan in the Kashmir province soon after the 1962 war with India. China denounced India's intervention in the vivisection of East Pakistan in 1971 and India's test of a nuclear device in 1974 as reflecting New Delhi's hegemonic ambitions in South Asia and sought to actively counter India. Beijing helped Islamabad acquire its own nuclear-weapon and missile capabilities from the early 1970s.[39]

China also intensified its outreach to the smaller nations of the subcontinent. While the scale of the assistance was a lot less in scope and content than that offered to Pakistan, it was enough for China to gain significant political ground within South Asia. As China became the second-largest economy in the world and its comprehensive national power rose rapidly in the twenty-first century, its salience in the subcontinent likewise increased dramatically. As in so many regions across the world, China has become a major economic partner for all countries in South Asia, including India. China has a long record of investing in strategic-infrastructure projects in the subcontinent. In the 1960s, China built the 'friendship highway' from Tibet to Nepal. And in the 1970s, it built the Karakoram Highway between Xinjiang and the Pakistan-controlled Kashmir region – a very demanding project in terms of terrain and engineering – triggering much strategic unease in India.[40] That record of regional infrastructure-building acquired new weight at the turn of the twenty-first century, thanks to the growing financial and technical resources at Beijing's command.[41] Many of these past projects provided templates for more expansive ideas on transborder economic corridors with Pakistan (China–Pakistan Economic Corridor, or CPEC) and Nepal (China–Nepal Economic Corridor, or CNEC). China also steadily began to raise its profile as a security actor in the region thanks to its arms supplies to India's neighbours and willingness to help them balance against New Delhi. China's soft power, too, has rapidly grown in the subcontinent as Beijing devotes special energies to cultivate a range of elites – from the political classes to the media and religious establishments.[42]

Through the second half of the twentieth century, China – despite its growing ties with India's neighbours – was not the dominant power in South Asia's international relations. Notwithstanding China's transfer of nuclear-weapon and missile technologies to Pakistan, the West remained the most influential partner for Islamabad. That has changed significantly in the twenty-first century. The first two decades of the twenty-first century saw the US pour billions of dollars into Pakistan to pursue its nation-building and counter-terror interests in Afghanistan. But the US neglected other foreign-policy interests in the region.[43] If US policy towards Pakistan became unidimensional, Beijing steadily emerged as a more comprehensive partner to Pakistan – extending growing economic, political, diplomatic and military support to Islamabad.[44] If the US partnership was seen as transactional and episodic, Pakistan's political class and the establishment viewed China as a more reliable and sustained partner.

As elsewhere in the world, China's ability to engage with the smaller South Asian countries benefited from its policy of 'non-intervention' in the internal affairs of the developing world.[45] It certainly stood in contrast to India's deep involvement in the domestic politics of its neighbours and the United States' emphasis on human rights and democracy promotion. With its growing international clout and status as a permanent member of the UN Security Council, China could offer South Asian states considerable international protection against Indian and American pressures on their domestic politics. In Sri Lanka, for example, Beijing has helped Colombo resist Western and Indian pressures to grant Tamil minority rights.[46]

For its part, India has struggled to extend its influence in the region through economic integration. Once South Asia adopted the Washington Consensus on growth – a set of policy recommendations that called for economic liberalisation and globalisation – in the 1990s, regional economic integration in the subcontinent should have been a natural consequence. Although all countries have moved towards opening up their economies, the process has been uneven and slow and has not led to deeper regionalism. The notion that South Asia is the 'least integrated region' of the world acquired even greater salience because the rest of the world took to regionalism at a fast clip in this era of renewed economic globalisation. There are, of course, good historical reasons for the entrenched resistance to regionalism in South Asia.

The subcontinent under the Raj was a single economic space. The tragic political partition of the subcontinent need not have been followed by an economic partition. But New Delhi's adoption of a socialist and inward-oriented economic path found its echo eventually among most of its neighbours. This made trade and export promotion marginal to the economic-development strategies of India and its neighbours, which in turn meant they had little interest in facilitating trade or maintaining the connectivity inherited from the Raj in good repair. The deterioration of India's relations with Pakistan and Bangladesh and the securitisation of the borders between them steadily made even minimal trade difficult.

The worsening of India–Pakistan relations in the 1990s saw Islamabad adopt a deliberate policy of 'economic non-cooperation' with New Delhi until the dispute over Kashmir is resolved. Even when it suited Pakistan's immediate commercial interests, and despite occasional encouragement from the US to reconsider, Islamabad stuck to this policy. Most other countries in the region, too, were hesitant to engage in deeper economic integration with India. The rise in anti-India nationalism and the perceived need to balance against India in these neighbouring states led to the domestic politicisation of major commercial projects with New Delhi and significant internal opposition to deeper economic ties with India. The situation began to ease only in the second decade of the twenty-first century. The return of Sheikh Hasina to power in Bangladesh in 2008 and the convergence of political interests between New Delhi and Dhaka laid the foundation for the steady expansion of economic engagement between the two countries.[47] Hasina's removal in 2024 has, however, raised questions about the future of this relationship.

As it woke up to the growing Chinese economic influence in its neighbourhood, New Delhi began reversing its complacent attitude towards regional integration. Under the Modi government, New Delhi has intensified its efforts to compete with China on connectivity projects.[48] India has also begun to shed its past reluctance to encourage its private-sector companies to participate in regional projects.[49] One of India's top businesses, the Adani Group, secured the tender for Colombo port's West International Terminal project in Sri Lanka. Earlier, Adani had won the bid to develop a joint power plant with Bangladesh and a port contract and special-economic-zone contract in

Thilawa, Myanmar.[50] Although the promotion of private-sector projects brought greater efficiency to India's regional economic diplomacy, it was controversial at home because of the close ties between the Adani Group and the Modi government. In the end, though, these controversies were overtaken by the shifting domestic politics in the neighbourhood that cast a shadow over some of these projects. In Sri Lanka, Adani withdrew from a wind-energy project after the government in Colombo changed hands in 2024. In Bangladesh, the ouster of Hasina's government in 2024 led to fresh scrutiny of the terms of power projects with Adani. And in Myanmar, US sanctions against entities controlled by the military junta led to Adani's withdrawal from the Thilawa port.[51]

Since India's resources are inadequate to compete with China commercially, New Delhi has explored collaboration with Tokyo in bidding for regional infrastructure projects.[52] Although no major contract has yet been won, it has created the basis for more Indian openness to partnering with others. In the past, New Delhi actively sought to keep Western powers out of regional economic cooperation. It is now ready for strategic economic coordination with the US and Japan within the region. US grants, for example, supported the construction of power-transmission lines between Nepal and India.[53]

The impact of a rising China was not limited to the changing military balance on the disputed Sino-Indian frontier or the scale of Beijing's economic profile in the subcontinent. As China invested ever more in its defence modernisation, its ability to extend military assistance, provide arms and cultivate institutional relationships with the armed forces of India's neighbours steadily increased. This led New Delhi to launch long-neglected defence diplomacy with its neighbours in the twenty-first century. It began to supply defence equipment, institute regular high-level military exchanges and develop joint mechanisms for security coordination.[54] Although India's military diplomacy widened its reach among neighbouring states, it also whetted the appetite of these neighbours to leverage for their own benefit the military competition between New Delhi and Beijing.

Indian Ocean

The growing and multidimensional challenges to India's security and regional interests from China and New Delhi's turn to the US and its allies to balance against China are even more strongly manifested in the broader Indian Ocean region. Historically, China's economic, political and military maritime interactions with India were episodic rather than continuous. After all, India faces the Indian Ocean and China faces the Pacific, and the Himalayas are a large barrier between the continental masses of China and India. Buddhism travelled to China by sea as well as overland across the Himalayas. Southern India's engagement with southern China acquired significance under the Chola kingdom, which ruled in the current Tamil Nadu region in the tenth and eleventh centuries.[55] Zheng He's expeditions to the Indian Ocean under Ming rule in the thirteenth and fourteenth centuries saw significant direct Chinese engagement with the Indian Ocean polities.[56] While the Qing dynasty oversaw the significant expansion of China's overland empire, its maritime ambitions remained limited.

The consolidation of a coherent state in China in the second half of the twentieth century and the rapid rise of China's comprehensive national power in the early twenty-first led to Beijing's growing influence not only across the Himalayan frontier in South Asia, but also in the waters of the subcontinent. As part of its military modernisation, China began to build a substantive navy in the twenty-first century.[57] The initial focus of the PLA Navy (PLAN) was on the western Pacific, where it had been on the back foot throughout the twentieth century thanks to US domination of the first island chain, from Japan to Taiwan, the Philippines and Indonesia.[58] Chinese interest in the Indian Ocean was relatively low in the twentieth century, but it was not completely off their radar. Although it was not defined in maritime terms, Mao's China sought friendly ties with island nations such as Sri Lanka; it also undertook significant infrastructure projects in East Africa, such as the Tan-Zam Railway, as part of an effort to expand its influence across the developing world in the 1960s and 1970s.[59] It was not until the mid-1980s, though, that the PLAN showed up in the Indian Ocean, when a small contingent of Chinese ships called on South Asian ports – Dhaka, Colombo and Karachi.

Although the normalisation of Sino-US relations reduced the immediate pressures on Taiwan from the late 1970s, China's ambition to integrate the island into the mainland demanded Beijing's preparation for that contingency. As its naval capabilities grew from the turn of the twenty-first century, China's ambitions expanded beyond the western Pacific into the Indian Ocean. At that time, many observers of Chinese maritime strategy argued that Beijing was unlikely to focus on the Indian Ocean given the scale of the challenges – the massive US military presence in the western Pacific and its East Asian alliances. Yet, in the first decade of the twenty-first century, China adopted a 'two-ocean strategy' and pursued it with deliberation.[60] The justification for its presence in the Indian Ocean was articulated in 2005 in terms of a 'Malacca Dilemma', which was rooted in the importance of the Indian Ocean's mineral and energy resources for China's economic growth.[61] Beijing argued that the flow of vital resources through the Malacca Strait – there are not many alternative routes from the eastern African coast and the Gulf to China's industrial heartland on the Pacific coast – could be choked by its adversaries.[62]

This argument also spurred Beijing to promote large-scale infrastructure projects linking China to the Indian Ocean within the broad framework of the Belt and Road Initiative (BRI).[63] The CPEC, linking Xinjiang with the Arabian Sea coast, was launched in 2015 and became the signature BRI project. Beijing also unveiled plans for the China–Myanmar Economic Corridor (CMEC) in 2018, which would connect Yunnan province with the Bay of Bengal.[64] China has also explored various proposals to cut through the Malay Peninsula to reduce dependence on the Malacca Strait.

Even as it sought to reduce vulnerabilities in moving natural resources from the Indian Ocean to China, Beijing began to explore the prospects of boosting its in situ naval presence in the Indian Ocean. This has involved a multi-pronged effort. One approach has been to grow the presence of the PLAN in the Indian Ocean.[65] There have been regular deployments of Chinese naval squadrons into the Indian Ocean since 2008 for counter-piracy missions. Although piracy has diminished, these deployments have continued.[66] China's forays into the Andaman Sea and the Bay of Bengal have become frequent, and the Indian Navy has had to occasionally chase away PLAN ships from the waters around the Andaman and Nicobar Islands.[67] The PLAN's deployment of research ships in the Indian Ocean has also steadily risen. Additionally, China has begun initial work on a site for deep-seabed mining in the central Indian Ocean.

A second prong has been the building of dual-use facilities – like ports – that could serve both commercial and military purposes for China.[68] In what was widely described as the 'string of pearls' strategy, China built several ports at critical locations in the Indian Ocean.[69] These include ports and related facilities at Sittwe (Myanmar), Hambantota (Sri Lanka), Gwadar (Pakistan) and elsewhere in the Indian Ocean littoral.

Thirdly, China has been looking for military bases and facilities in the region. The first Chinese base was unveiled in Djibouti in 2017. This is unlikely to be the last. In 2021, China began establishing a miliary presence at Cambodia's Ream Naval facility. The PLAN, according to the US Department of Defense, is also reportedly looking for additional military and dual-use bases and facilities in the region to aid its power projection into the Indian Ocean. Among the Indian Ocean countries reported to be under consideration in Beijing are Indonesia, Kenya, Myanmar, Pakistan, the Seychelles, Singapore, Sri Lanka, Tanzania, Thailand and the United Arab Emirates. China has also apparently made overtures to Vanuatu and the Solomon Islands in the South Pacific. According to the Pentagon, 'the PLA is most interested in military access along the SLOCs [sea lines of communication] from China to the Strait of Hormuz, Africa, and the Pacific Islands'.[70]

Fourthly, China has increased its engagement with the critically located Indian Ocean island states – especially Maldives, Mauritius, the Seychelles and Sri Lanka. This has been of growing concern to New Delhi, given the deep historic connections between India and these island states.[71] Unlike in the past, when China largely stayed away from intervening in the domestic politics of small states, it now actively engages in the internal politics of strategic island states. In Maldives, for example, there has been speculation that Beijing has been actively supporting the anti-India factions and whipping up the 'India out' campaign.[72] Competing political formations within Maldives have actively drawn Chinese and Indian interventions in their favour. If the government that took charge in 2018 under Ibrahim Solih favoured an India First policy, the Mohamed Muizzu government that was elected in 2023 has sought to distance itself from New Delhi, at least initially.

The scale and scope of PLAN activity in the Indian Ocean have steadily grown in the twenty-first century. Although the PLAN does not yet have long enough legs to operate as a fighting force in the Indian Ocean, New Delhi is aware that the security challenges presented by the Chinese maritime and naval engagement in the Indian Ocean region will continue to grow. This, in turn, has added an expansive dimension to India's China problem. Although maritime geography continues to favour the Indian Navy, China's capacity to blunt India's naval capabilities by supporting its neighbours has grown. China's maritime and naval diplomacy also provides a basis for deepening security ties with India's maritime neighbours.

The Indian response has been twofold. On the one hand, it has ramped up its own maritime engagement in the region. On the other hand, due to the gap between its own resources and the pace of Chinese expansion in the region, India has embarked on a strategy of building coalitions through a range of bilateral and 'minilateral' means, as well as new multilateral initiatives. None of them are more important than the deepening partnerships with the US and its allies.

Multilateral arena

China's challenge to India has inevitably gone beyond the disputed border, the immediate South Asian neighbourhood and the extended Indian Ocean region to the international domain. It has also undermined one of the central propositions of India's earlier China policy – that India can cooperate with China in the international and multilateral domains despite their unresolved boundary dispute and the geopolitical friction in the near and extended neighbourhood. This proposition was rooted in the ideas discussed earlier – Asian solidarity and the belief in the need and potential to transcend the Western international order. At a time when the West was isolating Mao's China, New Delhi insisted on engaging with Beijing and encouraged its neighbours in the subcontinent and in Asia more widely to do the same. India took the lead in inviting communist China to participate in the Afro-Asian conference at Bandung in 1955, despite criticisms from the West.

The 1962 war with China did not alter India's One China policy nor the core assumptions behind the idea of solidarity among non-Western nations. After India began to normalise relations with China at the turn of the 1990s, New Delhi once again bet on the prospects for deeper multilateral engagement with Beijing. While the border remained relatively tranquil, there were new issues to address, such as China's support for Pakistan's nuclear and missile development. However, India did not let these new obstacles get in the way of expanding international cooperation. New Delhi was convinced that deeper economic engagement and international cooperation with Beijing would build more bilateral trust and create an environment conducive to resolving the boundary dispute and mitigating other simmering tensions. These hopes, however, turned out to be a mirage. In 2021, India's External Affairs Minister, Subrahmanyam Jaishankar, publicly highlighted China's opposition to India's effort to secure a permanent seat on the UN Security Council and membership in the Nuclear Suppliers Group. He also highlighted Beijing's resistance to the UN designation of Pakistani individuals as international terrorists for their involvement in violent attacks against India.[73] China also supported Pakistan's efforts to bring the Kashmir question before the UN Security Council in the aftermath of India's 2019 decision to change Kashmir's constitutional status.[74]

By the 2020s, the edifice of India's imagined multilateral cooperation, pursued unilaterally and with much ideological enthusiasm in New Delhi, began to crumble. For an India that insisted on recognising the People's Republic of China as the legitimate representative of China in the 1950s and 1960s and turned down offers to take Beijing's seat in the 1950s, it was galling to see China undermine India's own aspirations for a larger international role.[75] If India had viewed China through the power-political prism, New Delhi would have known that Beijing had no reason to let other Asian powers, especially New Delhi and Tokyo, become permanent members of the UN Security Council. Whether it is reforming the UN Security Council, or defending its core interests on Kashmir, terrorism and nuclear issues, India today is ranged against China in the multilateral system. India has also been battling Chinese discourse power in the United Nations and other multilateral forums.[76] Sharply critical of the BRI, India now prevents Chinese efforts to inject positive references to the BRI into collective declarations at multilateral forums like the Non-Aligned Movement or avoids endorsing them when they cannot be blocked.[77] While India had supported China's entry into the World Trade Organization at the turn of the 2000s without asking for much in return, and backed the creation of a BRICS bank in 2014 and the establishment of the Asian Infrastructure Investment Bank in 2015, it walked out of the RCEP at the end of 2019, as its economic contradictions with China became sharper.

The new competitive dynamic between New Delhi and Beijing has expressed itself even more sharply in the regional domain. Consider two regional institutions of major importance to India – the South Asian Association for Regional Cooperation (SAARC) and the Indian Ocean Rim Association (IORA). India's neighbours have sought to bring China into the fold of SAARC, but New Delhi has fiercely resisted the move. While New Delhi could not block China from becoming an observer of SAARC in 2005, India encouraged the US and Western states to join SAARC as observers too. India has also blocked China's entry into the IORA as a full member; Beijing is setting up its own Indian Ocean forum.

The collapse of the illusion of multilateral cooperation between India and China at the global and regional levels underlines the deeper structural divergence between the two countries. India's hopes of managing the boundary dispute with China, minimising regional friction in South Asia and the Indian Ocean, deepening economic ties and actively collaborating in global governance have all come to nought, and New Delhi is now actively engaged in a rivalry with Beijing on all these fronts. It is also turning to Washington to cope with the multiple structural challenges presented by China. The next chapter will explore India's growing engagement with the US in a range of domains.

CHAPTER THREE

The US partnership

Introduction

Since the middle of the twentieth century, a triangular dynamic has operated between India, China and the United States. It was only rarely that all three countries enjoyed productive relations with each other. During the 1950s, the US did not recognise the People's Republic of China and was eager to gain India's support to isolate the regime of Mao Zedong and overcome the communist threat to Asia. But India was trying to befriend China in the 1950s and therefore was critical of Washington's China policy. New Delhi also made light of the communist challenge and opposed US Cold War alliances in Asia.[1] When Sino-Indian relations entered a crisis mode with the Chinese attack on India at the end of 1962, New Delhi turned to Washington for support. President John F. Kennedy was eager to seize the moment to build a new partnership with India to counter China.[2] But that effort stalled amidst India–US differences over Kashmir and New Delhi's continuing criticism of American policy in Southeast Asia. By the early 1970s, with the break-up of the Sino-Soviet compact, the US began engaging with China. New Delhi's ties with Beijing worsened and its warmth towards Moscow grew. India began to normalise ties with China in the late 1980s, as Beijing and Washington embarked on an expansive partnership. Sino-US ties rapidly became dense and far more consequential than New Delhi's relations with Washington or Beijing.

It was only in the twenty-first century that the idea of India as a potential balancer to a rising China in Asia once again gained ground in Washington.[3] In New Delhi, too, there was a new readiness to look at this idea closely. As China's relations with the US and India deteriorated in the second decade of the twenty-first century, the strategic partnership between New Delhi and Washington began to acquire greater traction. Central to the new bonhomie is the shared need to rebalance an Asia destabilised by China's assertiveness. This chapter examines the evolution of this partnership and the challenges that remain in consolidating it. The first section reviews the expanding defence cooperation between New Delhi and Washington. The subsequent sections examine the structural issues facilitating and complicating bilateral ties. They include differences between India and the US on perceptions of and policies towards Pakistan, the emergence of the Indo-Pacific construct, and the formation and development of the Quadrilateral Security Dialogue (Quad).

Defence cooperation

If the first decades after India's independence saw New Delhi drift away from Washington towards Moscow, there was an attempt in both New Delhi and Washington to recalibrate bilateral ties after the Soviet invasion of Afghanistan in 1979. Moscow's growing isolation in the region after the invasion, New Delhi's emphasis on diversifying its great-power relations and Washington's quest to loosen India's ties to the Soviet Union in the 1980s provided the context for rethinking India–US relations. The 1980s saw Indian prime ministers Indira Gandhi and

Rajiv Gandhi respond positively to overtures from US president Ronald Reagan to reset bilateral ties. India's priorities were to regain access to US technologies and explore the possibilities of acquiring advanced weapons technologies. As India embarked on the Light Combat Aircraft programme in the mid-1980s, the US agreed to offer engines and help develop flight-control systems. This was a break from past US policy towards India and highlighted the possibilities for future defence cooperation.[4] The easing of US–Soviet relations under Soviet leader Mikhail Gorbachev saw New Delhi begin an institutional engagement with the US defence establishment.

The early 1990s saw several new developments in India–US defence cooperation. These included annual *Malabar* naval exercises, which began in 1992, and exchanges between the two armies under the so-called Kicklighter proposals. The visit of US defense secretary William Perry to India in 1995 saw the finalisation of a structured engagement between the armed forces, civilian military leaders and the defence-research establishments of the two states. If India was tentative and hesitant thanks to the lingering legacy of suspicion of the United States among the political class and bureaucracy, the sanctions Washington imposed after India's nuclear tests in May 1998 cast a shadow over the bilateral defence relationship. The shadow was lifted when George W. Bush became president and devoted special attention to building a new defence partnership.[5]

Several critical developments in the early 2000s laid the foundation for an expanding defence partnership. The Bush administration's emphasis on treating India as a major power that could shape the wider Asian balance of power and 'de-hyphenating' US ties with India and Pakistan made a profound difference to New Delhi's perceptions of the potential for partnership with the US.[6] The Bharatiya Janata Party (BJP) government, in turn, sought to shed the overweight baggage of non-alignment and declared the US a 'natural ally' of India in 2003.[7] The BJP, in its original avatar as the Bharatiya Jan Sangh (1951–77), was critical of India's tilt to the Soviet Union under prime ministers Jawaharlal Nehru and Indira Gandhi and of the efforts of the Indian National Congress to cultivate China. Its conservative social values and deep suspicion of communist ideology made it more amenable to engagement with the United States. In the wake of the 9/11 attacks on New York and Washington, New Delhi offered the US access to its military facilities for a potential armed response. Although Washington did not take up that offer, it signalled a new Indian approach to security cooperation with the United States.[8] New Delhi also actively considered Bush's request to send troops to Iraq in 2003.[9] Although India did not in the end deploy forces, old political taboos in New Delhi were clearly being loosened under the Atal Bihari Vajpayee government. When the 2004 Boxing Day tsunami hit the eastern Indian Ocean, the Indian Navy was the first to arrive and begin relief operations. It was soon joined by the navies of Australia, Japan and the US to intensify the relief effort. This four-way cooperation provided a real basis to visualise the outline of a quadrilateral security forum.[10]

The George W. Bush administration's second term built on these bilateral developments. Condoleezza Rice, who moved from the National Security Council to take charge of the State Department, travelled to India in March 2005 to offer a comprehensive partnership to New Delhi.[11] At its core was the proposition that the US was ready to support India's rise as a major power in the international system without asking for anything specific in return from India. Although this US claim was viewed with widespread scepticism in New Delhi, the Bush administration was quite clear that assisting India's rise was in the United States' interest and that it would help secure a new balance of power in Asia and the world in favour of freedom.[12] This new US approach provided the basis for the framework for defence cooperation between the two countries (June 2005) and the historic civil-nuclear initiative (July 2005).[13]

The 2005 defence framework set out an ambitious agenda for bilateral security cooperation, as well as the institutional arrangements to implement it over a decade. It covered a range of subjects, including collaboration between the armed forces, counter-terrorism, disaster relief and humanitarian operations, military exercises to promote inter-operability, regular dialogue between civilian leaderships of defence establishments, intelligence sharing, arms transfers and collaborative defence-industrial production.

The civil-nuclear initiative was even bolder in seeking to reintegrate India into the global nuclear order. Bush believed that helping grow India's national power was a worthwhile objective, and the nuclear deal was a critical step towards winning New Delhi's confidence. He was willing to invest a significant amount of political capital in implementing it.

The civil-nuclear deal sought to end India's prolonged disputes with the US and the global nuclear non-proliferation regime. India agreed to separate its civil- and military-nuclear programmes, put a significant section of the civilian programme under international safeguards and support global efforts to limit the spread of nuclear weapons. The US, for its part, promised to reverse its previous policy of rolling back India's nuclear-weapons programme, accept the reality of India as a nuclear-weapons state and lift US and international restrictions on civilian-nuclear cooperation with India. The last promise demanded major changes to US domestic non-proliferation law and the international norms governing civilian-nuclear commerce. There was considerable resistance from the arms-control establishment in Washington, which saw the initiative as undermining the Nuclear

Non-Proliferation Treaty (NPT), which India had never joined, legitimising India's nuclear-weapons programme and promoting the expansion of India's atomic arsenal (as international support for its civil-nuclear activities would allow for greater indigenous resources to be devoted to its military-nuclear activities). Bush, however, would have none of it, and did the heavy political lifting to get the deal through the US Congress, the International Atomic Energy Agency and the Nuclear Suppliers Group during 2005–08. Even in this relatively early period, Bush and key members of his administration perceived India as an indispensable part of their long-term China strategy and were willing to go to considerable lengths to assuage traditional Indian suspicions of the US.

In New Delhi, both the defence and nuclear agreements became politically controversial as the leftist parties – a critical section of the ruling United Progressive Alliance (UPA) coalition – expressed strong reservations about deeper strategic cooperation with the United States.[14] The five-state naval exercises in the Bay of Bengal that the Indian Navy convened in September 2007 drew not only vehement protests from Beijing but also popular demonstrations by leftist parties across India.[15] Domestic opponents of the US–India agreements argued that they would undermine India's non-alignment and independent foreign policy. Beyond the communist parties, some sections of the Congress Party were also very uncomfortable with the Manmohan Singh government's tilt towards the United States and were apparently successful in getting the leadership – Sonia Gandhi and Rahul Gandhi – to raise doubts. The Congress Party leadership was eager to withdraw from the nuclear deal, but Manmohan Singh's threat to resign over the issue obtained their reluctant acquiescence. As the leftist parties withdrew their support for the government, it had to obtain a vote of confidence in the upper house in 2008.[16]

While the government survived, the Congress Party's political resistance to engagement with the US only increased.

This expressed itself most vigorously in the defence domain as the UPA government dragged its feet on signing the so-called foundational agreements (see below) and went slow on the implementation of the 2005 defence framework. Although formal high-level talks took place between New Delhi and Washington, there was a political stasis in defence engagement. It is not clear whether the UPA government, had it returned to power in 2014, would have renewed the ten-year framework agreement signed in 2005. However, the National Democratic Alliance (NDA) government, led by Narendra Modi, had fewer political inhibitions in engaging with the United States. Modi invited US president Barack Obama to the Republic Day celebrations in January 2015, renewed the defence-framework agreement for another ten years and signed a broad declaration with Obama on their shared interests in the Indian Ocean and the Asia-Pacific.[17] The NDA government also signed the foundational agreements – the Logistics Exchange Memorandum of Agreement (LEMOA), Communications Compatibility and Security Agreement (COMCASA), Basic Exchange and Cooperation Agreement (BECA) and Security of Supplies Agreement (SOSA) – to facilitate greater cooperation between the armed forces of the two countries.[18] While the Pentagon had repeatedly pressed for the signing of these agreements since the early 2000s, the UPA government had been hesitant to move forward. The NDA government ended that political hesitation and put the engagement between the two armed forces on a stronger foundation.

The US–India defence relationship made steady progress under the administrations of Obama (2009–17) and Donald Trump in his first term in office (2017–21). By the end of the 2010s, the US conducted more military exercises with

India than any other partner, and the NDA government has overseen their increasing sophistication.[19] India's arms contracts with the United States since 2008 have been valued at US$20 billion.[20] The Indian defence establishment had its reservations about importing arms from the US; the fear of US sanctions and Washington's reluctance to abide by agreements by invoking new political considerations were a major dampener. But painstaking effort at the political level steadily nudged the arms relationship along. There was also a reverse flow, as Indian firms like the Tata Group became part of the supply chain for US defence majors like Lockheed Martin. As a result, the US has emerged as the largest destination for Indian defence exports, which are growing from a very low base.[21] On the Indian side, there was disappointment that the US remained hesitant in transferring military technologies. The Obama administration's Defence Trade and Technology Initiative was widely viewed in New Delhi as inadequate, especially in responding to India's demands for defence-technology transfer. Washington, in turn, was disappointed with India's continuing reluctance to support US operations in Asia and the Indian Ocean. Although the political resistance within the government to defence cooperation with the US has come down significantly under Modi, bureaucratic obstacles have persisted and prevented the fullest utilisation of the existing frameworks for deeper defence cooperation.

As challenges mounted from China for both India and the United States, there was a determined effort to overcome these obstacles as part of the effort to elevate the strategic partnership to a higher level. Prime Minister Modi's visit to Washington in June 2023 showcased important progress in defence relations. The US agreed to license a significant level of technology transfer in the manufacture of the GE 414 engines for fighter jets to India's Hindustan Aeronautics Limited. This landmark decision was part of the new defence-industrial road map that sought to 'provide policy direction to defence industries and enable co-production of advanced defence systems and collaborative research, testing, and prototyping of projects. Both sides are committed to addressing any regulatory barriers to defence industrial cooperation.' India, in turn, agreed to become a hub for the 'maintenance and repair for forward deployed U.S. Navy assets and the conclusion of Master Ship Repair Agreements with Indian shipyards. This will allow the U.S. Navy to expedite the contracting process for mid-voyage and emergent repair.' Modi and president Joe Biden agreed 'to work together for the creation of logistic, repair, and maintenance infrastructure for aircrafts and vessels in India'.[22] If Biden bent the US bureaucracy to liberalise defence-technology transfer to India, Modi overcame New Delhi's entrenched resistance to offer logistic facilities for the United States.

In an important move of long-term significance, the two leaders launched the US–India Defence Acceleration Ecosystem (INDUS-X) to widen the interface between the two defence establishments. Described as 'a network of universities, startups, industry and think tanks', INDUS-X sought to 'facilitate joint defence technology innovation, and co-production of advanced defence technology between the respective industries of the two countries'.[23] For India, the injection of US defence technology was intended to create a credible pathway for modernising its defence-industrial base. For the US, it was hoped that the new arrangements would help wean the Indian military establishment away from Russia and enhance New Delhi's deterrent capabilities against China over the longer term.

Pakistan

A critical factor that facilitated the transformation of India–US relations in the 2000s was Washington's disentanglement of its dealings with New Delhi from those with Islamabad. In the 1990s, the Clinton administration put two issues at the top of the agenda: resolving the Kashmir dispute between India and Pakistan and rolling back the nuclear-weapon and missile programmes of New Delhi and Islamabad.[24] These two issues were not seen as separate but as part of a single problem – Kashmir was the most dangerous nuclear flashpoint in the world. This framework also fitted with the long tradition of viewing India and Pakistan as a pair and on a par with each other.

The George W. Bush administration broke this paradigm by de-hyphenating US relations with Pakistan and India.[25] This was a demanding effort, especially at a time when the US sought Pakistan's support on stabilising the post-Taliban regime in Afghanistan and pursuing the war on terror in the immediate aftermath of the 9/11 attacks on New York and Washington. This new approach survived successive administrations, providing a basis for reducing the salience of the Pakistan factor in US relations with India.

The policy of de-hyphenation in the 2000s helped reduce New Delhi's entrenched suspicion of Washington's regional intentions in the subcontinent. That suspicion was rooted in the US decision to be led by Britain, the former colonial power of the subcontinent, on the question of Kashmir and other regional issues in the late 1940s and 1950s. If India saw Britain as biased towards Pakistan, the US inherited that stigma in the Indian political discourse. This was reinforced by several key US foreign-policy decisions. During the Cold War, US military support for Pakistan was an important obstacle to improving India's relations with the United States. Adding to this was the failed US effort to directly mediate on the Kashmir dispute in the early 1960s and Washington's tilt towards Pakistan during India's intervention to secure Bangladeshi independence.[26] If the US approach to the region in the 1990s accentuated Indian discomfort, policies enacted since the George W. Bush administration began to reduce the accumulated distrust.

Several dimensions of the new policy consensus in Washington can be delineated. The first is the decision to reverse US activism on Kashmir. While the Bush administration continued to defuse the military tensions between India and Pakistan in the early 2000s, it emphasised that the Kashmir problem was something to be negotiated between New Delhi and Islamabad. This counter-intuitively coincided with one of the more productive phases in India–Pakistan diplomatic engagement, when New Delhi and Islamabad came close to several agreements, including on Kashmir.[27] The return of the Democrats to power in 2009, however, raised the prospect of a return to the more traditional framework on South Asia.[28] The idea of linking the Kashmir and Afghan questions came to the fore once again.

The argument that India's rivalry with Pakistan was a critical factor in the unwillingness of Pakistan to fully support US objectives in Afghanistan gained some traction in Washington in the early years of the Obama administration. Giving satisfaction to Pakistan on Kashmir, through Indian concessions, was widely seen as a critical factor in changing Pakistan's unhelpful Afghan policies.[29] The appointment of Richard Holbrooke as special envoy on Afghanistan and Pakistan seemed to give this idea some bureaucratic momentum in the administration.[30] The initial idea was to have Holbrooke focus on Kashmir as well. But pressure from India saw this idea discarded. Although Kashmir was not designated as part of Holbrooke's job, it remained a lingering thought in US Afghan policy. For his part, Obama repeatedly resisted the traditional temptation to mediate on Kashmir.

President Trump, during his first term in office, went the other way by publicly denouncing Pakistan's duplicity on Afghanistan – supporting the Taliban while receiving significant economic and military support from the US. Trump cut off both civilian and military assistance to Pakistan, leading to a new crisis in bilateral relations. Additionally, early on in its tenure, the Trump administration unveiled a regional strategy document on South Asia.[31] While the focus was on Afghanistan and Pakistan, the new South Asia strategy consolidated and advanced the separation of US policies towards India and Pakistan.[32]

Evidence of a fundamental shift in US policy towards India and Pakistan came when the Trump administration offered vital support to India at two critical junctures. The first was the Pulwama terror attack against Indian forces in Kashmir in February 2019.[33] When New Delhi and Islamabad came to blows after the Indian retaliatory attack on a terrorist camp in Pakistan, the US stepped in quickly to defuse the conflict; it also put some pressure on Pakistan to release the downed Indian pilot, Wing Commander Abhinandan Varthaman, who found himself on the wrong side of the border after a brief air skirmish between the two air forces.[34] The second and even more consequential move was the US diplomatic support given to India on Kashmir at the United Nations Security Council in the summer and autumn of 2019. India had passed constitutional amendments to change the special status of Kashmir in the Union, leading to a visceral condemnation from Pakistan and vigorous questioning by China.[35] When Beijing (at the prompting of Islamabad) called for a discussion on Kashmir at the UN Security Council during August and September, the Trump administration stood solidly behind New Delhi in fending off the challenge.[36] This episode marked a major reversal of the traditional US policy on Kashmir.

The second dimension on which US policy has shifted since 2001 is terrorism. If president Bill Clinton's policy was ambivalent on Pakistan's support for terrorism in India, George W. Bush's focus on the 'global war on terror' after 9/11 meant the US was more sensitive to New Delhi's concerns about terrorism and began to put some pressure on the Pakistan Army to address India's apprehensions. While this effort was not necessarily successful, Washington's good faith was quite evident to New Delhi and appreciated by it. Further, the US began to deepen counter-terror cooperation with India, which created the basis for substantive US engagement with India's highly influential internal-security establishment.[37]

The third aspect of Washington's new approach to the region is the political management of US arms transfers to Pakistan, which had long created a huge public uproar in India. The US began to address this problem by opening the door for arms sales to India from the early 2000s. In a paradox not fully appreciated by many analysts of South Asia's international relations, the US decision to renew the supply of F-16s to Pakistan in the second term of the George W. Bush administration – as a reward for Islamabad's support for US policy on Afghanistan – provided the immediate impetus to outline a separate grand bargain with India. The objective was to limit India's negative reaction to the F-16 sale and develop more substantive engagement with New Delhi. The bargain was unveiled when US secretary of state Condoleezza Rice visited India in March 2005, paving the way for the aforementioned defence framework and civil-nuclear initiative.[38] Sections of the Indian establishment preferred to criticise the US arms supplies to Pakistan rather than take advantage of the new openings offered by the US.[39] They were sceptical of the US plan to support India's rise. But realists in the Manmohan Singh government prevailed, and India accepted the bargain.

Finally, the defence and nuclear agreements with New Delhi were part of Washington's new geopolitical vision for India. If his immediate predecessors saw India through the narrow prism of South Asia, George W. Bush framed India within the larger concept of the Asian balance of power. In the twenty-first century, the growing convergence between New Delhi and Washington on the challenge posed by a rising China to the regional balance of power was accompanied by the steady decline of bilateral friction over Pakistan. Moreover, the withdrawal of US troops from Afghanistan in August 2021 ended more than four decades of US focus on Afghanistan, which had given Pakistan an important place in US policy towards the subcontinent. Under the first Trump and Biden administrations, Obama's pivot to Asia evolved into a more decisive China strategy that put India at the heart of the Indo-Pacific, disentangled from its Pakistani neighbour. The Biden administration's 2022 National Security Strategy (NSS) did not even mention Pakistan.[40]

The Indo-Pacific

The idea of India playing a critical role in shaping the Asian balance of power, revived in the George W. Bush era, was translated into an effective regional framework by Japanese prime minister Abe Shinzo. The Bush administration's initial plans to balance against China in Asia had to be put on the back burner as it grappled with the war on terror in Afghanistan after the 9/11 attacks and focused more broadly on the Middle East, including its invasion of Iraq. It was Abe and his colleagues who conceptualised the new geography of the Indo-Pacific and proposed a new regional institution centred on Asian democracies, which eventually became known as the Quadrilateral Security Dialogue, bringing together Australia, India, Japan and the United States. Abe articulated these ideas in his address to the Indian parliament in August 2007, suggesting a framework to consider the two oceans – the Indian and Pacific – as an integrated space.[41]

Expansive bilateral relations between China and each of the four countries led to political ambivalence and hesitation in responding to Abe's grand-strategic design. In Japan,

Abe's successors had less time for geopolitical engineering in Asia. In Australia, the Labor Party, which came to power in 2007, dismissed the Indo-Pacific framework. The US interest in the Indo-Pacific concept, too, turned out to be tentative under the Obama administration. And in New Delhi, there was much scepticism about the Indo-Pacific idea – some saw it as a strategy of entrapment in US foreign policy, while others viewed it as a distraction from the much-needed engagement with China to resolve the boundary dispute.[42]

Yet the implications of China's rapid rise for the Asian balance of power would not go away. Abe, who returned to power in Tokyo at the end of 2012, put the issue back on the agenda by outlining a new strategy to promote a 'Free and Open Indo-Pacific'.[43] Australia, which had rejected the idea in 2008, now embraced it decisively, adopting its own Indo-Pacific framework in 2013.[44] But India remained ambivalent until the summer of 2018, when Prime Minister Modi articulated an Indo-Pacific policy at the IISS Shangri-La Dialogue.[45] The shift in India's position was driven by two major developments – the intensification of military tensions on the Himalayan frontier in 2017, on the Doklam plateau (where the borders of Bhutan, China and India converge), and a decisive turn in US strategy towards the Indo-Pacific under the first Trump administration.

The US surprised Asia by replacing the familiar term 'Asia-Pacific' with the new moniker 'Indo-Pacific' during President Trump's swing through the region to attend the East Asia Summit in 2017.[46] Underlying this terminological shift was a bigger change in conceptualising US national-security challenges. The NSS issued in December 2017, soon after Trump's Asia trip, argued that the principal feature of the global landscape was renewed great-power rivalry. The post-Cold War policy of engagement with other great powers was replaced with the need to confront the simultaneous challenges from

China and Russia. Equally importantly, the US recognised the need to build a solid strategic partnership with India. The NSS welcomed 'India's emergence as a leading global power and stronger strategic and defence partner'.[47]

The Indo-Pacific framework flowing out of the NSS (declassified at the end of the first Trump administration) laid out in greater detail the new approach to India amid the determination to push back against Chinese expansionism in Asia. It assumed that 'a strong India, in cooperation with like-minded countries, would act as a counter balance to China'. The 'end-state' sought by the Trump administration was the emergence of the US as the 'preferred security partner' for India. It hoped that New Delhi and Washington would 'cooperate to preserve maritime security and counter Chinese influence in South and Southeast Asia and other regions of mutual concern'. It also desired that India 'maintains the capacity to counter border provocations by China'. Regionally, the framework also hoped that 'India remains pre-eminent in South Asia and takes the leading role in maintaining Indian Ocean security, increases engagement with Southeast Asia, and expands its economic, defence, and diplomatic cooperation with other U.S. allies and partners in the region'. To achieve these objectives, the US would align its diplomatic strategy with those of India, Japan and Australia and 'create a quadrilateral security framework', with New Delhi, Tokyo, Canberra and Washington as its hubs.[48] The NSS and the Indo-Pacific framework marked a sweeping change in the US approach to India. The US decided to help accelerate India's rise, strengthen its military capabilities to play a larger role in the Indo-Pacific, address New Delhi's continental challenges from China, develop inter-operability between the US and Indian armed forces, and deepen both bilateral defence trade and regional economic, political and security cooperation.[49]

Although the modern idea of the Indo-Pacific, first articulated in New Delhi by Abe, put India very much at the centre of that conception, the idea was not endorsed by the then-ruling UPA government.[50] The succeeding NDA government only slowly and cautiously moved to make the Indo-Pacific idea its own. Modi avoided confronting China explicitly, called his Indo-Pacific concept 'inclusive' and insisted on putting the Association of Southeast Asian Nations (ASEAN) at the centre of it. But the shift in New Delhi's approach was unmistakable by 2018, when Modi publicly adopted the Indo-Pacific concept in his address to the annual IISS Shangri-La Dialogue in Singapore.[51] It acquired even greater salience in 2020 after the Galwan crisis. This crisis saw the US make good on the policy articulated in the 2017 NSS by supporting India's ability to stand up to China. This involved providing material and intelligence support for the Indian armed forces to respond to Chinese aggression in eastern Ladakh. Within the United States, it was unclear if Trump's focus on great-power rivalry and deep commitment to the Indo-Pacific and to India would survive his administration. However, the Biden administration reaffirmed the need to confront the Russian and Chinese challenges, strengthened Washington's commitment to the Indo-Pacific, underlined the importance of India for its Asian strategy, and pushed for stronger security and defence ties with New Delhi.

The Quad

The period of 2017–20 saw the first Trump administration seek to revive the Quad, which had lain largely dormant since its first meeting in 2007. The origins of the Quad go back to the Boxing Day tsunami in 2004, when India cooperated with Australia, Japan and the United States to provide humanitarian assistance and disaster relief in the Indian Ocean region. This cooperation, in turn, fed into the Japanese debate taking place around the same time on 'building an arc of freedom and prosperity' around the Eurasian landmass.[52] In his aforementioned 2007 address to the Indian parliament, Abe called for a new coalition of democracies, including Australia, India, Japan and the United States, to work together to promote peace and prosperity in the region. Abe concluded his bold articulation with a rhetorical question: 'From now on let us together bear this weighty responsibility that has been entrusted to us by joining forces with like-minded countries, shall we not ladies and gentlemen?'[53]

It is not clear if the enormity of what Abe was suggesting to India made an impact on the members of parliament gathered there. The Indian political class was already engaged in an intensive debate on the political and strategic merits of the historic civil-nuclear deal with the United States and its impact on India's independent foreign policy. The UPA government was torn internally by the massive political opposition to the deal on the left and right of the political spectrum. Abe's ideas on the Indo-Pacific and the Quad ran into the well-entrenched anti-American sentiment and perennial neutralist temptations of the Indian political class, as well as bureaucratic resistance to new formulations. The consolidation of domestic opposition and Chinese objections contributed to the UPA government developing cold feet on the Indo-Pacific construct and the Quad. Much of the blame for killing the Quad has been laid at the door of Kevin Rudd, who was the Labor prime minister of Australia in late 2007 and publicly dissociated Australia from the Quad.[54] But the Indian government, too, appears to have been pressured by domestic opposition and China to walk back. This fact was confirmed in 2023 by the External Affairs Minister, Subrahmanyam Jaishankar, who in 2007 was a senior official in charge of the US desk in the Ministry of External Affairs.[55]

The government led by Narendra Modi took important steps early on to deepen engagement with the United States but was unwilling to rush into a revival of the Quad. It was only after the 2017 clash with Chinese forces on the Doklam plateau along the Bhutan–China–India border that India was motivated to revive the Quad. By that time, Trump was in office and was very focused on addressing the China challenge. In November 2017, a few months after the Doklam crisis was defused, senior officials of the four Quad countries met for the first time since 2007. Even then, India was reluctant to issue a joint statement, suggesting separate statements that hinted at a broad unity of purpose on maritime security in the waters of Asia.

Two years later, in 2019, the four foreign ministers met on the margins of the UN General Assembly. The first stand-alone meeting of the four foreign ministers took place in October 2020, amid the stand-off between the Indian and Chinese armed forces, which had begun in the spring.[56] At the end of 2020, India ended its reluctance to have Australia participate in the annual *Malabar* exercises. Nevertheless, New Delhi remained quite squeamish about calling the Quad an alliance mechanism. It was also reluctant to support the Trump administration's suggestion to give the Quad an organisational structure in the form of a secretariat. Nor was New Delhi enthusiastic about expanding the Quad to include other members. While sections of the US establishment were hoping for a tight military alliance, New Delhi's focus was on flexibility. Given its long legacy of non-alignment, that was not surprising. Military alliances involve formal commitments to mutual security and India's foreign-policy ideology shunned joining alliances. (The one exception was India's security treaty with the Soviet Union in 1971, amid the unfolding crisis in East Pakistan. Once the crisis passed, with Bangladesh's independence from Pakistan in December 1971, the treaty lost much of its practical relevance.)

The Biden administration quickly elevated the Quad forum to the leaders' level. Within a few weeks of coming to office, president Biden convened a virtual summit of the Quad leaders in March 2021.[57] As the Biden administration doubled down on the Indo-Pacific framework outlined by the first Trump administration, it also chose to boost the Quad. Unlike Trump's, Biden's strategy was to rebuild US alliances and partnerships, and the Quad was a natural candidate for Washington's stronger attention. An in-person summit was held in September 2021, and the leaders gathered again in Tokyo in 2022 and in Hiroshima in May 2023.[58] Also unlike Trump, Biden did not insist on turning the Quad into a military alliance and was willing to cut India much greater slack. Biden's focus was on the Quad's possibilities as a provider of regional public goods, which suited India well in pursuing an incremental expansion of the regional partnership with the United States.

The Indo-Pacific Strategy issued by the Biden administration in 2022 outlined the US ambition to 'strengthen the Quad as a premier regional grouping' and ensure it 'delivers on issues that matter to the Indo-Pacific'.[59] Besides contributing to the management of the COVID-19 pandemic, the Biden administration saw the Quad leading the 'work on critical and emerging technologies, driving supply-chain cooperation, joint technology deployments, and advancing common technology principles.' The Quad, the Biden strategy promised, will also 'build a green shipping network, and will coordinate the sharing of satellite data to improve maritime domain awareness and climate responses. Its members will cooperate to provide high-standards infrastructure in South and Southeast Asia and the Pacific Islands and work to improve their cyber capacity.'[60]

By any measure, this was a sweeping public-goods agenda in the Indo-Pacific. Critics complained it was so vast and incoherent that it lost the original objective of blunting Chinese power.[61]

They would have liked to see a definitive and explicit military alliance to counter Beijing's expansionism. Others, however, argued that by refusing to frame the Quad as a military alliance, the US and India both won significant geopolitical room for themselves.[62] Firstly, it blunted Chinese propaganda claiming that the Quad was the 'Asian NATO'.[63] Secondly, framing it as a public-goods coalition helped address regional anxieties about the Quad and its potential to undermine ASEAN's key role in the regional security architecture.[64] The Quad's leaders have made a point of repeatedly emphasising 'ASEAN centrality' in the strategic future of the Indo-Pacific, yet ASEAN leaders are not naive enough to buy into these declarations. If they see the Quad as enduring and not a flash in the pan, they will inevitably come to terms with its existence and growing strategic salience.

Thirdly, although the Quad has not been defined as a military alliance, it has begun to focus on a range of activities that include significant cooperation between the armed forces, including maritime security, as well as humanitarian assistance and disaster relief.[65] These activities have helped create a political comfort zone for New Delhi, which would like to avoid the perception of the Quad as a military alliance while expanding cooperation among the four armed forces for regional security. Fourthly, the Quad's 'benign' posture has been complemented by deepening bilateral military cooperation between the four members of the Quad, as well as the creation of new regional security structures, such as AUKUS (announced between Australia, the United Kingdom and the US in 2021). India, which in the past objected to US alliances in the region, is now offering quiet support for AUKUS in international fora to counter the Chinese campaign against it.[66] While India is not being offered the opportunity to cooperate with AUKUS on nuclear naval propulsion, there is speculation about potential cooperation on the second pillar of AUKUS – developing new strategic technologies.[67]

Fifthly, perhaps the greatest accomplishment of the Quad has been to draw India into a loose regional coalition with the US that includes some military activity. That it has developed deep bilateral military cooperation with the US and its Asian allies today is a historic shift in India's geopolitical orientation. That it sits with the US in a major regional security forum – the Quad – is no less significant. Moreover, the regional strategic convergence has not been limited to East Asia and the Pacific. It also includes the Middle East, where India and the US have unveiled a new regional 'minilateral' forum called I2U2 with Israel, the United Arab Emirates and the US.[68] India has also joined hands with the European Union, Saudi Arabia, the United Arab Emirates and the United States to develop the India–Middle East Corridor.[69] Although the Gaza conflict that exploded in October 2023 cast a shadow over these initiatives, they underline India's new willingness to work with the US in the Middle East. India has also dropped its historical resistance to Western military-strategic activity in the Indo-Pacific by joining hands with many European countries, as well as the EU, in promoting peace and stability in the littoral states of the Indian Ocean. The Quad's definition in non-military terms, its open-ended agenda and its flexible structure give time and space to both India and the US to consolidate their strategic cooperation in the Indo-Pacific.

At the turn of the century, India responded positively if cautiously to the US effort to build a new bilateral strategic partnership. As the effort acquired greater traction, India's historical hesitations began to ebb thanks to the sustained US effort to address New Delhi's concerns on Pakistan, Kashmir and nuclear issues. Yet New Delhi appeared reluctant to push forward to an intensive security engagement with the United

States. That reluctance changed with the relentless pressure from China on India's core security concerns. Within India too, the continuing decline of the leftist parties has expanded the domestic space for engaging with the United States. Although there is considerable antipathy to the US and the West on the Indian political right, Modi's dominance over this space and his deft projection of a confident India negotiating a sensible framework with the US have helped reduce the opposition of the nationalist right to a deeper partnership with Washington. Meanwhile, the steady deterioration in the US–China relationship since the 2010s has incentivised Washington to tighten the strategic bonds with New Delhi. Although the China factor has been critical in nudging India and the US closer, the structure of engagement now being built is likely to transcend the potential shifts in each country's bilateral ties with China. The intensifying collaboration between India and the US has now acquired a deep regional and an increasingly global character. But the potential for the expansion of the strategic partnership appeared to come into doubt as Donald Trump was re-elected as president of the United States at the end of 2024 with an agenda that seemed to challenge many of the traditional assumptions about US foreign and security policies.

Trump 2.0

For nearly a quarter of a century, it was Washington that pressed for a deeper and wider security partnership with New Delhi; the latter was reluctant to take bold steps forward, thanks to the lingering ideology of non-alignment in the Indian political class and the persistent distrust of the United States in the security establishment. It was the first Trump administration that elevated the strategic engagement with India with its emphasis on the Indo-Pacific geography, the revival of the Quad and an explicit balancing against China in Asia. The Biden administration continued with this policy and added an engagement track with China.

Trump returned to power with a message that was mixed. On the one hand, Trump appointed several 'China hawks' to his national-security team and a section of the Republican foreign-policy establishment insisted on the US pivoting away from its security commitments to Europe and devoting its resources to redressing the Asian balance of power disturbed by the rise of China. There was another section of the Trump coalition that demanded a retrenchment of US global commitments and a focus on the challenges at home and in its hemispheric neighbourhood. Trump himself often spoke of his positive personal relationship with Chinese leader Xi Jinping and the need to get along with Beijing. As with Europe, Trump has demanded greater burden-sharing from its Asian allies; he has also often questioned the wisdom of trying to defend Taiwan against potential Chinese aggression. Even more consequentially, Trump's principal focus has been on reducing trade deficits, ringing alarm bells for Asian leaders about their long-term commercial ties to Washington. While the debates in Washington in early 2025 have left much of Asia confounded on the direction of US policy, Trump's first meetings with Asian leaders suggested a measure of broad continuity in security policy with an added emphasis on rearranging trade ties.

On his first day in office in January 2025, US Secretary of State Marco Rubio met the foreign ministers of the Quad countries. After the meeting, the four leaders affirmed the 'shared commitment to strengthening a Free and Open Indo-Pacific', opposed 'any unilateral actions that seek to change the status quo by force or coercion' and underlined the importance of collaboration on 'regional maritime, economic, and technology security in the face of increasing threats'.[70] A meeting between the US defense secretary, Pete Hegseth, and the Australian deputy prime minister and defence minister, Richard Marles, discussed progress on the AUKUS initiative. A trilateral meeting of the foreign ministers of Japan, South Korea and the United States on the margins of the Munich Security Conference signalled that the Trump administration will persist with the Biden initiative to consolidate the East Asian alliances.[71] The message was also similar in President Trump's meetings with Japanese Prime Minister Ishiba Shigeru and Prime Minister Modi in February 2025.

A closer look at the outcome of the discussions between Modi and Trump points to an important twist in the story of policy continuity. Prime Minister Modi's visit to the United States in February 2025 marked the reaffirmation of the strategic partnership developed over the last two decades, with an added emphasis on a 'results-driven agenda with initial outcomes this year' to demonstrate the level of trust and seriousness of commitment to the partnership.[72] In the past, the US took the initiative to present new ideas for the relationship and New Delhi took its time to respond. Trump now wants to see quick action and has signalled that his patience is limited. India moved quickly to address Trump's concerns on immigration and trade. It also undertook several commitments to deepen the energy, defence and technological partnership. New Delhi now recognises the centrality of the United States in its strategic calculus, especially in Asia. Although there are concerns that Trump might make up with China, there is a recognition that the answer must be in doing more with Washington.

Modi and Trump relaunched many of the old initiatives under a different name – the 'U.S.–India COMPACT (Catalyzing Opportunities for Military Partnership, Accelerated Commerce & Technology) for the 21st Century'. The emphasis on accelerated commerce is driven by Trump, and Modi agreed to negotiate a new trade deal before the end of the year and raise the volume of annual bilateral trade to US$500 million by

2030. India agreed to import more hydrocarbons from the US to deepen their energy partnership as well as reduce the trade deficit with the US. Modi also promised to revive civil-nuclear energy cooperation and remove domestic regulatory impediments. Trump is eager to sell more weapons to India, and Modi has sought to liberalise defence-technology export guidelines. The two leaders agreed to renew their ten-year framework for defence cooperation, updating the agreements of 2005 and 2015.

Trump and Modi also pledged to 'accelerate defense technology cooperation across space, air defense, missile, maritime and undersea technologies' and committed to 'support and sustain the overseas deployments' of the two militaries in the Indo-Pacific. While the former element is about the US helping ramp up India's defence-technological capabilities, the latter is about New Delhi backing US military operations in the Indo-Pacific. In the past, India has been hesitant to support US military operations in the region, but it now appears open to partnering with the US more actively in shaping regional security. The two leaders also agreed to develop an Indian Ocean initiative to coordinate their regional policies and to step up cooperation in the Middle East.

As India moves closer to the US on regional security issues, the Trump administration appears more empathetic to India's concerns about cross-border terrorism originating in Pakistan and more willing to endorse a larger Indian role in the subcontinent. Yet Trump's apparent neutrality in the India–Pakistan military conflict of May 2025 and his offer to mediate between the two sides have renewed anxieties in New Delhi about the re-hyphenation of India–Pakistan relations.[73] The talk about spheres of influence in Trump's second term and a potential accommodation with China also generates concerns in New Delhi.[74]

India, for its part, has held its nerve and refused to engage Trump in public argumentation. It has maintained a sustained focus on trade negotiations, which are a high priority for the US president. In the formal interactions between the two establishments, the signs of continuity are real and suggest that the bilateral strategic partnership is likely to survive the turbulence unleashed by Trump. The next chapter examines the intersection between the India–US partnership and the regional situation.

CHAPTER FOUR

Regional dynamics

Introduction

This chapter explores the intersection between India's changing triangular dynamic with China and the United States, on the one hand, and India's engagement with key regional actors, on the other. The rise of China in Asia and India's cooperation with the United States to balance against China have had ripple effects across the region. Regional states and major international powers have had to navigate the new currents. India has drawn closer to Australia and Japan, and the salience of its ties to Russia has seen a relative decline. New Delhi has welcomed growing European interest in the region and sought deeper cooperation with European states and institutions in South Asia. The major-power rivalries have changed the dynamics of regional international relations and affected domestic politics in smaller states in Asia. In sum, India's approach to the region today is dramatically different than it was during the Cold War.

Australia and Japan

Given the Quad's political visibility since 2017, it is easy to imagine that Australia and Japan are India's natural partners in Asia. Yet the opposite was true in the second half of the twentieth century. As the political distance between India and the US grew – largely over their differing assessments of the Asian geopolitical situation – New Delhi became alienated from Canberra and Tokyo. In the evolving rigidity of Asian Cold War politics, India's criticism of US regional policies was at odds with the views of Australia and Japan. If a shared heritage from the British empire, in terms of political values and common legal traditions, could not overcome the geopolitical divergence between India and Australia during the Cold War, New Delhi's focus on Asian solidarity and its considerable goodwill towards Japan (both before and after the Second World War) were insufficient for building a productive bilateral relationship with Tokyo. Following the Sino-Indian border clashes of 1962 and Chinese leader Mao Zedong's focus on the promotion of regional revolutions in Asia in the 1960s, it seemed possible for New Delhi, Canberra and Tokyo to cooperate in countering the Chinese threat to Asian stability. Ideas for trilateral cooperation were discussed among the strategic communities of the three countries.[1] But the shifting regional dynamics marked by the Sino-Soviet split, New Delhi's entente with Moscow and, later, the Sino-Soviet normalisation left no scope for such cooperation between India and US allies in Asia. It was only in the early twenty-first century that a formal Australia–India–Japan trilateral dialogue was established in parallel with the evolution of the Quad.[2]

Although the end of the Cold War opened new possibilities for India's engagement with Australia and Japan, there were new problems as well. The question of nuclear proliferation quickly became a deeply divisive issue between India, on one side, and Australia and Japan, on the other, in the 1990s. As a non-signatory of the Nuclear Non-Proliferation Treaty (NPT) and a country determined to keep its option of building nuclear weapons, India became a major target of the non-proliferation regime – of which Australia and Japan were major champions – from the 1970s. India's nuclear tests of 1998 and its self-declaration as a nuclear-weapons power sharpened these tensions. Canberra and Tokyo reacted harshly against India's tests and imposed a range of punitive measures.[3] In the early 2000s, the US, which had led the world's condemnation of India's nuclear tests, began to seek a resolution of the non-proliferation problem with India, and this engagement became a vehicle for restructuring relations between New Delhi and Washington.[4] US president Bill Clinton's visit to India in 2000 was soon followed by the visits of the Australian prime minister, John Howard, and the Japanese prime minister, Mori Yoshiro, which set the ball rolling for the recalibration of bilateral relations. As president George W. Bush made a big move to end the nuclear dispute with India during 2005–08, Australia (enthusiastically) and Japan (somewhat hesitantly) rallied round to put the nuclear question aside and begin to develop bilateral strategic partnerships with India.[5]

The more fundamental changes in Indo-Australian and Indo-Japanese bilateral ties would emerge only a few years later amid the construction of a new strategic geography, the Indo-Pacific, which in turn was a response to China's growing ambitions in Asia. Much of the credit for the recognition of the China challenge, imagination of the Indo-Pacific geography, articulation of a critical role for India in the region and promotion of the idea of the Quad goes to Abe Shinzo, who served as Japan's prime minister during 2006–07 and 2012–20. None of these ideas were self-evident in the first decade of the twenty-first century. Abe initially outlined his vision of the Indo-Pacific – the 'confluence of the two seas' and 'a diamond of democracies' to promote regional peace and prosperity – in a speech to the Indian parliament in August 2007.[6] At the time, there was little strategic resonance in New Delhi for Abe's new strategic vision, and the United Progressive Alliance (UPA) government was deeply divided on both the Indo-Pacific framework and the idea of a coalition of Asian democracies. Abe, who returned to power in 2012, advocated for the Indo-Pacific and the Quad far more vigorously. Meanwhile, Abe's long tenure and personal investment in improving ties with India encouraged a steady expansion of bilateral engagement between Tokyo and New Delhi.

Australia under the Liberal government embraced Abe's ideas when he first propounded them, but the Labor government that followed distanced itself from the framework.[7] In 2012, Canberra published a White Paper on 'Australia in the Asian Century' that articulated its own concept of the Indo-Pacific, which retained a positive outlook on China.[8] However, Australia's views on China began to evolve in the years following its announcement of a strategic partnership with China in 2014. The return of the Liberal Party to power in 2013 helped shift Australian perceptions of China, and the 2017 White Paper on foreign policy spelt out a clearer view of the emerging China challenge to Australia.[9] The same years also saw an expanding emphasis on engagement with India. The Australian debate on Asian security took a decisive turn when Donald Trump's first administration adopted the Indo-Pacific nomenclature at the end of 2017. This provided a more conducive atmosphere for the improvement of the India–Australia strategic partnership.

The revival and consolidation of the Quad from 2017 also led to the solidification of India's bilateral relations with both Japan and Australia. For the first time since India's independence, the two relationships acquired significant regional strategic salience, thanks to growing convergence on the question of balancing against Chinese power in Asia. The historic revision of Japanese defence policies in 2022, which called for a more muscular regional security strategy, has opened space for even more expansive defence cooperation.[10]

The big question is about the ability of the three countries to align their regional diplomatic, political and military strategies through the Quad and bilateral means to counter Chinese strategic forays. Each country brings unique strengths in different geographies, and collaboration among them will help them effectively pursue shared interests. To be sure, individual action by a large and purposeful state like China is far more effective than coordination within a coalition. Yet common approaches to regional development, security and order by three weighty regional players are bound to have a cumulative impact on challenging Beijing's putative primacy in Asia.

Russia

If shifting relations with the US and China helped reinforce India's strategic partnerships with Japan and Australia in the twenty-first century, they steadily reduced the relative weight of India's long-standing strategic partnership with Russia, even as New Delhi and Moscow managed to keep the partnership going. Top Indian officials have insisted that solid ties with Russia have been an enduring and time-tested element in independent India's international relations. While other major-power relations in Asia have varied widely since the Second World War, the argument goes, India–Russia relations have held steady.[11] For a moment after the Cold War, post-Soviet Russia seemed more interested in building ties with the US and Europe than with its traditional friends in the non-Western world, like India. Despite Moscow's westward turn, New Delhi actively sought to sustain the bilateral relationship, replacing the defunct 1971 security treaty with a new bilateral agreement in 1993, resolving the rupee–rouble trade issue (a unique national-currency trading system developed by India and the Soviet Union during the Cold War that became unviable after the rouble's value crashed in the post-Soviet era) and sustaining defence cooperation with Russia.[12] The decision to hold onto the Russian connection was driven by New Delhi's fear of the post-Cold War unipolar moment, which in South Asia saw the US seeking to cap, roll back and eliminate India's nuclear-weapon and missile programmes and – from New Delhi's perspective – meddling in the Kashmir dispute between India and Pakistan.

If the enthusiasm to sustain bilateral ties with Russia in the post-Soviet era initially came from New Delhi, Moscow began to show equal interest by the mid-1990s. As nervousness about Russia's relations with the West began to resurface in Moscow, the Russian prime minister, Yevgeny Primakov, formally proposed the idea of constructing a 'strategic triangle' with India and China that would ensure a measure of balance against US hegemony.[13] This idea would form the basis for the creation of the Russia–India–China (RIC) and Brazil–Russia–India–China–South Africa (BRICS) forums. The ascension of Vladimir Putin to power in 1999 led to even greater interest in Moscow in restoring traditional ties with New Delhi. As Russian relations with the West became testy in the twenty-first century, India along with China became an important part of the Russian quest to promote a multipolar world and to develop a post-Western order.

Several developments, however, began to slowly diminish Russia's salience for India. One was the changing nature of the Indian economy after the reforms that began in the 1990s. As it discarded the Soviet model of economic development in the 1990s and became more market-friendly and open to the world, Russia's weight in the Indian economy began to diminish. Structural changes in India's economy towards greater freedom for capital brought to the fore the natural synergies between the Indian and Western markets. Russia, in turn, was focused on reforming its economy and building stronger commercial ties with Europe and the United States. Meanwhile, as reforms accelerated India's growth, its projected GDP in 2025 stood at US$4.1 trillion – twice that of Russia's at US$2trn.[14]

Yet although recent decades have witnessed a significant divergence between the sizes of the Russian and Indian economies and between the volume of India's trade with the US and that with Russia, Moscow remains economically significant for New Delhi. This is partly due to a recent shift in energy trade: Russia has emerged as a major supplier of oil to India since Moscow's invasion of Ukraine in 2022, thanks to the discounted prices that have been on offer. This, in turn, has led to a significant surge in bilateral trade, which reached US$65.7 billion during 2023–24. This development has further skewed trade relations in Russia's favour, with India barely exporting US$4.2bn-worth of goods to Russia.[15] In the future, it is possible that India's economic dependence on Russia might not be limited to oil. India's External Affairs Minister, Subrahmanyam Jaishankar, has talked about Russia as a major supplier of other natural resources as India's industrialisation marches ahead.[16] After all, Russia is among the world's richest states in natural resources.

Despite India's growing economic power, it also remains dependent on Moscow for its defence needs, given the large inventory of Russian weapons in the Indian arsenal that has accumulated since the 1960s. Though both the quantity and proportion of equipment India has procured from Russia has declined in the twenty-first century, significant dependencies remain.[17] Of the Indian Army's armoured fighting vehicles, 94% are of Soviet or Russian design; the same is true of 64% of the air force's multi-role fighter and ground-attack aircraft.[18] A little before Russia's war in Ukraine, Prime Minister Narendra Modi began to emphasise the importance of reducing defence imports and producing more weapons at home. He has also sought to draw private and foreign capital into India's defence production, which has long been the preserve of the public sector, and to promote exports.[19] Although progress has been slow, Modi is determined to alter the nature of the Indian defence-production system. Since the Ukraine war, the US has offered to help India reduce its defence dependence on Moscow.[20] While Indian reliance on Russian weapons cannot be undone overnight, the Ukraine war might have accelerated the process of diversification and the domestic production of armaments.

The changing triangular dynamic between the US, China and Russia, which in the final third of the twentieth century facilitated the New Delhi–Moscow partnership, today weakens it. The Soviet Union's confrontation with the US and China in the latter decades of the twentieth century coincided with New Delhi's difficulties with Washington and Beijing. Moscow was a critical partner for New Delhi's Asian strategy in the latter part of the twentieth century as the two sides shared several objectives in the region, including the need to balance against the US and China. Today, India–Russia relations have become less significant for New Delhi amidst its improving ties with Washington and its sharpening contradictions with Beijing. Russia, on the other hand, is getting closer to China and is locked in a confrontation with the US and the West. Russia has therefore increasingly become a problem for New Delhi's Asia strategy in the twenty-first century. India's embrace of the Indo-Pacific framework and the Quad stands in sharp contrast to Moscow's repeated denunciation of both these constructs.[21] While the contradictions between the Indian and Russian views of Asian security are profoundly at variance, optimists hope that New Delhi and Moscow can learn to live with these differences and insulate their own partnership from them. The Modi government has felt that New Delhi must do what it can to limit Russia's drift into the Chinese orbit. As Russia, squeezed out of Europe after the Ukraine war, looks to Asia for greater economic, political and military engagement, the Modi government has often said that Moscow must have options other than Beijing, and New Delhi is eager to provide them.[22]

This optimism about potential relations with Moscow is rooted in the entrenched goodwill for Russia in New Delhi, continuing faith in Russia's role as an independent great power and residual distrust of the West. Moscow did sustain arms supplies to India when New Delhi and Beijing were locked in a military confrontation in the summer of 2020 in the Ladakh sector. But might Russia be so obliging as it comes under greater Chinese influence in the years ahead?[23] During the Ukraine crisis, neither the Indian government nor the political opposition was willing to criticise Russian aggression. Critical sections of the foreign-policy elite were heard channelling Russian arguments about being provoked into a war. While insufficient to derail US (and broader Western) drives towards closer relations with New Delhi, India's reaction to Russian aggression reminded many in Western capitals that such relations were likely to be of a transactional nature.

While Russia's relative weight in India's strategic calculus is likely to diminish in the years ahead, amidst India's rise and widening strategic options, the Indian political leadership continues to talk up the importance of the ties with Moscow. New Delhi has set itself a new target of US$100bn in annual trade with Russia by 2030 and hopes to step up engagement on energy and defence in the coming years.[24] All that said, while New Delhi and Moscow might retain a semblance of their partnership amid global and regional turmoil, the relationship is unlikely to occupy the Indian strategic mind in the manner that it did in the latter part of the twentieth century.

President Trump's attempt to construct a cooperative partnership with Russia in his second term certainly reduces pressure from Washington on New Delhi to downgrade ties with Moscow. Any new entente between Trump and Putin would be likely to sharpen contradictions between Russia and Europe and would present an enduring challenge to New Delhi as it seeks to deepen ties with the old continent.

The United Kingdom and Europe

One of the remarkable transformations of the Asian security landscape has been the return of the UK and other European states to the regional geopolitical stage. The US has encouraged its European allies to balance against China in the region, and India has broken with tradition to embrace greater European engagement in Asia. There is a significant debate on the credibility and durability of the European strategic interest in the region, but the very discussion underlines the new context. After the decolonisation of Asia following the Second World War, Europe became marginal to the regional security calculus. European countries' attempts to regain their colonial possessions in Asia – which had been lost to Japan during the Second World War – were foiled by the intensity of local Asian nationalisms and European decline triggered by the two world wars. France retained some territorial possessions in the region. Britain, which dominated the Indo-Pacific from the early nineteenth to the mid-twentieth century, lingered on as a major player after the Second World War, but eventually withdrew from 'East of Suez' from the late 1960s. The US replaced the Europeans as the dominant power in the region, while the Soviet Union began to offer some strategic competition to the West. If the residual colonial connections between Europe and Asia endured weakly in the cultural domain, they became irrelevant in the strategic domain. In the economic sphere, the United States became the dominant economic partner among Western countries to much of Asia.

Despite its reasonably good relations with European powers, including Britain, independent India saw little role for them in the Asian order. Indian prime minister Jawaharlal Nehru focused on the ambitious agenda of building a new post-colonial and post-Western Asian order. Rejecting a security role for Europe and the West in Asia became one of the central tenets of his Asianist and non-aligned ideologies, which gained ground in the post-war era. Today, we see the reversal of both European and Indian positions on Asian security. Leading European countries, including France, Germany, the Netherlands and the UK, as well as the European Union, have outlined Indo-Pacific strategies.[25] India, discarding its anti-colonial ideological baggage, now welcomes a larger role for Europe in Asia.

Several factors contributed to this convergence of interests. One was the pull factor of the region. Although Britain and France retained a relatively small presence in the region, European recognition that Asia was emerging as the principal economic and geopolitical theatre led to the regeneration of their strategic interest in the region. Within Asia, it was, ironically, Japan that recognised the importance of bringing European powers back into the region. If Imperial Japan had driven the Europeans out of East and Southeast Asia in the 1940s, Tokyo was now inviting them back to cope with the expansive Chinese challenge in the early twenty-first century.[26] Since then, there has been a steady expansion of European activity in the Indo-Pacific.[27]

The second was the push factor – the encouragement from the United States to its European allies to take a greater interest in Asia. The US National Security Strategy of 2022 made explicit the US strategy of drawing its European allies into Asia – as well as encouraging its Asian allies to contribute to European security, especially after the Russian invasion of

Ukraine. The Biden administration argued that the Asian and European theatres were deeply interconnected and promised to seek out 'new ways to integrate our alliances in the Indo-Pacific and Europe and develop new and deeper means of cooperation'.[28] As it nudged European powers to engage with the Indo-Pacific region, it also encouraged its Asian allies to collaborate with NATO in Europe. NATO's Madrid Summit in 2022 saw the participation of four Asian countries – Australia, Japan, New Zealand and South Korea – at the highest political level. NATO, for its part, has been stepping up its engagement with Asian states on regional security.[29] As Trump's outreach to Russia at the beginning of his second term casts a shadow over the future of NATO, it remains to be seen how the four Asian powers will engage with the largely European alliance.

Two complications, however, have raised questions about a credible European role in Asia in the 2020s. One is the continuing war in Ukraine, which is bound to consume a lot of Europe's energy and limit the intensity of its Indo-Pacific engagement. The second is the profound European ambivalence on managing China's growing power. Given Europe's deep economic ties to China, it is wary of following the US into a confrontation with Beijing. This view is quite widespread in the German business community and was articulated with some vigour by French President Emmanuel Macron during his visit to Beijing in April 2023. Macron's position, seeking strategic autonomy from the US on China, caused much consternation within the West.[30] There are other equally strong views in Europe. For example, President of the European Commission Ursula von der Leyen gave a sharp speech on China different in tone and orientation from Macron's, calling on Europe to fundamentally rethink its relationship with Beijing.[31] The debate within Europe and between it and the United States on China is far from settled and will continue to be animated.

India is quite realistic in its expectations of a European role in Asia. New Delhi recognises, however, that any European contribution to stability and security in Asia – from the normative to the political, economic or military – would be of great value. Although Europe does not have a huge military to directly bring to bear on the balance of power, it remains a major producer of weapons and could contribute to the capacity-building of Asian partners and thus to local deterrence against Chinese expansionism. Since Macron's 2018 visit to India, New Delhi and Paris have actively collaborated in the western Indian Ocean and, more broadly, on maritime security issues in the region. Both New Delhi and Paris face challenges from the rising Chinese maritime profile in the Indian Ocean.[32] Britain's 'Indo-Pacific Tilt', first unveiled in 2021 and updated in 2023, emphasised closer strategic cooperation with India in the region. Defence and security cooperation is now an important pillar of the official edifice of India–UK cooperation.[33] The focus on the maritime domain has also begun the de-hyphenation of Britain's relations with Pakistan and India. London's presumed preference for parity in its relations with India and Pakistan has long irritated New Delhi. Maritime cooperation is also emerging as a major priority for India's engagement with other European countries, including Germany and Italy. Meanwhile, India has begun defence and security consultations with the EU.[34] New Delhi is also beginning to shed its traditional reluctance to engage, if quietly, with NATO, the premier European security institution.[35] Although the new possibilities for India–Europe security cooperation need to be fleshed out, an important barrier has been crossed in their post-colonial engagement.

South Asia
The rapidly changing relations over the last decade among China, India, Russia and the US are creating new power dynamics in South Asia. During the latter years of the Cold

War, South Asia's international relations had settled into a relatively stable framework. The US involvement in Afghanistan from the late 1970s inevitably ensured a Pakistan First policy towards the region. The Soviet Union, in turn, built a regional policy centred on India. China was an interested but relatively minor player in the subcontinent's geopolitics. But Beijing had already established a solid strategic partnership with Pakistan and was making forays into the rest of the region. South Asia's international politics were centred around two axes – the US–Soviet rivalry and the India–Pakistan contest. The rest of the subcontinent seemed marginal to the major powers.

More than three decades after the end of the Cold War, we now have a profoundly transformed structure of regional geopolitics. Compared to the Soviet Union's significant influence in the subcontinent in the twentieth century, Russia's weight in the region has diminished. The decline of Russia has been accompanied by the emergence of China as an important external actor in South Asia. Geographic proximity to the subcontinent, massive economic size, substantive diplomatic influence in global forums (including the United Nations Security Council as a permanent member) and growing military capabilities have made China the most important external great power in South Asia. The residual influence of the UK, as the former colonial power, has steadily diminished over the decades. As a large economic entity, Europe retains a measure of commercial weight in South Asia. The US remains a powerful external force but its attention at any given time is focused on a couple of concerns at best rather than pursuing a steady region-wide engagement. As the US faces up to the China challenge, this geopolitical dimension has begun to colour US engagement with the subcontinent. The US withdrawal from Afghanistan in August 2021 might have looked rather ugly, but it has liberated the US to focus on the Indo-Pacific and to transition from two decades of counter-insurgency in Afghanistan to competing with China in Asia. Meanwhile, the acceleration of India's economic growth since the early 1990s has significantly elevated India's standing in the region. The growing Sino-Indian rivalry and the US–China confrontation have produced a very different template for the geopolitics of the region.[36]

Within the region, the heightened rivalry between China, on one side, and the US and India, on the other, has affected these countries' bilateral relations with South Asian states. Pakistan has been struggling to navigate the rivalry between Washington and Beijing, whereas previously it had benefited from good relations with both.[37] The withdrawal of the US from Afghanistan appeared to reduce Washington's interest in Pakistan significantly. Moreover, Pakistan's economy has declined steadily relative to its neighbours. India's aggregate GDP, at US$3.9trn in 2024, is ten times larger than that of Pakistan. Bangladesh, long considered almost as a colony of Pakistan, now boasts a GDP that is nearly US$100bn bigger than Pakistan's.

In Nepal, the rise of communist parties in the 1990s resulted in growing warmth with China and some hostility towards India and the United States. With its growing economic heft and purposeful political engagement, Beijing has rapidly elevated its standing in Kathmandu. But New Delhi, whose stakes in Nepal are high (given their close ethnic and cultural connections and a history of political association), and Washington, which is taking a greater interest in China's periphery, are pushing back. India's continuing weight in Nepal and its new commitment to connectivity and economic integration with Nepal are beginning to have some impact.[38] However, the US effort to re-engage with Nepal within the Indo-Pacific framework was seen by the communists in Kathmandu as an anti-China move.[39] The US managed to overcome the communist resistance to a US grant of US$500 million under the Millennium Challenge Corporation with the support of the centrist parties.[40] (The grant funds the deepening of power connectivity between Nepal and India.) Even as China devotes greater attention to Nepal, political elites in Nepal are learning to leverage the new possibilities arising from Beijing's confrontation with New Delhi and Washington.

More broadly, the Himalayan ring separating the subcontinent from Tibet and China is regaining its strategic significance amid the renewed geopolitical contest among China, India and the US. In the early decades of the Cold War, the US actively sought to undermine the People's Republic of China by supporting the Tibetan separatist movement. India and China had their own differences on Tibet and its border with India, and on the political orientation of Himalayan states. These conflicts eased with the Sino-US rapprochement from the 1970s and the relaxation of tensions between India and China in the 1990s. Renewed rivalries between Washington and Beijing and between India and China have turned the Himalayas once again into a contested zone. As China increases the pressure on Bhutan to settle their boundary dispute and to develop a relationship with Beijing like the one it has with New Delhi, India is under considerable pressure to raise its game in Thimphu.[41] Meanwhile, the question of Tibet's relationship with Beijing and the succession of the ageing Dalai Lama are coming into sharp view, challenging the Indian policy that has been static for decades.[42]

Moving further east, Bangladesh and Myanmar have long been a contested zone between New Delhi and Beijing. The Obama administration's attempt to normalise ties with Myanmar in the early 2010s and the Trump administration's outreach to Bangladesh within the Indo-Pacific framework suggested the US was ready to join India in challenging growing Chinese influence in both countries.[43] But the Biden administration imposed severe sanctions on Naypyidaw in early 2021, when the army ousted the civilian government and took charge of the country. This move has allowed the Chinese to return as a powerful actor in Myanmar. For its part, India has had a hard task matching Beijing's influence and impact in Myanmar, despite its desire to balance against China there.[44] In Bangladesh, the Biden administration questioned the democratic credentials of the Sheikh Hasina government, and New Delhi was suspicious of the US role in promoting the popular revolt against the Hasina government in the summer of 2024. The gap between Washington's and New Delhi's enthusiasm for Hasina's opponents put the US at odds with India, which had worked closely with Hasina to transform the Indo-Bangladesh relationship and lay the basis for stronger economic integration in the eastern subcontinent.[45]

Policy differences between India and the US on Bangladesh and Myanmar might make it harder to deal with the growing Chinese forays into the Bay of Bengal, which is adjacent to the South China Sea and is at the heart of the Indo-Pacific region.[46] However, the Indian and US positions are more closely coordinated on the island states of the subcontinent – Maldives and Sri Lanka – which have emerged as a focal point in China's naval and maritime expansion into the Indian Ocean.[47] India has been engaged in consultations with both the US and other Quad partners to address multiple internal challenges in these island states, as well as to coordinate efforts to balance against China's attempts to acquire a stronger strategic position in the heart of the Indian Ocean.[48]

Southeast Asia
The transformation of US–China relations from partnership to rivalry in the twenty-first century has created opportunities and challenges for India's relations with Southeast Asia.

India's renewed engagement with Southeast Asia in the 1990s was facilitated by the Association of Southeast Asian Nations (ASEAN), which provided a solid institutional basis for a diverse range of interactions with the region. Unlike in the 1950s, when Nehru's India was animated by the idea of being a natural leader of the region, New Delhi renewed its focus on the region in the 1990s with the recognition that India had fallen behind its Asian compatriots in economic growth. ASEAN had deepened and widened its institutional architecture in the 1990s amidst a new wave of economic globalisation and relative harmony among the great powers of the world. For India, this provided a conducive environment to reconnect with Asia and integrate into ASEAN-led institutions. ASEAN itself was enthused by New Delhi's economic reforms – as the then-prime minister of Singapore, Goh Chok Tong, put it, India could provide the 'second engine' for ASEAN's future economic growth, which was increasingly tied to the rapid economic transformation of China. For ASEAN, engaging with India was not just about expanding Southeast Asia's economic possibilities. Integrating a rising India into the regional architecture fitted well with the ASEAN framework of providing an institutional basis to mediate and manage potential tensions among the major powers.[49] The notion that India would bring greater stability and balance to the region's major-power relations was a key factor behind the invitation to New Delhi to join the East Asia Summit in 2005 as a founding member.

This quiet but happy convergence on ASEAN-led regionalism began to come under a cloud in the 2010s. When the Trump administration and the Modi government revived the moribund Quad in 2017 as a response to Chinese assertiveness in Asia, there was some disquiet in ASEAN. Given the thriving partnerships with both China and the US, ASEAN did not want to choose between them.[50] The speed at which US–China relations deteriorated was certainly unexpected in ASEAN capitals. Equally, India's quick and uncharacteristic pivot to the United States also surprised them. In his formal articulation of India's Indo-Pacific policy in 2018 at the annual IISS Shangri-La Dialogue in Singapore, Modi took pains to emphasise India's 'inclusive approach' to the Indo-Pacific as well as the centrality of ASEAN in the Indo-Pacific.[51] The message has been repeatedly reaffirmed since then. Yet it has not been easy to get it across. To be sure, nudged by Indonesia, ASEAN did adopt in 2019 a framework document on the Indo-Pacific.[52] However, the dominant perception among ASEAN members remained that the Quad challenged 'ASEAN centrality'.[53]

Two factors appeared to be changing ASEAN's perception of the Quad in the early 2020s. Firstly, the Biden administration's heavy political investment in the Quad and the Indo-Pacific framework began to convince the region that the new strategic constructs were here to stay. The region is also coming to terms with the fact that neither the Sino-US nor Sino-Indian rivalries are likely to disappear, and must be dealt with. Secondly, the Biden administration downplayed Trump's first-term goal of turning the Quad into a military alliance that went beyond existing levels of military cooperation. Indian opposition to making the Quad a military instrument played a key role in this change. According to the analysts Sharon Seah and Kei Koga, the Quad 'reframed its purpose from exclusively countering China to a broader vision that ASEAN countries were comfortable with'.[54] The emphasis on the provision of public goods such as healthcare, mitigation of climate change, infrastructure development and regional disaster management has helped reduce some of the negative perceptions of the Quad. The Quad's decision to slow down on the military front, it was argued by an analyst from Southeast Asia, might allow it to 'go further' in the region.[55] The question of the Quad's contribution to military security in the Indo-Pacific is likely to return to centre stage in President Trump's second term.

Moreover, the signal from the Quad leaders' Hiroshima summit was that the Quad aimed to complement and strengthen the various pre-existing regional forums. In the joint statement issued after a brief meeting in Hiroshima on the margins of the G7 meeting, the Quad leaders underlined their support for 'the region's development, stability, and prosperity through the Quad's positive, practical agenda'. They added that 'respect for the leadership of regional institutions, including the Association of Southeast Asian Nations (ASEAN), the Pacific Islands Forum (PIF), and the Indian Ocean Rim Association (IORA), is and will remain at the centre of the Quad's efforts'.[56]

In an interview with the *New Straits Times* in May 2023, then Indonesian president Joko Widodo said ASEAN 'should view the Quad and AUKUS as partners, and not competitors'.[57] India and its Quad partners, however, have no reason to take ASEAN for granted and need to intensify their efforts to engage with ASEAN on a sustained basis and address its potential concerns.

Meanwhile, there are indications that ASEAN perceptions of India, which were damaged in the wake of New Delhi's withdrawal from the Regional Comprehensive Economic Partnership trade arrangement in 2019, are turning positive. An annual survey of elite regional opinion found that preference for India as a partner for regional security has grown.[58] The survey, conducted by the ISEAS–Yusof Ishak Institute in Singapore, showed a growing number of respondents from the ten ASEAN countries choosing India, after the EU and Japan, to act as a bulwark against uncertainties arising from the US–China strategic rivalry. India, which ranked last in 2022, doubled its approval from 5.1% to 11.3% to take the third spot out of six, followed by Australia, Britain and South

Korea. Further, the survey also showed an increase in levels of trust in India in almost all the ASEAN countries, with overall trust jumping from 16.6% in 2022 to 25.7% in 2023, and levels of distrust dropping in tandem. The survey also saw 18.2% of respondents agreeing that India's military power can be an asset for global peace and security, up from 6.6% a year before. Although India's ranking and perceptions have improved in these annual surveys, India has a great distance to go before it emerges, on its own, as a consequential player in Southeast Asia; but in alliance with other powers, it could make a considerable difference to regional security.

Asian reset

On the face of it, India's deepening contradictions with China and growing strategic partnership with the United States from the mid-2000s appeared at odds with the dominant regional perceptions of China's rise and inevitable leadership of Asia and of the irreversible US decline in the region. India's drift away from non-alignment and its Asianist worldview and shift towards the US was not dramatic or sudden enough to convince many in India and the region of the unfolding structural change in New Delhi's geopolitical orientation. But fears of India's increasing strategic isolation from the rest of Asia, as it drew closer to the US, have turned out to be unfounded. Three factors are at work. Firstly, India is not alone at the receiving end of Beijing's muscular policies. Chinese assertiveness on regional issues has affected Beijing's other neighbours as well. But China has been utterly confident that its neighbours can do little to cope with the massive and growing power imbalance between it and them.

Secondly, the surprising resilience of US policy towards Asia has altered the regional calculus. Although the first Trump administration raised questions about its commitment to NATO and European security, it devoted special emphasis to Asian security by embracing the Indo-Pacific framework, strengthening traditional bilateral alliances and building new partnerships. While reaffirming its commitment to Europe, the Biden administration built on Trump's Indo-Pacific initiative by stepping up the military, political and diplomatic engagement with the region. Biden also mobilised the United States' European allies to support its initiatives in the Indo-Pacific: modernising bilateral alliances, upgrading the Quad coalition, unveiling the AUKUS partnership, and making a special effort to connect bilaterally and multilaterally with ASEAN members and the Pacific islands. Washington was back in Asia as a force to be reckoned with in the first Trump and Biden administrations.[59] President Trump's second term has regenerated misgivings about Washington's commitment to Europe, with its approach to peace in Ukraine and new warmth towards Russia, but its emphasis on Asia and the Indo-Pacific appeared to endure in early 2025, as seen in the formal outcomes of President Trump's summit meetings with the Japanese and Indian prime ministers.

The third factor was the slow but definitive change in the region's attitudes. From trying to wish away the emerging contest between Beijing and Washington, Asia is learning to navigate the new regional dynamic. Even as great-power rivalry becomes intense in Asia today, it provides opportunities as well as challenges for the smaller states of the region. As former Singaporean diplomat Bilahari Kausikan put it: 'The complexity of twenty-first-century competition provides sovereign states more space to maneuver than did the binary of US–Soviet competition during the Cold War. Of course, states must have the intelligence, agility, and courage to recognize the opportunities to use their agency.'[60] Although much of Asia wants good relations with China and is worried about the consequences of the US–China rivalry, there is also a clear recognition that sustained US and allied activism in the region will enhance their bargaining power vis-à-vis China, which looms large over the region.

The rivalry between the US and China and Washington's determination to balance against Beijing in the Indo-Pacific has set the stage for productive relations between New Delhi and the region's capitals, but under a very different framework from India's historical engagement with Asia. In the past, India's policy was premised on limiting the United States' post-war dominance over Asia or remaining neutral between the US and China. Today India is moving closer to the US in order to balance against China. To be sure, the deepening tensions with China impose significant constraints on India's freedom of action. Yet the sustained US outreach to India, including Washington's offer to strengthen New Delhi's ability to stand up to Beijing and reduce its dependence on Moscow for weapons, has offered new possibilities for India. But New Delhi's effort to develop a strategic partnership with Washington, in the face of Beijing's opposition, has put India on a new geopolitical trajectory that it has long sought to avoid. India's attempt to build a partnership with Russia and China to develop a multipolar world to prevent the global dominance of the United States in the 1990s seemed to be a continuation of India's traditional anti-Americanism and Third-Worldism. But India under Modi has not allowed the rhetoric on multipolarity to get in the way of building a deeper strategic partnership with the US and its Asian allies.

At the same time, India's embrace of the Indo-Pacific framework has given it the solid regional anchor it has lacked in the last six decades. If its idea of Asian unity and solidarity took a knocking in the early 1960s, New Delhi's attempt to re-engage with Asia since the early 1990s has produced significant results.

India's initial emphasis was on integrating into ASEAN structures. But as a large and rising state, it was inevitable that India would outgrow ASEAN and would have to develop a strategy of its own towards the region. The Indo-Pacific framework was in that sense a blessing: although New Delhi has had to reassure ASEAN that the Quad will not undermine its centrality in the region, India's options for regional engagement have significantly widened.

To be sure, India's new association with the US does create certain problems in post-colonial Asia. Yet New Delhi's careful delineation of a path that avoids a formal alliance and highlights strategic independence has helped limit the potential damage. At the same time, the partnership with Washington has made it easier to build stronger ties with US allies like Australia, Japan, the Philippines and South Korea, which New Delhi had deliberately shunned in the second half of the twentieth century. Expanding partnerships with US allies have deepened India's engagement with the Indo-Pacific. While New Delhi's growing ties with Washington have generated much unease in Moscow, Russia would not or could not abandon its partnership with India, one of its long-standing and consistent friends in the world. India's capacity to bargain with Russia has significantly improved with the increased diversity of its strategic options, arising out of greater collaboration with the West. For instance, faced with competition from the US in India's arms and hydrocarbon markets, Moscow is offering New Delhi better terms on energy and defence cooperation. The US mobilisation of its European allies to contribute to Asian security has opened the door for a more broad-based relationship between India and Europe. It has also reinforced India's own special relationships with some European countries like France. Europe is likely to contribute far more significantly to India's comprehensive national power than a declining Russia in the twenty-first century. Yet New Delhi will have to carefully navigate the sharpening tensions between Europe and Russia amidst a putative rapprochement between Washington and Moscow in Trump's second term. Although the general trend within the West towards a more confrontational posture vis-à-vis China is creating a new basis for India's economic and military engagement with both the US and Asia, New Delhi is likely to remain anxious about a potential entente between the West and China.

CHAPTER FIVE

India as the balancer

Introduction

In the first few decades after India's independence, New Delhi and Washington held opposing views on Asia's regional order, largely due to differing approaches to China. India, under Jawaharlal Nehru, sought to build close ties with communist China and create a post-Western order in Asia. The United States, in contrast, pursued the containment of communist China in Asia through a range of alliances. During the Cold War, India's alignment with the Soviet Union and its ideological focus on anti-imperialism widened the gap with Washington. The US, meanwhile, normalised relations with China in the 1970s in order to isolate the Soviet Union in Asia. It was no surprise that the occasional efforts to build a sustainable partnership between India and the US foundered.

After the Cold War, India–US tensions lessened, but frictions emerged over issues like Kashmir and nuclear policy in the 1990s. India grew wary of the global unipolar moment and sought to limit US dominance by engaging with China and Russia. However, as China's regional assertiveness intensified – including on the disputed border with India – New Delhi began distancing itself from Beijing's vision of a China-led

Asian order. Discarding its earlier Asianist and post-Western ideals, India embraced a vision of a multipolar Asia, aligning more closely with the US. Now, India is more willing to challenge China's regional dominance and collaborate with the US and its allies to shape a balanced Asian order. At the same time, India seeks to retain its strategic autonomy and avoid becoming a treaty ally of the United States.

Meanwhile, the idea that India can play a critical role in stabilising the security order in Asia and the Indo-Pacific has taken firm root in the United States' national-security establishment. Washington, for its part, adjusted its policies on Kashmir and nuclear non-proliferation to build better ties with India. US policy to help accelerate the rise of India and boost its national capabilities – despite New Delhi's reluctance to become an ally – enjoys bipartisan political support in Washington. A strong India, even if it is non-allied, is viewed as serving US interests in rebalancing Asia, which is perceived to be at risk of falling under Chinese dominance. Given Washington's weight in allied capitals, many of its European and Asian allies are beginning to develop similar policies towards India. While most countries in Asia are averse to taking sides between the US and China in their unfolding competition, many of them are investing in closer ties with India to give themselves greater room for manoeuvre in the unfolding Sino-US rivalry.

This chapter looks at four broad areas in which India could contribute to the rebalancing of Asia – ideological, economic, technological and military. In thinking about New Delhi's role in balancing against Beijing, it is often pointed out, rightly, that India is far weaker than China. The claim here is not about parity between the two; in fact, the gap between the capabilities of India and China is likely to endure for the near future. The argument is that India's growing national capabilities will be an important part of any effort to rebalance the region, which has been destabilised by an assertive China. Those efforts are natural given the difficulty that the US and many of China's neighbours face in accepting and accommodating Chinese dominance over Asia.

Ideological balance

The view of India as a democratic alternative to communist China was an important element of US foreign-policy discourse on Asia in the first decades after the Second World War. However, India did not see the triangular dynamic with the US and China from the perspective of democracy but from a post-colonial one.[1] Sino-US normalisation and India's drift towards the Soviet Union in the 1970s meant there was little room for building a solid partnership between New Delhi and Washington based on shared democratic values. There was a brief effort to do so in the 1980s, when the more ideological administration of Ronald Reagan made a pitch to woo India based on shared values.[2] Yet the idea of 'estranged democracies' summed up the state of the indifferent India–US relations during the Cold War.[3] On the face of it, the end of the Cold War and the collapse of the Soviet Union during 1989–91 provided a new context in which shared democratic values once again seemed to offer a durable basis for building an India–US partnership. The rhetoric that the US was the oldest democracy and India was the largest once again dominated the discourse on bilateral relations. But translating that into practice turned out to be hard.

Like other previous Democratic administrations, Bill Clinton's put a special emphasis on democratic values in US foreign policy. Flush from their Cold War triumph, the US and Europe saw fewer constraints on the pursuit of an ideological agenda in the world. The Clinton administration's general interest in human-rights promotion and preventive diplomacy led to its focus on Kashmir in its regional approach to South Asia. But Clinton's activism on Kashmir – raising questions about human rights in the restive province and enthusiastically seeking to resolve the dispute between India and Pakistan – came at a difficult time for India, when it was coping with massive internal turbulence in the province and battling external support from Islamabad for Kashmiri militants. US questioning of Kashmir's accession to India and its reluctance to confront Pakistan's support for cross-border terrorism generated a great deal of political resentment in New Delhi against Washington.[4] But the US focus on human rights in India did lead to changes in India's policy. New Delhi passed a human-rights act in 1993 and set up a statutory commission for their protection in the same year. India also started training its armed forces on respecting human rights while coping with the insurgency in Kashmir and beyond.[5] Even as India adapted to the new Western emphasis on human rights, it began to figure out that the US was quite open to balancing human-rights concerns with its other interests.

Beijing's crackdown on the Tiananmen Square protests in 1989 and the end of the Cold War in 1991 led to the US political class raising human-rights concerns to a higher political level. During his presidential campaign in 1992, Clinton called the Chinese Communist Party leaders 'the butchers of Beijing'.[6] But as US commercial engagement with China dramatically expanded in the 1990s, Clinton made a U-turn in China policy by stepping up political engagement with China, granting it most-favoured-nation status and supporting Beijing's entry into the World Trade Organization (WTO), which eventually took place under George W. Bush in 2001.[7] Clinton also unveiled a strategic-partnership agreement with China during his visit to Beijing in 1998; a joint statement issued during that visit called for greater collaboration in stabilising various regions, including the subcontinent. Concurrently, during his second term, Clinton began to soften the political tone on nuclear and human-rights issues in relation to India and chose to visit New Delhi in 2000, celebrating the shared values between the two countries.[8]

Clinton's Republican successor, George W. Bush, retained this emphasis on democracy promotion in US foreign policy during his tenure. Yet, unlike the Clinton administration's liberal internationalism, Bush sought to meld both realist and idealist goals in developing a strategy to promote a 'balance of power that favours freedom', as then-national security advisor Condoleezza Rice put it.[9] The Bush administration's attempts at democracy promotion and nation-building ran aground in Afghanistan and Iraq. With India, though, the emphasis on shared values and common interests in producing a stable Asian balance of power helped reduce the salience of the Kashmir question, de-hyphenate US relations with India and Pakistan (that is, delink US policies towards India and Pakistan) and present Indian democracy as a counter to Chinese autocracy. Bush, it has been reported, had a particular fascination with Indian democracy and was determined to support its rise despite the reluctance of large parts of the US bureaucracy, which was driven by concerns about nuclear non-proliferation.[10]

In a public speech at the historic Old Fort in New Delhi in 2006, George W. Bush underlined the importance of democracy as a binding factor between the US and India. He insisted:

> [The] partnership between the United States and India has deep and sturdy roots in the values we share. Both our nations were founded on the conviction that all people are created equal and are endowed with certain fundamental rights, including freedom of speech, freedom of assembly, and freedom of religion.[11]

President Barack Obama sought to build on the foundations of a deeper partnership with India that George W. Bush had laid. But emerging American concerns about the state of India's democracy were something that Obama had to deal with when Narendra Modi was elected as India's prime minister in 2014. In 2005, the George W. Bush administration had denied a visa to Modi, then-chief minister of Gujarat, on the allegation that Modi was responsible for the 2002 riots in the state. Obama ended Modi's visa ban and invited him to the US in September 2014, recognising the importance of boosting engagement with India. But during Obama's visit to India in January 2015 to join the Republic Day celebrations, Obama publicly warned about the dangers of New Delhi departing from its democratic roots amid the rise of Modi and the assertive Hindu nationalism of his party. In a speech just before he concluded his visit, Obama pointed to the risk of religious intolerance, arguing that nowhere was the freedom of religion more important than in India given the diversity of faiths that made up its society. 'India will succeed so long as it is not splintered along the lines of religious faith – so long as it's not splintered along any lines – and is unified as one nation.'[12]

US discomfort with the emerging fault lines in India's democracy began to grow in Modi's second term, which began in 2019. As the Bharatiya Janata Party (BJP) took a range of bold steps – including constitutional changes in Kashmir and the Citizenship Amendment Act – liberal opinion in the US and the West was highly critical. The argument that India is either an illiberal democracy or an electoral autocracy began to gain ground. However, Donald Trump's first administration chose to largely look away from the question of India's presumed democratic backsliding. The Hindu–Muslim riots in New Delhi during Trump's visit to India in early 2020 seemed to highlight the emerging tension between the US geopolitical interest in drawing India into an Asian coalition to balance against China and weakening democratic values in India under the Modi government.[13] But the Trump administration held its peace, given its focus on developing the Indo-Pacific framework in partnership with India through the Quadrilateral Security Dialogue (Quad).[14]

Joe Biden entered the White House with a much greater emphasis on the ideology of democracy than his predecessor. Taking charge amid the Republican questioning of the US election results, the 6 January 2021 attack on Capitol Hill by Trump supporters, and the deepening US contestation with authoritarian Russia and China, Biden made the question of democracy quite central to his international policy. He framed the global situation as a contest between 'democracies and autocracies' and convened an international Summit for Democracy in December 2021. Although the idea resonated with a large section of the US foreign-policy establishment, there were sceptical voices too.[15] As the US began to grapple with the challenges that China presented, the image of India as a leading democracy fit even more firmly within Biden's worldview. The Russian invasion of Ukraine in 2022, the deepening strategic bonds between Russia and China, and the explicit attack on Western democratic values by Russian President Vladimir Putin and Chinese leader Xi Jinping appeared to raise India's strategic value in the perceived ideological contestation.

Modi was given prime speaking slots in two of the annual Summit for Democracy gatherings, which took place in December 2021 and March 2023. 'Shared democratic values' became a consistent theme in US pronouncements on India in bilateral and 'minilateral' settings such as the Quad.[16] Biden's tenure seemed to bring about an unprecedented fit between the geopolitical interests and democratic values of India and the United States.

However, the US liberal disenchantment with Indian democracy under Modi is real.[17] Will it make a difference to US engagement with India? Unlikely. Some analysts have argued that the continuing decline in the quality of Indian democracy might 'undermine the foundations' of the emerging strategic partnership between India and the US.[18] Yet, despite the growing chorus in the US about India's weakening democracy, the Biden administration was careful not to openly criticise developments within India.[19]

The allegations in 2023 of official Indian involvement in the killing of a Canadian citizen of Indian origin in Canada and the formal launch of legal proceedings in the US against an Indian citizen, said to be operating under official Indian institutions, for attempting to murder Gurpatwant Singh Pannun, a US citizen of Indian origin, in the US have raised new concerns in Washington and other Western capitals about the nature of India's policies and the prospect of its participation in illegal trans-jurisdictional actions. Commentary in the Western press questioned the mutual trust and fragility of the partnership between New Delhi and Washington.[20] New Delhi, for its part, has declared that killing dissidents abroad is not government policy.[21] In October 2024, India arrested a former Indian intelligence official, Vikash Yadav, who is accused by the US of orchestrating the murder plot against Pannun. The arrest, however, was on unrelated charges and it remains to be seen if New Delhi will extradite him to the US when a New York court hears the case at the end of 2025.[22]

Indian commentators have raised concerns about Western powers, especially the developed anglophone countries, turning a blind eye to anti-India activity by separatist groups on their soil. The intersection of India's domestic politics with growing diaspora groups in the anglophone world is likely to emerge as a problem in the future that New Delhi will have to manage with its friends in the Five Eyes intelligence-sharing partnership of Australia, Canada, New Zealand, the United Kingdom and the US.[23] These five countries are among the top destinations for Indian immigrants. The public outcry in the West might also serve to caution the adventurists in the Indian security establishment.

India's presumed democratic infractions, such as they are, have so far not threatened its partnerships with the US or its Western allies. Although the issue has cast a shadow over India's ties with Canada, there appears to be a determination in New Delhi and Washington to prevent the issue from derailing the progress in bilateral relations. Mark Carney – who became the prime minister of Canada in March 2025, following the resignation of Justin Trudeau, and won a popular mandate in April 2025 – has talked of a reset in bilateral relations. He is expected to reduce some of the political toxicity in the Indo-Canadian relationship. India, too, appears eager to look beyond the difficult years of Trudeau's leadership and rebuild the relationship.[24]

Realists would argue that democracy has never been the sole element in defining the trajectory of US foreign policy. While the ideology of democracy has endured in US discourse, Washington has had to consistently balance it against other pressing interests, whether economic or geopolitical. More broadly, the US has begun to temper its rhetoric on democracy. As the US National Security Strategy of 2022 stated, the new global coalitions that Washington wants to build include 'countries that do not embrace democratic institutions but nevertheless depend upon and support a rules-based international system'.[25] This finessing of the initial dichotomy of democracy versus autocracy suggests the Biden team gave higher priority to the more pressing task of balancing against China in Asia.

Washington is acutely aware that China's threat to Western democratic values is far greater than that from India's supposed democratic backsliding.[26] As Beijing seeks to export its version of authoritarianism to the Global South, India's democracy – warts and all – will remain a valuable part of US strategy in Asia and beyond for liberals.[27] While Trump and his America First ideologues reject the US pursuit of external adventures in the name of democracy and other political values, the idea of democracy as a shared value with India is unlikely to disappear in the second term of the Trump administration. For example, the joint statement issued by Modi and Trump in February 2025 declared upfront:

> As the leaders of sovereign and vibrant democracies that value freedom, the rule of law, human rights, and pluralism, President Trump and Prime Minister Modi reaffirmed the strength of the India–U.S. Comprehensive Global Strategic Partnership, anchored in mutual trust, shared interests, goodwill and robust engagement of their citizens.[28]

Economic rebalance

As Mao Zedong's China and Nehru's India entered the international system as independent states, their contrasting political and economic systems were of considerable interest to the rest of the world. In the decades of intense anti-communism in the West, a democratic India stood as a natural political alternative to the People's Republic of China. In the economic domain too, there was a great deal of Western hope that India's economic development would demonstrate democracy's systemic superiority over communist China. This hope, in turn, led to a perceived stake in India's economic success.

But history unfolded in many complex turns. Although India was a democracy, it took a 'socialist' orientation that limited the possibilities for economic growth and for a sharp contrast with China on economic ideology.[29] Yet the US and Europe poured large amounts of economic aid into India to shore up its economic possibilities. This picture began to change in the 1970s, as New Delhi embraced radical economic populism at home and deepened strategic ties with Moscow. The framing of the New Delhi–Beijing dynamic in terms of economic ideology steadily dissipated as China opened up its markets to the West. Many in Asia, especially the emerging 'Asian tigers', like Singapore, saw India's chaotic democracy as an essential factor in its economic underperformance. Even more fundamentally, it was argued in non-communist Asia that economic development must be given greater priority over democracy. The dominant view in Asia was that democracy could follow but not precede development.

In the era of economic globalisation, capital went to the most attractive destinations rather than preferred political systems. A late entrant to the world of economic liberalisation, India began to demonstrate high growth rates only in the reform era, which began in the early 1990s. But China, which had begun its reforms in the late 1970s, was racing ahead. The Indian and Chinese economies were broadly on a par until the early 1990s; the nominal per capita GDP in 1990 was US$368 in India and US$318 in China.[30] But the gap between the two began to grow rapidly after that due to China's sustained high growth rates. The steady expansion of commercial engagement between Beijing and its East Asian neighbours, as well as the West, made China a more familiar and promising place for global capital. India's slow and cautious reform made it much less inviting and more demanding in terms of patience in overcoming multiple policy, regulatory and political hurdles.

Although India was growing at a much quicker pace from the 1990s relative to its own past performance, China was growing even faster. The widening gap between the two economies meant that, at the turn of the millennium, few in the world saw India as an economic alternative to China. A reforming India was seen as an additional opportunity, full of promise, given the potential size of its economy.

India itself saw China as a major opportunity. The idea of 'Chindia' – combining the strengths of the two economies – was a popular slogan in India in the early twenty-first century.[31] India also believed that growing economic engagement with China would create the conditions for resolving the political and security issues between the two sides. The rise of a China-centred economic boom seemed to herald the long-dreamt-of Asian century. However, much of this enthusiasm in India came crashing down by the late 2010s, as the mounting trade deficit with China became part of the problem in bilateral relations, in addition to the growing tensions on the boundary. New Delhi took two momentous decisions that sought to actively limit India's economic exposure to China. One decision was to oppose China's Belt and Road Initiative (BRI) in 2017, and the other was to withdraw in 2019 from the Asia-wide trade-liberalisation agreement, the Regional Comprehensive Economic Partnership (RCEP).[32]

While the BRI decision had little immediate consequence for the rest of the region, India's rejection of the RCEP appeared to take India out of any potential role for regional economic balancing. Association of Southeast Asian Nations (ASEAN) states, Australia and Japan were all deeply disappointed by India's decision to pull out of the RCEP at the very last minute. Many in the region argued that India's presence would have served as a useful counterweight to China in the RCEP and improved the bargaining power of the region vis-à-vis Beijing.

That argument did not cut much ice with New Delhi, which was determined to protect its manufacturing sector from being hollowed out by cheap Chinese imports. India's External Affairs Minister, Subrahmanyam Jaishankar, underlined the economic threat from China without naming it:

> In the name of openness, we have allowed subsidised products and unfair production advantages from abroad to prevail ... The effect of past trade agreements has been to deindustrialise some sectors. The consequences of future ones would lock us into global commitments, many of them not to our advantage. Those who argue stressing openness and efficiency do not present the full picture.

Jaishankar added that India was not 'turning its back on the world' but strengthening itself.[33]

New Delhi's growing discomfort with China-led Asian economic integration found a parallel in Washington. The 2016 US presidential campaign saw the Republican candidate, Donald Trump, argue against free trade by claiming that China was taking away US manufacturing jobs. One of the first acts of the first Trump administration was to walk out of the negotiations on the Trans-Pacific Partnership (TPP), a Pacific trade pact that was originally conceived as the US answer to China's growing economic salience in Asia. Trump was convinced that such free-trade agreements were at the expense of the American working class.[34] His decision was pilloried by US partners in Asia, as well as large sections of the US financial elite who were proponents of free trade. Many had hoped that the 2021 return to power of the Democrats – who had previously, under the Clinton and Obama administrations, strongly championed globalisation – would reverse Trump's policies.

But president Biden quickly dashed those hopes. In fact, the Biden administration embarked on a more systematic revision of global economic rules as a complement to the strategy of developing vigorous competition with China on the economic front and regaining strategic primacy in Asia. The then-US national security advisor, Jake Sullivan, summed up Biden's economic vision as reversing neo-liberal economic globalisation. He challenged the conventional wisdom on a number of counts. These included faith in the markets as efficient allocators of capital, the idea that all growth is good and will benefit all sections of American society, the proposition that economic interdependence would lead to peace and the notion that multilateral institutions like the WTO are effective in preventing the weaponisation of trade.[35]

In challenging the conventional economic wisdom, highlighting the deep interconnection between economics and national security, underlining the importance of active competition with China and emphasising the imperative of rearranging the global economic order, Sullivan fused American geopolitics and geo-economics. If China and large parts of East Asia were the main beneficiaries of the old Washington Consensus, India figured prominently in the Biden administration's effort to build a 'new Washington Consensus' that emphasised encouraging equitable economic growth at home, increasing the role of the state in allocating capital, reducing economic exposure to China and restructuring the global economic order. The ideas of resilient supply chains, cooperation in the development of critical technologies and collaboration in the transition to a 'greener' world figured prominently in the India–US bilateral agenda, as well as that of the Quad.[36]

The economic wheel, then, has turned full circle from the 1950s, when India was seen as an economic alternative to China. Today's context, however, is quite different, with China having the second-largest economy and being a powerful commercial force in the world. Although New Delhi is unlikely to match Beijing's economic weight in the foreseeable future, its rapid economic growth will have a strategic salience of its own for the evolving Asian economic architecture. In 2025, India's GDP was expected to be US$4.1 trillion and China's US$19trn; therefore, even if India grows faster than today and China slows down, the economic gap between the two will endure. But India is in striking distance of overtaking Japan (whose GDP is currently at US$4.2trn) as the second-largest economy in Asia.[37]

Three factors are likely to shape India's role in the economic rebalancing of Asia. One is India's prospects for continued high growth in the coming decades. According to the International Monetary Fund, India remains the world's fastest-growing large economy and is expected to contribute nearly 15% of global growth in the second half of the 2020s. China's contribution is estimated to be 23% in the same period.[38] India's share is widely expected to rise in the years ahead and its economic heft will be of value to the US and its allies. Secondly, as global capital adapts to new problems arising out of the US–China confrontation, India figures in the 'derisking' strategies of the major powers. While the idea of 'China plus one' – that is, focusing on other high-growth Asian economies in addition to China – has long animated global investors, the attractiveness of India has continued to rise. To be sure, most of the industries moving out of China are not relocating to India. But we have seen some interesting shifts from Apple and its associates, which are moving an increasing share of their production from China to India.[39] Thirdly, India continues to seek out new trade opportunities. India joined the US regional initiative, the Indo-Pacific Economic Framework for Prosperity (IPEF), which was announced at the Quad summit in Tokyo in early 2022.[40] The return of Trump to the White House in January 2025 and his launch of a tariff war has, however, made IPEF irrelevant. Even more consequentially, Trump is departing from the Biden administration's focus on friend-shoring (relocating supply chains to friendly partners) in favour of onshoring (relocating them to the US mainland). Trump has opposed Apple's decision to move some iPhone manufacturing to India.[41] Amid the uncertainties generated by Trump's trade policies, New Delhi has focused on fast-tracking trade talks with the second Trump administration and is expected to be among the first countries to sign a new bilateral trade agreement.[42]

On the face of it, there are many big 'ifs' associated with the three factors that could make India a potential economic force to be reckoned with in the rebalancing of Asia. Yet the probability of such an outcome is not insignificant; it is rooted in current efforts to reorientate the economic order that has worked until now in China's favour. US efforts to restructure the global economic order, even if not entirely successful, are bound to have a significant impact on the Asian economic architecture. While China will remain the dominant economic force in the region, the seeds of an alternative framework in which India is an important part are beginning to be visualised. India's accelerating economic growth and China's slowdown in the mid-2020s are reinforcing that hope.[43]

Technological rebalance

As in the political and economic domains, India is emerging as an important element in the reorganisation of the technological order in Asia away from excessive dependence on China. Western support for India's technological advancement dates back to the 1950s, as part of their efforts to stem the rising tide of communism in Asia. Three factors shaped this support. Firstly, the building of a scientific establishment in India after independence was led by the likes of Homi Bhabha and Vikram

Sarabhai, who easily leveraged their deep connections with Western scientific establishments to boost the development of advanced technology in India.[44]

Secondly, in the era of scientific internationalism and empathy for India's development aspirations, there was an openness in the West to supporting New Delhi's technological ambitions. The early progress in India's nuclear and space programmes was a result of US and European technological cooperation. Thirdly, an interest in demonstrating that democratic India could do better than communist China saw the US think boldly about assisting India's nuclear development. US President John F. Kennedy, some Indian diplomats have claimed, offered to help India develop a nuclear weapon in the early 1960s. Washington was aware of the impending Chinese nuclear test and eager to prevent India from lagging behind. There was, indeed, a section of the US establishment in the early 1960s that believed that helping allies acquire nuclear weapons made strategic sense. But Nehru apparently turned down that offer.[45] Instead, the US moved to sell a civilian nuclear power station (with two reactors) to India in 1963, in order to boost India's prestige relative to communist China.[46] The Tarapur power station made India the first country in Asia to generate civilian nuclear power six years later in 1969. India's first space satellites were American, and the US has supported India's use of its civilian space programme for education and other developmental purposes.[47]

The India–US romance in high technology soured once the Nuclear Non-Proliferation Treaty (NPT) came into force in 1970. With China acknowledged as a formal nuclear-weapons power in the NPT framework (thanks to Beijing's first nuclear test in 1964), the political balance between New Delhi and Beijing began to change in the US bureaucratic calculus – the former an outlier and the latter a privileged part of the NPT system.

New Delhi's inability to conduct a nuclear test before 1968 made it a permanent outsider to the non-proliferation regime. India's first nuclear test in 1974 made matters worse for New Delhi in the United States. As the US began to strengthen the NPT system, the prior high-technological cooperation between the two came under the shadow of non-proliferation sanctions, which continued to mount in the decades that followed. The nuclear dispute became one of the major obstacles to the improvement of bilateral relations. Attempts to overcome it in the 1980s during the Reagan administration once again focused on finding ways to expand technological cooperation between New Delhi and Washington.[48]

It would take nearly four decades after the NPT was signed to resolve, if only partly, the nuclear dispute between India and the United States relating to India's status in the global nuclear order and its access to civilian-nuclear technology. Here again, considerations of balancing against China were front and centre in overcoming the nuclear barrier between New Delhi and Washington. Although the room for India–US engagement expanded rapidly after the Cold War, the question of non-proliferation thoroughly complicated the relationship, as the Clinton administration sought to halt and roll back the nuclear-weapons programmes of India and Pakistan.[49] While Clinton saw New Delhi through the South Asian non-proliferation lens, George W. Bush's administration viewed India through the prism of China's rise and the Asian balance of power. This altered the strategic perspective in Washington, and Bush committed enormous political capital to modify domestic non-proliferation laws and change the global rules on nuclear commerce to facilitate American and international civilian-nuclear cooperation with India.[50] This also involved an implicit acceptance of India's nuclear-weapons programme, thus overriding the non-proliferation purists in the US political and bureaucratic system. The change in the domestic and international rules on nuclear cooperation were exclusively for India, and the Bush administration rejected Pakistan's entreaties for a similar arrangement.

China was clear-eyed in seeing the strategic rationale behind the historic US–India civil-nuclear initiative and understanding it as a transformative moment in US–India relations and a major shift in India's foreign policy. Beijing moved to mobilise international sentiment in favour of the view that NPT norms should not be modified in an ad hoc manner in favour of just one country. Although China could not block the revision of global nuclear rules in favour of India in 2008, it succeeded in blocking an Indian effort to seek formal membership in the Nuclear Suppliers Group in 2017.[51] Although the public argument was framed in terms of the nuclear non-proliferation regime, Beijing recognised, rightly, that the Indo–US nuclear deal was about building a deeper strategic partnership between New Delhi and Washington. India, for example, has not yet bought a single American nuclear reactor since the deal, but the bilateral partnership has continued to advance nevertheless.[52] In the second term of the Trump administration, there is an intensified political effort in New Delhi and Washington to remove the barriers to allow India to purchase US nuclear reactors.[53] For Washington, the civil-nuclear initiative sought to overcome a major dispute between the two countries that was preventing deeper engagement with India. For New Delhi, this deal was proof that Washington could now be a trusted partner.[54] Beijing's brazen attempt to block the US effort to end India's dispute with the global nuclear non-proliferation regime brought new clarity to New Delhi on who its friends and rivals were.

The civil-nuclear agreement also set the stage for India to join a range of global technology-control regimes, including the Missile Technology Control Regime, the Australia Group on chemical and biological weapons, and the Wassenaar Arrangement on managing the commerce of conventional arms and dual-use technologies.[55] Besides getting India into a set of regimes that had long sought to constrain New Delhi's strategic programmes, Washington also began to liberalise domestic rules on the transfer of advanced technologies to India. Taken together, the civil-nuclear initiative ended a long-running battle between India and the US as well as the global nuclear non-proliferation regime. And it set the stage for a potentially more consequential technological partnership between the US and India for regional security in Asia and the Indo-Pacific.

As Sino-US and Sino-Indian tensions worsened from the late 2010s, deeper and wider technological cooperation became a central pillar of the US approach to India. This involved two different strands. One was to elevate the bilateral technological partnership with India. Based on the appreciation that the two sides needed something substantive to lift up the partnership, there was an effort to significantly enhance India's access to US technology. At a bilateral meeting on the margins of the Quad summit in Tokyo in May 2022, Modi and Biden unveiled the US–India Initiative on Critical and Emerging Technology. After intensive consultations between the two establishments, the national-security advisers issued an ambitious framework in early 2023 to significantly enhance India's access to sensitive US technologies, as well as to clear the ground for comprehensive technological cooperation between the defence establishments, commercial entities and academia. The framework covered several areas from innovation in civilian and defence domains to telecommunications, space and semiconductor production.[56] Modi's visit to Washington in June 2023 saw political agreement between the two sides on putting technology at the very heart of the strategy to transform bilateral relations.[57] This was reinforced during the talks between Modi and Trump at the White House in February 2025, pointing to the continued centrality of advanced technologies in the bilateral relationship.

A second strand of the efforts to increase US–India technological cooperation was to lend it a regional and global dimension. The Quad meetings throughout 2020–24 highlighted the regional dimension of the expanding technological cooperation between New Delhi and Washington. The scale and intensity of the challenges presented by the COVID-19 pandemic, which hit the world in early 2020, underlined the problem of over-reliance on China in medical supply chains. It also pointed to the answer: diversifying supply chains and deepening cooperation among trusted partners. The pandemic induced a big India–US effort to develop bilateral and regional cooperation in producing vaccines in India and delivering them across the Indo-Pacific region.[58]

As the global roll-out of fifth-generation telecommunications technology (5G) became a bone of strategic contention between the US and China, India and the Quad became quite central to the challenge against the domination of the Chinese firm Huawei. New Delhi eventually kept Huawei out of its own 5G plans and joined hands with the Quad partners in building 'clean networks' through vendor diversification and the development of an open, diverse and inter-operable telecommunications ecosystem.[59] As part of an ideological contestation against China in the technological domain, the Quad members also outlined a broad set of principles to help ensure that ways in which 'technology is designed, developed, governed, and used' would be 'shaped by our shared democratic values and respect for universal human rights'.[60] This ambition was driven by the shared conviction that China's model of technological development would reinforce authoritarianism and autocracy.

More broadly, the emphasis on India–US technological cooperation, bilaterally and regionally, is now considered an essential part of competing with China in Asia and across the world in developing a more resilient and sustainable economic and technological future. Beyond the Quad, the US has also been promoting triangular technological cooperation between Washington, Seoul and New Delhi.[61] President Trump, in his second term, has reiterated the commitment to deeper technological cooperation with India, but the political context in which that operates could become a lot more transactional. India, for its part, is looking beyond the US to develop deeper technological ties with Europe and other major actors like Israel.

Military rebalance

The idea of military balancing was quite alien to the post-independence Indian leadership in its engagement with Asia. India's first prime minister, Nehru, discarded the expansive expeditionary role of the Indian Army inherited from the British Raj and distanced the armed forces from the imperial role of ensuring regional security. Rooted in the liberal-internationalist tradition and moralpolitik imbibed in the interwar period, Nehru believed that independent India did not face any military threats.[62] His effort to construct an 'area of peace' around India complemented his vocal opposition to Western military alliances in Asia to counter the perceived communist threat in the region. Nehru called instead for dialogue and the peaceful resolution of disputes. He offered India's good offices to resolve major Asian conflicts, especially in the Korean Peninsula and Indochina.[63] The emphasis on development at home and disarmament abroad meant Nehru did not devote many financial resources to defence. Alarmed by the prospect of militarism in post-colonial Asia, Nehru also weakened the salience of the Indian armed forces in independent India's security policymaking.[64]

Yet Nehru also envisioned India becoming one of the few consequential powers in the international system and a critical player in Asia. In the immediate aftermath of independence, Nehru sought to develop a range of bilateral and trilateral security partnerships with like-minded countries such as Burma (now Myanmar), Egypt, Indonesia and Yugoslavia.[65] India also retained some of its links with Britain; for example, it participated in the British-led joint naval exercises off Trincomalee, along with Pakistan. But as India weakened in the 1960s and put itself on a path of relative decline, the political will for regional military cooperation steadily declined. New Delhi, for example, simply did not respond to the request from newly independent Singapore for military support. Similarly, early Indian initiatives of defence-industrial collaboration with fellow non-aligned nations like Egypt – for example, for the development of a jet engine and a fighter aircraft – came to nought.[66]

As India adopted left-wing populism at home, it also embraced more radical anti-Western positions in the 1960s and 1970s. Yet New Delhi was not only suspicious of Western alliances in Asia; it was also wary of the Soviet Union's proposals for collective security in Asia. Despite growing bilateral security ties to Moscow, New Delhi was unwilling to endorse Soviet leader Leonid Brezhnev's 1969 plan for collective security in Asia.[67] At the end of the Cold War, military isolationism was a deeply held policy in India's international relations.

But soon after the Cold War came to an end, New Delhi began to dismantle its military isolation and initiate wide-ranging defence engagement with a number of countries.[68] The new but tentative approach involved a number of elements. One was conducting joint military exercises. Defence engagement with the United States was first off the block and has been discussed in Chapter Three. India's new defence engagement was eventually extended to all the major powers, including France, Russia, the UK and the European Union. India did not limit itself to the great powers and also focused on renewing military contact with a number of countries in India's extended neighbourhood. Bilateral naval exercises with Singapore were among the earliest and began in 1994. Over time, India expanded its military cooperation with most Southeast Asian nations. India's bilateral and trilateral exercises with ASEAN countries eventually culminated in the first joint India–ASEAN maritime exercise in 2023.

A second feature of India's military diplomacy was offering training support to other armed forces in the region. India's large and long-standing military establishment lent itself to this important purpose. A third element was launching political-military dialogues with various countries. While the Indian Ministry of Defence was not entirely comfortable with this engagement, the Ministry of External Affairs and the National Security Council Secretariat took up much of the slack in nudging this forward.[69]

The post-1991 era also saw India shed its past reluctance to engage in multilateral security forums. India's Look East policy, initiated in the early 1990s, inevitably involved taking part in the emerging ASEAN security institutions. India became a member of the ASEAN Regional Forum in 1996 and a founding member of both the East Asia Summit in 2005 and the ASEAN Defence Ministers' Meeting-Plus in 2010. India has also initiated its own multilateral defence forums since the 1990s. This includes the MILAN biennial naval exercises around the Andaman and Nicobar Islands, the Indian Ocean Naval Symposium, the Regional Maritime Information Fusion Centre in New Delhi, and regular dialogue among the national-security advisers of India, Maldives and Sri Lanka. This wide-ranging engagement has helped socialise India's armed forces and the civilian-defence establishment with their counterparts in the rest of Asia. These new military-diplomatic instruments have been routinely used in India's engagement across the extended neighbourhood of the Indo-Pacific, including the Indian Ocean.

India's emerging capability for power projection in the Indo-Pacific became evident with its growing emphasis on evacuation operations. Domestic pressures to bring home Indian citizens caught in war zones translated into regular evacuation operations by Indian armed forces, which demonstrated India's capabilities and reach in the region.[70] India also sought to become the first responder in regional humanitarian crises and disasters. Humanitarian assistance and disaster relief (HADR) operations have increasingly become integral to India's regional military engagement.[71]

Power projection across distances in the vast Indo-Pacific has demanded that India seek military-access arrangements with friendly countries. New Delhi, which long campaigned against foreign military bases in the region as part of its promotion of non-alignment, was now seeking similar military access for itself. This is a major transition in India's perception of regional security from that of idealist internationalism to great-power realpolitik.[72] Although there has been much speculation about India acquiring bases in other countries, such as Mauritius, New Delhi does not have overseas military bases in the traditional sense of the term. Unlike China, which secured its first overseas military base in Djibouti, India's emphasis has been on negotiating operational turnaround facilities for the Indian Navy, developing joint facilities for HADR operations and maritime surveillance of exclusive economic zones of partner states, and setting up radar installations, space tracking stations and communication facilities.

Even this modest Indian strategy has often run into trouble, for example in Maldives, when nationalist sentiment was aroused against the Indian military presence. Soon after he took charge in November 2023, Maldivian President Mohamed Muizzu demanded the removal of all Indian personnel from the island nation. India complied with the request, even as it managed to improve relations with the Muizzu government.[73] It was a lesson for India in dealing with the prickly nationalist sentiment of small states, which all great powers have had to overcome in the past. Unlike distant China, which needs bases to develop a solid military presence in the Indian Ocean, India is not under great pressure to acquire formal military bases in the Indian Ocean. Its central location, a long coastline along a peninsula that juts into the Indian Ocean, and two far-flung island territories in the Arabian Sea and the Bay of Bengal give the Indian Navy sufficient reach from its own home territory. Its naval diplomacy is therefore focused on the development of access arrangements that are less controversial than formal bases.

In the post-Cold War era, New Delhi also sought to overcome one of its main weaknesses – its limited ability to export arms, which provide a critical instrument to build long-term security partnerships in the region. That shortcoming, in turn, was tied to the weaknesses of India's defence-industrial infrastructure. In the Modi years, we have seen a major effort to raise the domestic production of arms and arms exports.[74] This reform effort is beginning to show some results. In 2024–25, India's defence exports rose to a historic high of ₹23,622 crore (approximately US$2.76 billion), marking a 12% increase over the previous year's exports of ₹21,083 crore. The equipment exported to about 80 countries included a wide range of items from ammunition to arms, sub-systems/systems, parts and components. India's private sector, which is now being encouraged to enhance defence production at home, is producing a significant share of these exports.[75] India, however, remains a new player, finding its feet in the rough and tumble of the global arms bazaar.

The acceleration of India's military diplomacy was the result of two important factors. One was the impact of American ideas on Indian thinking about regional security, which came from the intense Indian engagement with the US military. For example, the idea of India as a 'net security provider' in the Indian Ocean region was first articulated by the US secretary of defense at the Shangri-La Dialogue in 2009 and became an integral part of Indian discourse within a few years.[76] As India's own regional ambitions grew and the US paid greater attention to India's potential role, there has been an osmosis of ideas from Washington to New Delhi.

Far more consequential for the acceleration of Indian military diplomacy was the second factor: the relentless military pressure from China – not only in the Himalayas, but also in the subcontinent and the Indian Ocean. The question of military balancing against China, through India's own national effort as well as through coalition-building, has over time become a key driving force for greater Indian military activism in the region in three dimensions – engagement with the US and its allies, bilateral engagement with key actors in the region and more active military multilateralism. Within the subcontinent and in the island states of the Indian Ocean, where India had traditionally enjoyed some influence, denying greater influence to China has become a major preoccupation. In Maldives, Mauritius, the Seychelles and Sri Lanka, New Delhi has been trying to blunt Chinese attempts to build stronger military ties with these states. This has not been an unqualified success in Maldives and Sri Lanka, which are unwilling to shut down their defence ties with China. The rising Chinese military profile, however, has compelled India to intensify its own defence diplomacy with these island states.

India has also reached out to countries where China already has a major military presence to gain a toehold for the Indian military. Bangladesh and Myanmar are two countries where New Delhi has made military forays with assistance packages of its own. While military exchanges with Bangladesh significantly improved during prime minister Sheikh Hasina's rule (2009–24), her ouster has left New Delhi–Dhaka defence ties under a shadow amid the general deterioration of bilateral relations. With Myanmar, India's military engagement has grown steadily.

India's incremental and slow-paced military diplomacy, however, is coming to a potential denouement with the deepening tensions between New Delhi and Beijing as well as between the US and China. The era when India could pretend that the military threats from China were minimal and that it did not need US support to counter them is now definitively behind us. Many have pointed to India's non-alignment as such a powerful ideology that it will continue to limit India's military cooperation with the US.[77] The US analyst Ashley Tellis has argued:

> India's significant weaknesses compared with China, and its inescapable proximity to it, guarantee that New Delhi will never involve itself in any US confrontation with Beijing that does not directly threaten its own security. India values cooperation with Washington for the tangible benefits it brings but does not believe that it must, in turn, materially support the United States in any crisis – even one involving a common threat such as China.[78]

Tellis's cautioning that Washington should not have illusions about the Indian role in a US conflict with China may be important, but the US appears to be quite realistic about India's potential contributions in balancing against China and its emphasis on strategic autonomy. Kurt Campbell, who directed US policy in the Indo-Pacific in the White House during 2021–23, stated publicly:

> India has a unique strategic character. It will not be an ally of the United States. It has the desire to be an independent, powerful state and it will be another great power. But I think there are reasons to believe that our strategic alignment is growing across the board in almost every arena.[79]

If some American analysts have questioned India's commitment to stand with the US against China, Trump's second term has raised questions about the US willingness to defend its allies against China.[80] Given the growing military capabilities of China – economic, technological and military – there will be inevitable hesitations among all major actors, including the US, to embark on a confrontation with China. Yet it is unlikely that the US and China's neighbours will simply roll over and accept Beijing's dominance over Asia.

It might be premature, therefore, to conclude on how exactly New Delhi's alignment with Washington might work out in a scenario of major conflict involving the US and China in the Indo-Pacific. A lot would depend on the specifics of the dynamics at that moment between the three powers. For one, the structural tensions between India and China show no sign of abating and New Delhi is increasingly conscious that a Taiwan contingency – a Chinese invasion of the island territory – could well turn out to be an Indian contingency – mounting pressure on the Himalayan border. The fall of Taiwan would leave the redemption of Chinese claims on the land border with India a high priority for Beijing. Preventing or delaying that outcome is increasingly viewed in New Delhi as in India's interest.[81]

Secondly, fighting alongside the US against China is not the only way India can contribute to the outcome of a major regional conflict. There could be multiple other ways – including allowing US forces the use of its logistical facilities and taking over some of the tasks of the US Navy in the Indian Ocean – in which New Delhi could shape the larger theatre using its military capabilities. In a major signal of Indian support for US operations in the Indian Ocean, three Indian ports have signed agreements with the US for the maintenance and repair of US naval ships.[82] Strategic coordination and effective burden-sharing arrangements across the theatre could hold the key to successful collaboration in dealing with different Indo-Pacific military contingencies against China in the future.

As India's military capabilities grow, including with the support of the United States, New Delhi's ability to contribute to the regional balance of power will become more salient. Yet several important questions arise from Tellis's argument that must be addressed. That India has a long, disputed and increasingly militarised border with China in the Himalayas imposes significant constraints on its willingness to support or join US military operations in a regional conflict. Given the Chinese capability to put pressure at any point of its choosing in response to what Beijing might see as a provocative Indian act in partnership with the US, New Delhi will necessarily have to consider the consequences for its own frontier in joining the US in a distant conflict. Recognising that its freedom of military action in the region is constrained, New Delhi is devoting significant energies to enhancing deterrence against China in the Himalayas, including deploying additional troops, activating new airfields, modernising its military infrastructure on the frontier, and deploying new technologies and weapons systems. Underlying the effort is the political recognition in New Delhi that a partnership with the US is critical in enhancing deterrence against China in the Himalayas. Washington, too, understands India's vulnerabilities in the north and is prepared to assist with New Delhi's immediate needs to cope with the challenge and to support the longer-term project of Indian defence modernisation, which will enhance deterrence in the Himalayas and liberate New Delhi to play a larger regional balancing role. This outcome, desired by both, cannot be achieved overnight. Academic critics are right to point to the current constraints, but policymakers and political leaders are focused on how to overcome them, if only over time.

Secondly, India's potential two-front military situation against Pakistan and China has long been a constraint on India's wider regional security role. Here again, there is some improvement, thanks to a change in US policies and the evolution of the regional situation. US military assistance to Pakistan and Islamabad's solid defence cooperation with Beijing were part of this two-front problem. The US decision to reduce military assistance and the transfer of advanced weapons to Pakistan in recent years, its growing military assistance to India and its tacit political support for India on the Kashmir question have together begun to reduce the military salience of Pakistan's security challenge to India. But it has not eliminated it. Meanwhile, Pakistan has experienced rapid economic decline – its GDP at US$375bn in 2024 compares poorly with India's GDP at US$3.9trn in the same year. This gap is expected to widen in India's favour, given Pakistan's economic stagnation since the late 2010s. Relative economic decline and a diminished partnership with the US have, in fact, increased Pakistan's strategic reliance on China, thereby exacerbating India's China challenge. The hostilities between India and

Pakistan in May 2025, precipitated by a terrorist attack on tourists in Kashmir, underlined that Pakistan's security challenge to India remains present. The reported success of Chinese-supplied Pakistani fighters against India's (French-supplied) aircraft further emphasised China's role in this dynamic.[83]

Moreover, since the withdrawal of US forces from Afghanistan in 2021, Pakistan has acquired a two-front problem of its own amid deteriorating relations with the Taliban in Afghanistan and fresh questions about the stability of the Durand Line that separates the sovereignties of Islamabad and Kabul in the Pashtun heartland.[84] The Afghan Taliban has also sought deeper cooperation with India and has opened the door for New Delhi to try to exploit Pakistan's emerging two-front problem. There are also growing tensions between Iran and Pakistan on their shared frontier in Balochistan.[85] Tit-for-tat airstrikes by Tehran and Islamabad in January 2024 against their respective Baloch insurgents underlined Pakistan's wider challenges in its western borderlands and highlighted India's enduring interest in strong political ties with Iran. The improved regional situation for India does not mean its difficulties with Pakistan have disappeared, but New Delhi is in a better position to manage them thanks to its growing partnership with the US.

While Western commentators have questioned the willingness of India to sail with US forces in the Taiwan Strait, Chinese analysts have worried about New Delhi joining hands with Washington to constrain China's access to the Indian Ocean. New Delhi and Washington have intensified their naval collaboration, at the bilateral as well as the Quad level, in tracking the growing Chinese naval presence in the Indian Ocean and enhancing intelligence sharing in general, and maritime-domain awareness in particular. Some Indian navalists see maritime collaboration with the US and its allies as a lever against the Chinese threat on the Himalayan border. They call for a powerful naval coalition with the US to mount pressure on Chinese supply lines in the Indian Ocean. They bet that the coalition's naval dominance in the Indian Ocean will generate greater flexibility for India in coping with the China threat on the land frontier.[86] India is strengthening its military presence around the Andaman and Nicobar Islands and is opening up the islands for naval visits from its strategic partners, including the US and its allies.

The assessment of India's balancing capabilities in the military domain has been inevitably clouded by the huge gap in military power between India and China. To be sure, according to the IISS *Military Balance 2025*, India was the sixth-largest defence spender globally, with an annual budget of about US$75bn, ranked after the US (US$968bn), China (US$235bn), Russia (US$146bn), Germany (US$86bn) and the UK (US$81bn).[87] The massive gap with China is amplified by the nature of India's spending – personnel takes up a large part at 53%.[88] It was only in the second term of the Modi government (2019–24) that New Delhi began a major effort to refashion its armed forces, reform the management of its defence institutions and modernise its defence-industrial base (for a comparative summary of defence budget, active personnel and population in 2024, see Table A1, p. 181). It has a long way to go in closing the gap with China. The 2024 Global Firepower ranking puts India at number four in the world after the US, Russia and China.[89] The gulf between India's significant military capabilities (in absolute terms for various metrics like the size of the armed forces, defence spending and the possession of advanced weapons) and its relative weakness in relation to China can only be bridged through intensive partnerships with other powers. If India relied on the Soviet Union and Russia in the past, it is now turning to the US and other Western countries to enhance its overall military capabilities. While India will never 'catch up' with China in terms of absolute capacity, it is New Delhi's growing relative weight across many sectors that contributes to the balance of power in favour of a multipolar Asia (see Figure A1, p. 181 for defence spending for India, China and Japan, 2008–25). In a similar way, Mao's China was an insignificant economic and military actor in relation to the Soviet Union in the 1960s and 1970s, but drawing close to China helped the US to complicate the Soviet calculus in Asia. For a Washington that is today seeking to rebalance the military equation in Asia, helping New Delhi to enhance its military capabilities is an important investment. Although it is not a treaty ally, India brings the mass and motivation in Asia to boost US plans to rearrange the regional security order.

The discussion of India's role in the military rebalancing of Asia is incomplete without reference to its nuclear weapons and its interactive dynamic with China. Nuclear politics has been quite central to the evolution of India's relations with China, Pakistan and the US; but the operational impact of India's nuclear weapons on Asian security remains limited, for now at least, to the conflict dynamics between New Delhi and Islamabad. This could, however, change in the future as the nuclear-weapons capabilities of the three countries continue to grow. American strategic considerations of China and the Asian balance of power informed the US decision to support the construction of India's first nuclear power reactor in 1962 and the civil-nuclear initiative four decades later. If China's nuclear-weapons test in 1964 triggered India's discourse on nuclear weaponisation, Beijing's support for Pakistan's nuclear-weapons programme between the 1970s and the 1990s pushed India over the edge in 1998, when it decided to test nuclear weapons.[90] Beijing's opposition to the US–India civil-nuclear initiative and its resistance to New Delhi's quest for membership in the Nuclear Suppliers Group is among a growing number of Indian grievances against China.

India's modest nuclear arsenal of about 180 weapons is substantially smaller than the Chinese arsenal of about 600 weapons. Pakistan's nuclear armoury stands at 170 warheads.[91] Beijing has long maintained a minimum-deterrence posture to deal with Washington's nuclear superiority. That approach appears to be changing as China accelerates its nuclear-weapons build-up; it is expected to build an arsenal of 1,000 nuclear warheads by 2030.[92] New Delhi is some distance away from acquiring a credible second-strike nuclear capability against Beijing. It does not have sufficiently long-range missiles to credibly threaten China with nuclear weapons. While it is incrementally increasing its delivery capabilities, India has not so far embarked on a nuclear-weapons race with China. Further, unlike Pakistan, which relies on the threat of nuclear escalation to deal with the growing conventional military imbalance with India, New Delhi has not gone down that road to deal with superior Chinese military power on the contested northern frontier. India's emphasis has been on developing conventional military capabilities to deter China.

In the two major military crises with China during 2017 and 2020, there was a lot of conventional brinkmanship but no resort to nuclear signalling or rhetoric by either side. This could, however, change in the coming years. As a former Indian diplomat involved in the development of India's nuclear policy put it: 'Even though India and China still do not see each other as existential threats, the likelihood of a limited, short, but high-intensity conflict has grown, and face-to-face deployments with constant probing could catalyse escalation pressures.' However, the danger of escalation to nuclear proportions may grow as 'the deployment or use of dual-capable missiles against air bases close to the border areas or increasing standoffs in the Indian Ocean region as both countries increase subsurface patrols create friction points'.[93]

CONCLUSION

In Asia and of Asia

Introduction

In this concluding chapter, we review the emergence of India as a consequential actor in Asia and its imperatives in dealing with the continuing radical changes in the region's geopolitical and economic environment. One of the unanticipated features of Asia's new geopolitics has been the return of India to centre stage. During the colonial era, British India played a decisive role in shaping the regional security order in the Indian Ocean and the abutting regions, underwritten by Britain from the early nineteenth to the middle of the twentieth century. Independent India deliberately chose to withdraw from such a security role in the name of non-alignment and its opposition to Cold War bloc politics. India compounded this geopolitical orientation by cutting links to Western capital in the name of socialism. Together, the choices steadily marginalised India in Asia – despite the centrality of the idea of post-colonial solidarity in Asia in independent India's foreign policy.

With the end of the Cold War, India began to move away from these ideas, which had been dominant in India's political class for more than half a century. As it opened its economy in the 1990s, India's growth rate picked up. By the early 2020s,

India was already the third-largest economy in Asia, only behind China and Japan. By the end of the 2020s, India is likely to overtake Japan to become the second-largest economy in Asia and the third largest in the world. India's economic transformation has been accompanied by growing defence expenditures, making it the sixth-largest defence spender in the world in 2024. It also has the world's third-largest armed forces. The twenty-first century has also seen the rapid growth of India's technological capabilities, with growing private-sector capabilities in emerging digital and related technological capabilities. Put simply, India's comprehensive national power – which was on a path of relative decline in the second half of the twentieth century – began to grow in both absolute and relative terms in the early twenty-first century.

Accretion of national capabilities alone does not a great power make. Post-war Germany and Japan stand out as examples of states endowed with large capabilities but constrained by domestic pacifism and the status of a junior partner in the United States-led alliance system. India, like China, aspires to be a major power. The rise of its national capabilities has been associated with a simultaneous discarding of the ideology of non-alignment. With material capabilities and a new political will, India's location at the crossroads of Asia and at the heart of the Indian Ocean makes it quite consequential for the balance of power in the region. In fact, the invention of the Indo-Pacific strategic geography is about putting India back into the heart of Asian geopolitics. Yet, as India's relative position in Asia improves, the broader political and economic context in Asia is undergoing rapid change. New Delhi's salience in Asia will be determined by its ability to effectively deal with these changes, limiting the potential negative consequences for its position and leveraging the changes to enhance India's weight in the regional order.

Assertive China, disruptive America

The first quarter of the twenty-first century began with a celebration of the economic rise of Asia, its growing internal integration and its deepening interdependence with the United States and the West. Asia, once home to endemic internal and external conflict, was largely at peace. If conflict between the great powers darkened its past international relations, relative harmony among them at the dawn of the twenty-first century promised unprecedented prosperity and peace. But by the middle of the 2010s, that framework had come under great stress. At the heart of this change was China's rise and the nature of its relations with other great powers, especially the US and Beijing's Asian neighbours.

Asia's strategic landscape was profoundly transformed in the late twentieth century by three developments: the normalisation of Washington's relations with Beijing in the 1970s; Chinese leader Deng Xiaoping's reforms from the late 1970s, which put China on the path to becoming the world's second-largest economy and a military power to be reckoned with; and the slow but steady process of regional institution-building. For much of the region, this new geopolitical and economic framework was immensely beneficial and appeared irreversible. However, confidence in the continuation of this framework was shaken by China's assertiveness towards its neighbours and the emergence of an enduring Sino-US confrontation from the mid-2010s. If the US effort to integrate China into the global trading system helped accelerate regional economic integration and growth for all, US policies attempting to reduce its exposure and that of its allies to the Chinese economy promise to rearrange Asia's economic order.

Thanks to the transformation of Chinese military capabilities, built upon the foundation of a rapidly expanding economy, conditions emerged for China's potential primacy in

Asian geopolitics. With its post-war dominance in Asia under threat from China's rise, the US began to rethink its traditional approach to Asian security. From the 2010s, the US has taken a series of steps to shore up its regional position; this effort has involved strengthening bilateral alliances, building new partnerships outside the treaty framework, and developing new strategic institutions and military strategies to deter Chinese expansionism in Asia. China's quest to claim what it sees as its natural primacy in the region also puts it at odds with its neighbours, many of which are not willing to accept Beijing's regional hegemony. Together, the two intersecting contradictions – between China and the US and between Beijing and its neighbours – have set the stage for a new contest in Asia.

How these two intersecting contradictions will play out has been complicated by the dramatic disruptions in US policy initiated by Donald Trump in his second term as president. To be sure, it was Trump's decision in the first term to break the mould on China that set the stage for a major shift in US policy towards Asia. The emphasis on great-power rivalry, the framing of the Indo-Pacific strategy, the revival of the Quadrilateral Security Dialogue (Quad) and the push for an active strategy to balance against China all were products of Trump's first term. This period also witnessed Trump's effort to redefine US alliances in Asia (as in Europe) and restructure America's trade relations with the region (as with other partners). Under Trump, there was also a deepening of the traditional Republican distrust of multilateral institutions.

There was a significant measure of continuity with these policies under the administration of Joe Biden, with some changes of its own. While Biden intensified the effort to balance against China, he also underlined the importance of sustained engagement – building guardrails to prevent the uncontrolled escalation of bilateral tensions. Biden also sought to strengthen the alliances and coalitions in Asia by elevating the Quad to the summit level, unveiling the AUKUS (Australia–United Kingdom–United States) partnership, and developing triangular cooperation between Japan, South Korea and the US. On trade, Biden did not resurrect the Trans-Pacific Partnership (TPP), from which Trump had withdrawn, but sought to offer a new alternative in the form of the Indo-Pacific Economic Framework for Prosperity (IPEF), which was not about market access. Biden did not remove tariffs imposed against China by Trump. He added a range of technology sanctions against China to retain the US lead and slow Beijing's strides to catch up and overtake the United States.

Trump's return to the White House in January 2025 has cast a shadow over the prospects of broad continuity in US policy towards Asia. Underlying the change is the overall political orientation of Trump's second term. One potential change is in the attitude towards China. Although many in Trump's coalitions are hawkish on China and want Washington to focus more purposefully on the challenge presented by Beijing, there are others who call for restraint and seek to avoid an unnecessary conflict with China. The initial emphasis of the second Trump administration's effort to redress the severe trade deficit with China was through the imposition of a massive tariff wall against Chinese imports.

In seeking a broader rebalancing of US commercial relationships, the second Trump administration has not spared its friends and partners in Asia. It imposed significant tariffs on most Asian countries including its Quad partners. Historically, the US has been willing to be the main sink for Asian exports – one reason for that was a strategic decision to build security partnerships with Asian states during the Cold War. That approach, Trump has made it amply clear, is no longer US policy. America's economic ties with Asia, as the argument in Trump's world goes, must stand and flourish on their own merit. This idea also extends to the security domain.

During his first term, President Trump criticised allies in Asia as free riders and demanded greater contributions from them for the common defence. Trump's scepticism of alliances has acquired a stronger tone in his second term, as seen in the cases of Ukraine and NATO in Europe. Extending that argument to Asia could have profound consequences for the regional order – especially for the credibility of the US security commitment, including extended deterrence. Questions have arisen about Trump's commitment to defend Taiwan against a Chinese attack.

Trump's penchant for great-power understandings – as seen in his administration's early efforts to negotiate with Vladimir Putin – could also express itself in relation to China. There is also some speculation about a potential 'grand bargain' between the US and China, defined by a so-called fourth communiqué, in which the US seeks to recalibrate and stabilise the increasingly fraught relationship with China.[1] The idea is rooted in the history of US–China relations, which were built in the latter third of the twentieth century based on three communiqués (in 1972, 1979 and 1982). The understandings reached in these foundational documents helped manage bilateral differences on Taiwan, security and trade. There is also a new argument in Washington that the US should focus on the defence of the Western Hemisphere – stretching from Latin America through the Panama Canal and the US (including an emphasis on border security) to Canada and Greenland – instead of frittering away its wealth and power in Eurasia.[2] It is by no means clear if Washington and Beijing can construct a grand bargain with a fourth communiqué, nor is it certain the US will completely abandon Eurasia in favour of 'hemispheric defence'. But the very prospect of Washington's movement in that direction sends a chill down the spine of many Asian countries, especially US allies. Meanwhile, Trump has reaffirmed his contempt for multilateral institutions, whether it is the World Health Organization and the G20 at the global level or IPEF at the regional level. The Quad and AUKUS, major US institutional innovations in Asia over the last decade, are coming under more rigorous scrutiny in Trump's second term. Although the administration has expressed its formal bureaucratic support for these institutions, US allies cannot take them for granted amid the internal political churn of the Trump administration.

The great triangle

India's new geopolitical role in the region is accentuated by a new triangular dynamic with China and the United States. Independent India began with an ambition to build a post-Western order in Asia in partnership with China; today, it is locked in a semi-permanent confrontation with Beijing on its long and disputed frontier in the Great Himalayas. As the economic and military balance of power between China and India shifted rapidly in favour of Beijing in the twenty-first century, Beijing began to assert itself on the disputed border and contest India's traditional primacy in the subcontinent. With a rapidly growing economy and deepening interest in the resources and markets of the Indian Ocean, Beijing began to raise its strategic profile in the waters that New Delhi had long assumed were far from China's reach. Beyond the region, China has blocked India's aspirations for a larger role in global institutions by opposing New Delhi's entry into the Nuclear Suppliers Group and its claim for permanent membership of the United Nations Security Council. India's expanding economic engagement with China did not help dampen the political friction between the two sides; instead, it generated new economic tensions, thanks to expanding trade deficits in favour of China.

As the long-held ideological goal of partnering with China in Asia soured, New Delhi turned to balancing against Beijing through internal policy changes as well as external collaboration with the US and its Asian allies after the military crises of 2017 and 2020. The US, long frustrated by Indian reluctance to engage in deeper military and strategic cooperation with the US, moved decisively to build on the new possibilities with India. The US adoption of the Indo-Pacific geographic framework and the Quad, and India's support for them, underlined their shared concerns about Chinese dominance over Asia. While India's movement towards balancing against China in partnership with the US was cautious and designed to not prematurely provoke Beijing into a bilateral confrontation, Washington was willing to be patient in building a strong security partnership with India.

To be sure, the US has made major upfront investments – including loosening export controls, adjusting its regional policies to accommodate India and building this relationship without expecting immediate reciprocity. For its part, New Delhi has moved, if slowly, to shed its historical hesitations about partnering with Washington and has expanded the ambit of regional security cooperation. Although both India and the US have sufficient incentives to maintain a reasonable relationship, their respective bilateral tensions with China are now structural and not amenable to early resolution. But tactical and ad hoc arrangements between Beijing and Washington for limiting conflict and pursuing shared interests are bound to unfold in the coming years. Even if the US and China resolve all their issues at some point in the future and New Delhi and Beijing find mutual political accommodation, the stake for India and the US in deepening their bilateral partnership is bound to grow. Put simply, the India–US partnership is not an extension of China's current problems with India and the US.

Yet Donald Trump's second term has posed some new questions about the current trajectory of India–US relations. Trump's unexpected return to activism on the Kashmir question and his neutrality in India's war against Pakistan-backed terror during the brief military hostilities between the two countries in May 2025 have revived Indian fears of Washington re-hyphenating relations between New Delhi and Islamabad. Far more consequentially, the fluidity in US domestic politics and the fundamental rethink of the US approach to the world under Trump means India will have to develop a dynamic policy of triangular engagement with Washington and Beijing. Given the persistent structural contradictions between India and China and the massive power gap between the two, India will need the US to effectively secure Asia and the Indo-Pacific. Until now, India had reason to presume that the US presence was here to stay and would even intensify. If there is uncertainty about the US commitment to the region in the long term, New Delhi will need to do more to ensure that the US remains in Asia.

At the same time, India is also hedging against a potential US withdrawal or a grand bargain with China. This has increased the incentives for India to ease the military stand-off with China since the summer of 2020 and resume political dialogue. India's management of great-power relations amid the current flux also includes a renewed emphasis on retaining its relationship with Russia. But the volatility in US-Russia relations since the Ukraine war has increased the political costs in the West of New Delhi's expanding Moscow connection, along with possible costs to New Delhi, exemplified by Trump's announcement of tariffs designed to curb India's imports of Russian oil. India is also eager to step up engagement with the United Kingdom and Europe to bring a greater range to its regional partnerships. Yet there are limits to this potential diversification. Russia has drawn increasingly closer to China; while Moscow is eager to retain its long-standing strategic partnership with New Delhi, it is likely to be constrained by its larger and more solid ties with Beijing. The UK and Europe, meanwhile, are keen to build their own partnerships with China as part of their diversification of partnerships, especially after the re-election of Trump. Managing this fluidity in great-power relations should not be too difficult for India as its own comprehensive national power continues to grow in the years ahead.

Alliances, autonomy and burden-sharing

India's opposition to US regional alliances during the Cold War, expressed in the form of non-alignment, has lingered on in New Delhi's emphasis on 'strategic autonomy' in recent decades. The dominance of the concept in Indian discourse runs headlong into US anxieties about the depth of India's military commitment to regional security and the value of the strategic partnership with New Delhi. But the argument has been turned on its head since Trump's return to the White House. It is the US that is now questioning the value of alliances and is willing to downgrade them as part of an 'America First' strategy. This renewed contempt for alliances in the Trump administration is arguably rooted in a new self-assurance about the United States' own strengths and the related conviction that it does not need either alliances or multilateral institutions to pursue its national interests.[3] Some former US policymakers worry that the America Firsters are underestimating Chinese power and the nature of the challenges that it presents to the US. They argue that Washington cannot address this challenge on its own and needs allies to generate the necessary political, economic, technological and military depth to balance against Beijing.[4]

The importance of allies in deterring China in Asia was articulated more narrowly by the Biden administration.

As then-US secretary of defense Lloyd J. Austin III told an Asian audience at the IISS Fullerton Lecture in Singapore during 2021:

> Integrated deterrence means using every military and non-military tool in our toolbox in lockstep with our allies and partners. Integrated deterrence is about using existing capabilities, and building new ones, and deploying them all in new and networked ways – all tailored to a region's security landscape and growing in partnership with our friends.[5]

Integrated deterrence, the Biden administration argued, demands the boosting of the military and technological capabilities of allies and partners and promoting greater inter-operability between armed forces, as well as developing coordinated diplomatic and economic approaches to challenges in the Indo-Pacific.[6] It is by no means clear if the second Trump administration will simply abandon this approach in Asia. Consider, for example, the debate in Washington on closing the large 'shipbuilding gap' between China and the US; the Trump administration has had no option but to turn to South Korean and Japanese shipyards to plug the massive shortfall in US shipbuilding.[7]

Yet the Trump administration's rhetoric against alliances is having political effects in Eurasia. In Europe, this has compelled many US allies to discover the virtues of strategic autonomy and greater self-reliance in the domain of defence. The debate is no less important in Asia, where many US allies wonder if 'Ukraine is the future of Asia'. 'What we are seeing in Ukraine today', then Japanese prime minister Kishida Fumio declared within weeks of Russia's invasion of Ukraine in February 2022, 'could be what is in store for East Asia tomorrow'.[8]

His argument was that accepting the Russian invasion of Ukraine could encourage Chinese territorial expansionism in Asia. Defending Ukraine's sovereignty, Kishida argued, was part of securing the territorial integrity of states in Asia. That the second Trump administration is encouraging Ukraine to accept the loss of territory in return for peace with Russia generates deep discomfort among US allies in Asia. The new ambiguities about US commitments to Taiwan under Trump reinforce that fear.[9] Equally important are questions about the credibility of US extended nuclear deterrence in Asia. This has triggered regional debates on the utility of national nuclear deterrents among US allies. The debate has been particularly sharp in South Korea. That Trump might revive nuclear diplomacy with North Korea adds to the concerns of US allies in Asia.[10]

New Delhi sees an opportunity in the US demand that allies take greater responsibility for regional security. New Delhi would like to explore the space between the concepts of 'alliances' and 'non-alignment' to pursue a larger role in Asia through strategic cooperation with the United States while seeking peaceful coexistence with China (if possible). That strategy has come under stress amid Trump's 'America First Trade Policy', and his impossible demands to open up India's agrarian economy to US exports.

India's Asian challenges

Beyond the grand-strategic questions about India's great-power relations and its national doctrines are practical questions about how India can play a larger role in Asia. The last three decades have shown that India has emerged as a power 'in Asia'. But can India be a power 'of Asia' – that is, integral to the future evolution of Asia? The answer lies in assessing how India might respond to five broad challenges in the coming years.

The first challenge concerns India's contribution to *peace and stability in Asia*. The proposition that India is a net security provider in the region is rooted in the reality of India's military heft – New Delhi has the largest armed forces in Asia after China. Its defence spending is also the second largest in Asia. Further, India has a large defence-industrial base and its military diplomacy has picked up steam in recent years. Yet its impact on regional security affairs is well below its full potential.

One reason for this underperformance lies in the reality that New Delhi has to operate in the shadow of China, which has emerged as the peer competitor of the United States within the Asian theatre. All-round military modernisation has put the People's Liberation Army well ahead of its large Asian neighbours, including India and Japan. It stands to reason that New Delhi can make up for this military imbalance with Beijing by joining its military forces with those of its strategic partners. India's continuing hesitation to participate in military coalitions with the US and its allies is another reason for New Delhi's underperformance. To be sure, India is willing to participate in a range of coalition activities involving non-traditional security threats in the Quad, but it has been unwilling to undertake joint military missions with its closest partners. Finally, there is a crying need to make India's military machine more effective for the pursuit of New Delhi's national and regional objectives. India needs to raise its defence spending, which has fallen below 2% of GDP over the last decade, as well as bring greater efficiency to its higher defence organisation and defence production and acquisition. India also needs to promote greater investment – public and private – in defence-related research and development. Ending the dominance of the public sector and encouraging a greater role for Indian and foreign private capital is critical for the accelerated modernisation of India's vast but rusting defence-industrial base.

India also needs to boost its military diplomacy to lend credibility to its regional security ambitions. Urgent action on all these fronts is necessary for India to emerge as an effective partner in regional military coalitions, as well as a credible independent security actor in Asia.

The second challenge relates to India's *regional economic integration and technological collaboration*. Since the era of reform and opening up, India's economic growth has accelerated – and so has its trade with Asia. But India's commercial ties with Asia, while impressive, are overshadowed by China's economic integration in Asia. India's trade with members of the Association of Southeast Asian Nations (ASEAN), for example, was about US$121 billion in 2023–24.[11] In 2024, China's trade with ASEAN was close to US$1 trillion.[12] This is not surprising given the gap in the size of the Chinese and Indian economies. The problem, however, comes from the fact that India's current strategy is to disentangle itself from the Chinese economic sphere in Asia. India walked out of the ASEAN-driven regional trade liberalisation under the Regional Comprehensive Economic Partnership (RCEP) in 2019. The fear of RCEP driving up India's already high trade deficit with China was one of the reasons. The strategy of derisking India's economic ties with China has acquired greater intensity since the military confrontation between the two sides in the Ladakh region in the summer of 2020. The strategy has not been successful so far, given the massive Indian dependence on Chinese inputs to expand its domestic manufacturing and exports. The same holds true in the technological sector as well. But the political direction is to distance itself from China-led regional economic and technological integration in Asia.

This strategy is reinforced by a significant new Indian effort to strengthen trade ties with the West. Its hopes of concluding a trade agreement with the US were seriously damaged by President Trump's August 2025 decision to impose 50% tariffs against India in an attempt to curb India's purchases of Russian oil. Nevertheless, India signed a free-trade agreement with the United Kingdom in May 2025, and accelerated trade talks with the European Union.[13] This approach seems to make sense, given the complementarity of the economies of India and the West. Unlike the Asian economies, Western economies are not in competition with the dominant Indian production lines. On the technological front, too, India is tied more closely to the US and the West rather than the East. Under the Quad, the strategy has been to develop alternative technology supply chains that bypass China. The direction of India's technological-talent flows is also to the West. Although India's Asian trade will continue to grow, India's new trade tilt to the West and its quest for separation from the Sinosphere raise broader questions about the future of India's economic and technological integration with Asia.

The third challenge concerns India's engagement with *Asia's regional institutions*. Engaging with Asian institutions was quite integral to India's economic reforms in the early 1990s, as well as to New Delhi's effort to reconnect with Asia under its Look East policy. East Asian outreach has produced significant gains for India. New Delhi is now part of all major Asian institutions except Asia-Pacific Economic Cooperation (APEC). As mentioned earlier, India withdrew from the RCEP and the future of IPEF is under a cloud. But India remains a member of various ASEAN-led institutions, including the East Asia Summit, the ASEAN Regional Forum and the ASEAN Defence Ministers' Meeting-Plus.

As we look ahead, three sets of issues cast a shadow over India's institutional engagement with the region. Although India has been a member of these forums, its impact has not been remarkable by any means. In comparison, China has begun to loom large over these institutions, given Beijing's centrality to regional political and security issues. Meanwhile, China's growing salience and influence over individual states, as well as renewed great-power rivalry within Asia, have undermined ASEAN's ability to mediate international competition. Equally, ASEAN's capacity to cope with regional crises, such as the civil war in Myanmar, has been found wanting. The weakening of ASEAN works against the interests of India. As the smaller power – in comparison to China and the US – India's preference is for a strong ASEAN. New Delhi needs to do its bit by raising the intensity of its own engagement with ASEAN-led institutions.[14] Finally, India has become part of the new regional institutional architecture, the Quad, being built by the US outside the ASEAN framework. New Delhi also has no quarrel with other institutions such as AUKUS. Although India has so far navigated the tension between the two sets of institutions, the former led by ASEAN and the latter by the US, India is conscious of the dangers of being seen as an extension of US strategy in the region.

A fourth challenge relates to *India's continuing difficulties with its neighbours*. Persistent tensions with Pakistan, which resulted in a fresh military confrontation in April–May 2025, and the rapid deterioration of India's relations with Bangladesh after the ouster of Sheikh Hasina in August 2024 underline the bitter legacies of the partition of the subcontinent on religious lines that linger nearly eight decades after decolonisation and independence. Meanwhile, India's relations with its smaller neighbours continue to go through cold and warm cycles. Even as India experiments with different instruments to strengthen structural ties with smaller neighbours, its relationship with Pakistan appears deadlocked. New Delhi's engagement with Dhaka, in contrast, has seen periods of intense cooperation and sharpened conflict. India's difficulty in stabilising its relations with its South Asian neighbours presents an open invitation to other powers to meddle in the subcontinent.

China's path to solid ties with the subcontinent has been smooth, given the structural contradictions between New Delhi and its neighbouring capitals – all China needs to do is step in to balance against India. New Delhi has sought to enhance its engagement with the region by trying to resolve its conflicts with ne ighbours and work with its Quad partners to improve economic and security ties and limit the influence of Beijing in South Asia. Meanwhile, tensions between India and Pakistan have put the only regional forum – the South Asian Association for Regional Cooperation (SAARC) – in limbo. India's effort to bypass Pakistan and develop the Bay of Bengal Initiative for Multi-Sectoral Technical and Economic Cooperation (BIMSTEC) to bring together the Bay of Bengal littoral states has not yielded significant progress in regionalism.[15] The problem is not with the organisational format but with India's enduring challenges in dealing with a complex region burdened by a history of animosity and lack of a political consensus on the virtues of regionalism. The lack of movement in South Asian regionalism will continue to act as a drag on India's larger Asian and Indo-Pacific goals.

The final challenge concerns *India's domestic political orientation* and its impact on India's regional engagement in Asia. Whether India has experienced 'democratic backsliding' has in essence been a debate within Western foreign-policy establishments. The growing Western criticism of the internal developments in India has not had a significant impact on Western policies towards India. It has never been easy for the West to put the ideology of democracy and human rights above other, more pressing interests in the domains of commerce, foreign policy and security. Even more difficult has been the problem of pushing for them in a consistent manner over time and space. Hence, the credibility of these policies has taken a big hit. Moreover, the post-Cold War hectoring of the world by Western liberals produced political friction with the leaders of non-Western societies, including India's. What is new, though, is the backlash within the West, especially in the United States, against liberal evangelism around the world. We have seen the force of that backlash and the political support behind it since Trump's return to the White House. The emphasis on 'America First' has challenged many familiar tenets of liberal internationalism in the West.

Notwithstanding these internal debates within the West, the issues of democracy and human rights have not had great resonance in the evolution of Asian geopolitics and economics. Realpolitik has been the dominant theme in shaping great-power politics and intra-state relations within Asia in recent decades. In that sense, a politically illiberal India, much like authoritarian China, is unlikely to enjoy less success in its efforts at regional political and economic engagement. However, growing hypernationalism in India – and its spread to diasporic communities – does produce negative reactions in a multi-religious and multi-cultural Asia.[16] Reining in hypernationalism and xenophobia at home must be a high priority for New Delhi in crafting a more weighty role for India in Asia and beyond.

APPENDIX

Table A1: **Defence budget (nominal and PPP), active military personnel and population, 2024**

2024	Defence budget (US$bn)	Defence budget (PPP US$bn)*	Active personnel (m)	Population (m)
Australia	36.3	38.4	0.06	26.77
China	235.1	478.5	2.04	1,416.69
India	75.8	313.8	1.48	1,409.13
Indonesia	11.0	36.9	0.40	281.56
Japan	52.5	85.2	0.25	123.20
North Korea	n.k	n.k	1.28	26.30
Pakistan	8.4	35.7	0.66	252.36
Singapore	15.6	25.9	0.05	6.03
South Korea	43.6	75.6	0.50	52.08
Vietnam	7.5	27.1	0.45	105.76
USA**	968.0	968.0	1.32	341.96

*constant 2015 US$
**2024 defence budget figure includes Supplementary Request for Israel, Ukraine and Indo-Pacific military aid.

Sources: Military Balance+, milbalplus.iiss.org; US Census Bureau

Figure A1: **Defence spending: China, India and Japan, 2008–25**

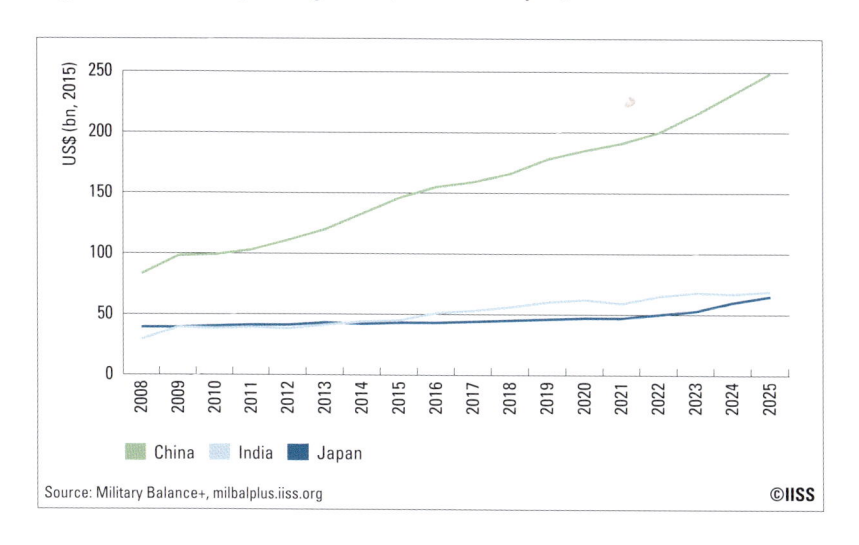

Source: Military Balance+, milbalplus.iiss.org ©IISS

NOTES

Introduction

[1] This term was used by Chinese Foreign Minister Wang Yi in 2018. Abhijnan Rej, 'China and the Quad: From Sea Foam to Indo-Pacific NATO', *Diplomat*, 15 October 2020, https://thediplomat.com/2020/10/china-and-the-quad-from-sea-foam-to-asian-nato/.

Chapter One

[1] C. Raja Mohan, 'India's Regional Security Cooperation: The Nehru Raj Legacy', Institute of South Asian Studies, 7 March 2013, https://www.isas.nus.edu.sg/papers/168-indiaocos-regional-security-cooperation-the-nehru-raj-legacy/; and Vineet Thakur, 'The Colonial Origins of Indian Foreign Policymaking', *Economic and Political Weekly*, vol. 49, no. 32, 9 August 2014, pp. 58–64, http://www.jstor.org/stable/24480792.

[2] Robert J. Blyth, *The Empire of the Raj: India, Eastern Africa, and the Middle East, 1858–1947* (London: Palgrave, 2003), p. 3.

[3] James Onley, 'The Raj Reconsidered: British India's Informal Empire and Spheres of Influence in Asia and Africa', *Asian Affairs*, vol. 40, no. 1, 2009, pp. 44–62.

[4] *Ibid.*, pp. 44–5.

[5] Ainslee T. Embree, 'The British Concept of South Asian Borders', in Peter Gaeffke and David A. Utz (eds), *The Countries of South Asia: Boundaries, Extensions, and Interrelations* (Philadelphia, PA: University of Pennsylvania, 1988), p. 98.

[6] George N. Curzon, *Frontiers: The Romanes Lecture 1907* (Oxford: Clarendon Press, 1907), p. 20.

[7] Bisheshwar Prasad, *Our Foreign Policy Legacy: A Study of British Indian Foreign Policy* (Delhi: People's Publishing House, 1965), p. 57.

[8] Embree, 'The British Concept of South Asian Borders', p. 94.

9   For a useful history, see T.A. Heathcote, *The Military in British India: The Development of British Land Forces in South Asia, 1600–1947* (New York: St. Martin's Press, 1995).

10 For a comprehensive account of all Indian expeditionary operations from the late eighteenth to the end of the nineteenth century in theatres as diverse as the Mediterranean and China, see Intelligence Branch, Army Headquarters, *Frontier and Overseas Expeditions from India*, vol. 6 (Simla: Government of India, 1907), reissued by Mittal Publications, Delhi, 1983.

11 Ashley Jackson, 'Britain in the Indian Ocean Region', *Journal of the Indian Ocean Region*, vol. 7, no. 2, 2011, pp. 145–60.

12 For a comprehensive account of the recruitment of Sikhs, see Thomas R. Metcalf, *Imperial Connections: India in the Indian Ocean Era* (Berkeley, CA: University of California Press, 2007), pp. 102–35.

13 Ashley Jackson, 'The Imperial Antecedents of British Special Forces', *RUSI Journal*, vol. 154, no. 3, 2009, pp. 62–8; see also T.R. Moreman, '"Small Wars" and "Imperial Policing": The British Army and the Theory and Practice of Colonial Warfare in the British Empire, 1919–39', *Journal of Strategic Studies*, vol. 19, no. 4, 1996, pp. 105–31.

14 David Omissi, 'The Indian Army in the First World War, 1914–1918', in Daniel P. Marston and Chandar S. Sundaram (eds), *A Military History of India and South Asia: From the East India Company to the Nuclear Era* (London: Praeger, 2007), pp. 74–87.

15 See Daniel Marston, 'A Force Transformed: The Indian Army and the Second World War', in Marston and Sundaram (eds), *A Military History of India and South Asia: From the East India Company to the Nuclear Era*, pp. 102–22.

16 David Omissi, Anna-Maria Misra and Nicholas Owen, 'Co-option and Coercion in India 1857–1947', *Contemporary Record*, vol. 6, no. 3, December 1992, pp. 536–52, https://doi.org/10.1080/13619469208581227.

17 C. Raja Mohan, *Crossing the Rubicon: The Shaping of India's New Foreign Policy* (New Delhi: Penguin/Viking, 2003), pp. 204–5; A. Wess Mitchell, 'The Curzonian Imprint on India Foreign Policy', *Hindustan Times*, 12 June 2021; and Mithilesh Jayas Mukherjee, 'Embracing Curzon's Political Vision to Secure India's Cultural and Political Borders', *Electronic Journal of Social and Strategic Studies*, vol. 2, February 2021, pp. 47–58.

18 Peter John Brobst, *The Future of the Great Game: Sir Olaf Caroe, India's Independence, and the Defence of Asia* (Akron, OH: University of Akron Press, 2005).

19 Jürgen Dinkel, *The Non-Aligned Movement* (Boston, MA: Brill, 2018); and Sandra Bott et al. (eds), *Neutrality and Neutralism in the Global Cold War: Between or Within the Blocs?* (London: Routledge, 2016).

20 Vojtech Mastny, 'The Soviet Union's Partnership with India', *Journal of Cold War Studies*, vol. 12, no. 3, July 2010, pp. 50–90, https://doi.org/10.1162/JCWS_a_00006; Peter J.S. Duncan, *The Soviet Union and India*, 1st ed. (London: Routledge, 2022), https://doi.org/10.4324/9781003349457; and Jyotsna Bakshi, *Russia and India: From Ideology to Geopolitics 1947–1998* (New Delhi: Dev Publications, 1999).

21 Avtar Singh Bhasin, *Nehru, Tibet and China* (Gurugram: Penguin/Viking, 2021); and Nirupama Rao, *Fractured Himalaya: India Tibet China 1949–1962* (Gurugram: Penguin/Viking, 2021).

22 Mohan, 'India's Regional Security Cooperation: The Nehru Raj Legacy'.

23 For India's search for arms, see

K. Subrahmanyam, 'Arms and Politics', Manohar Parrikar Institute for Defence Studies and Analyses, January 2005, https://www.idsa.in/strategicanalysis/ArmsandPolitics_ksubrahmanyam_0305.

24 Swapna Kona Nayudu, '"In the Very Eye of the Storm": India, the UN, and the Lebanon Crisis of 1958', *Cold War History*, vol. 18, no. 2, 3 April 2018, pp. 221–37, https://doi.org/10.1080/14682745.2018.1445997; and Manu Belur Bhagavan, *India and the Quest for One World: The Peacemakers* (Basingstoke: Palgrave Macmillan, 2013).

25 Francine R. Frankel, *When Nehru Looked East: Origins of India–US Suspicion and India–China Rivalry* (Oxford: Oxford University Press, 2020).

26 See Robert J. McMahon, *The Cold War on the Periphery: The United States, India, and Pakistan* (New York: Columbia University Press, 1994).

27 Tanvi Madan, *Fateful Triangle: How China Shaped US–India Relations During the Cold War* (Washington DC: Brookings Institution Press, 2020); and Bruce O. Riedel, *JFK's Forgotten Crisis: Tibet, the CIA, and Sino-Indian War* (Washington DC: Brookings Institution Press, 2015).

28 The many dimensions of the shifting great-power politics in South Asia are discussed in Barry Buzan and Gowher Rizvi (eds), *South Asian Insecurity and the Great Powers* (Basingstoke: Macmillan, 1986).

29 Vidya Nadkarni, 'India and Russia: A Special Relationship', in Sumit Ganguly (ed.), *Engaging the World: Indian Foreign Policy Since 1947* (New Delhi: Oxford University Press, 2016).

30 Zorawar Daulet Singh, *Power and Diplomacy: India's Foreign Policies During the Cold War* (New Delhi: Oxford University Press, 2019); and Mohan Guruswamy and Zorawar Daulet Singh, *India China Relations: The Border Issue and Beyond* (New Delhi: Viva Books, 2009).

31 International Monetary Fund (IMF), 'World Economic Outlook Database', October 2024, https://www.imf.org/en/Publications/WEO/weo-database/2024/October.

32 *Ibid*.

33 Harsh Pant, 'Unbungle up Bangladesh', *Economic Times*, 13 December 2024, https://economictimes.indiatimes.com/opinion/et-commentary/unbungle-up-bangladesh-delhi-has-reached-now-dhaka-needs-to-reciprocate/articleshow/116265219.cms?from=mdr.

34 The 'Bandung spirit' that Jaishankar referred to is the sweeping sentiment in favour of anti-colonial solidarity and regional cooperation that was articulated vigorously at the Afro-Asian Conference held in Bandung, Indonesia, in 1955. For a discussion of the ideas that were articulated in Bandung and which resonate even today, see Amitav Acharya and See Seng Tan, *Bandung Revisited: The Legacy of the 1955 Asian–African Conference for International Order* (Singapore: National University of Singapore Press, 2008).

35 See 'Rising but Divided: Asia's Geopolitical Future', speech delivered by Dr S. Jaishankar, Minister for External Affairs of India, New Delhi, 29 August 2022, https://asiasociety.org/video/rising-divided-asias-geopolitical-future.

36 *Ibid*.

37 Tanvi Madan, 'The Rise, Fall, and Rebirth of the "Quad"', *War on the Rocks*, 16 November 2017, https://warontherocks.com/2017/11/rise-fall-rebirth-quad/.

38 Happymon Jacob, 'Russia Is Losing India', *Foreign Affairs*, 22 September 2022, https://www.foreignaffairs.com/india/russia-losing-india.

39 IMF, 'World Economic Outlook Database', n. 31.

40 World Bank, 'World Integrated Trade Solution', https://wits.worldbank.

40. org; see also Embassy of India, Moscow, Russia, 'Brief on India–Russia Economic Relations', https://indianembassy-moscow.gov.in/overview.php.
41. On India's continuing dependency on Russian arms, see Sameer Lalwani and Tyler Sagerstrom, 'What the India–Russia Defence Partnership Means for US Policy', *Survival*, vol. 63, no. 4, 4 July 2021, pp. 149–82, https://doi.org/10.1080/00396338.2021.1956196.
42. Pieter D. Wezeman et al., 'Trends in International Arms Transfers, 2023', Stockholm International Peace Research Institute, March 2024, https://www.sipri.org/sites/default/files/2024-03/fs_2403_at_2023.pdf.
43. Pradip Sagar, 'India–Russia: Keeping an Arms Distance', *India Today*, 12 August 2024, https://www.indiatoday.in/magazine/defence/story/20240812-india-russia-keeping-an-arms-distance-2575646-2024-08-02.
44. For the continuity of India's non-alignment thinking, see Sunil Khilnani et al. (eds), 'NonAlignment 2.0: A Foreign and Strategic Policy for India in the Twenty First Century', *Centre for Policy Research*, 29 February 2012, https://cprindia.org/briefsreports/nonalignment-2-0-a-foreign-and-strategic-policy-for-india-in-the-twenty-first-century/.
45. Author's conversations with senior Indian officials on India's renewal of Global South diplomacy in September 2023, on the eve of the G20 summit in New Delhi.
46. 'A Conversation with Henry Kissinger', *The Economist*, 17 May 2023, https://www.economist.com/kissinger-transcript.
47. 'In Conversation with Subrahmanyam Jaishankar', *The Economist*, 15 June 2023, https://www.economist.com/asia/2023/06/15/in-conversation-with-subrahmanyam-jaishankar/.

Chapter Two

1. Stephen N. Hay, *Asian Ideas of East and West: Tagore and His Critics in Japan, China and India* (Cambridge, MA: Harvard University Press, 1970).
2. For a review of the engagement, see Madhavi Thampi (ed.), *India and China in the Colonial World* (London: Routledge, 2017), https://doi.org/10.4324/9781315101125.
3. Guido Samarani, 'Shaping the Future of Asia: Chiang Kai-Shek, Nehru and China–India Relations During the Second World War Period', Working Papers in Contemporary Asian Studies (Lund: Centre for East and South-East Asian Studies, Lund University, 2005).
4. Jawaharlal Nehru, *Independence and After: A Collection of the More Important Speeches of Jawaharlal Nehru from September 1946 to May 1949* (New Delhi: Publications Division, 2013), http://www.indianculture.gov.in/ebooks/independence-and-after-collection-more-important-speeches-jawaharlal-nehru-september-1946.
5. Tanvi Madan, *Fateful Triangle: How China Shaped US–India Relations During the Cold War* (Washington DC: Brookings Institution Press, 2020); Avtar Singh Bhasin, *Nehru, Tibet and China* (Gurugram: Penguin/Viking, 2021); and Vijay Gokhale, *The Long Game: How the Chinese Negotiate with India* (Gurugram: Vintage, 2021).

6. 'Sardar Patel's Letter to Nehru', Friends of Tibet, 7 November 1950, https://friendsoftibet.org/sardarpatel.html.

7. Frank O'Donnell and Mihaela Papa, 'India's Multi-alignment Management and the Russia–India–China (RIC) Triangle', *International Affairs*, vol. 97, no. 3, 10 May 2021, pp. 801–22, https://doi.org/10.1093/ia/iiab036; and Raj Verma and Mihaela Papa, 'BRICS Amidst India–China Rivalry', *Global Policy*, vol. 12, no. 4, September 2021, pp. 509–13, https://doi.org/10.1111/1758-5899.12977. For more, refer to special issue articles in *Global Policy*, vol. 12, no. 4, September 2021, https://onlinelibrary.wiley.com/toc/17585899/2021/12/4.

8. Vinay Kaura and Chakravarti Singh, 'India and the Geopolitics of UNSC Permanent Membership', *Strategic Analysis*, vol. 45, no. 4, 4 July 2021, pp. 271–85, https://doi.org/10.1080/09700161.2021.1938943.

9. Jonathan Holsag, 'The Persistent Security Dilemma Between China and India', *Journal of Strategic Studies*, vol. 32, no. 6, 17 December 2009, https://doi.org/10.1080/01402390903189592; and Rajesh Rajagopalan, 'Evasive Balancing: India's Unviable Indo-Pacific Strategy', *International Affairs*, vol. 96, no. 1, 1 January 2020, pp. 75–93, https://doi.org/10.1093/ia/iiz224.

10. Shyam Saran, *How China Sees India and the World* (New Delhi: Juggernaut Books, 2022).

11. Martin J. Bayly, 'Global Intellectual History in International Relations: Hierarchy, Empire, and the Case of Late Colonial Indian International Thought', *Review of International Studies*, vol. 49, no. 3, 11 October 2022, pp. 1–20, https://doi.org/10.1017/S0260210522000419; and Martin Bayly, 'The Histories of Indian International Relations', *Hindustan Times*, 29 April 2021, https://www.hindustantimes.com/opinion/the-histories-of-indian-international-relations-101619704903162.html.

12. S. Jaishankar, *Why Bharat Matters* (New Delhi: Rupa, 2024).

13. Mathew Mosca, *From Frontier Policy to Foreign Policy: The Question of India and the Transformation of Geopolitics in Qing China* (Stanford, CA: Stanford University Press, 2013).

14. Dawa Norbu, 'The Europeanization of Sino-Tibetan Relations, 1775–1907: The Genesis of Chinese "Suzerainty" and Tibetan "Autonomy"', *Tibet Journal*, vol. 15, no. 4, 1990, pp. 28–74; and Dawa Norbu, 'Tibet in Sino-Indian Relations: The Centrality of Marginality', *Asian Survey*, vol. 37, no. 11, 1997, pp. 1078–95, https://doi.org/10.2307/2645742.

15. Zorawar Daulet Singh, *Power Shift: India China Relations in the Multipolar World* (New Delhi: Pan Macmillan, 2020).

16. Manoj Joshi, *Understanding the India–China Border: The Enduring Threat of War in High Himalaya* (London: Hurst & Company, 2022).

17. See 'Statement by External Affairs Minister, Dr S. Jaishankar in Lok Sabha', speech delivered by Dr S. Jaishankar, Minister of External Affairs of India, New Delhi, 3 December 2024, https://www.mea.gov.in/Speeches-Statements.htm?dtl/38665/.

18. Vijay Gokhale, 'India–China Entering a Decade of Uncertainty', interview by Shashank Mattoo, *Mint*, 22 December 2022, https://www.livemint.com/economy/india-china-entering-a-decade-of-uncertainty-ex-foreign-secy-vijay-gokhale-11671987818878.html. For more excellent analysis, see Vijay Gokhale, 'A Historical Evaluation of China's India Policy: Lessons for India–China Relations', Carnegie India, 13 December 2022, https://carnegieindia.org/2022/12/13/historical-evaluation-of-china-s-india-policy-lessons-for-india-china-relations-pub-88621.

19 Sunil Khilnani et al. (eds), 'NonAlignment 2.0: A Foreign and Strategic Policy for India in the Twenty First Century', Centre for Policy Research, 29 February 2012, https://cprindia.org/briefsreports/nonalignment-2-0-a-foreign-and-strategic-policy-for-india-in-the-twenty-first-century/.

20 C. Raja Mohan, *Modi's World: Expanding India's Sphere of Influence* (Noida: HarperCollins Publishers India, 2015).

21 Gautam Datt and Abhishek Bhalla, 'Xi Warmth Freezes Over in Chumar', *India Today*, 23 September 2014, https://www.indiatoday.in/india/north/story/xi-jinping-narendra-modi-chumar-india-china-standoff-lac-indian-army-general-dalbir-singh-pla-293877-2014-09-22.

22 Daniel Kliman et al., 'Imbalance of Power: India's Military Choices in an Era of Strategic Competition with China', Centre for New American Security, October 2019, https://s3.amazonaws.com/files.cnas.org/CNAS-Report_ImbalanceofPower_DoS-Proof%20(1).pdf.

23 Yogesh Joshi and Anit Mukherjee, 'From Denial to Punishment: The Security Dilemma and Changes in India's Military Strategy Towards China', *Asian Security*, vol. 15, no. 1, 9 November 2018, pp. 25–43, https://doi.org/10.1080/14799855.2019.1539817.

24 'India Bans 54 Chinese Apps Citing Security Threats', *Business Today*, 14 February 2022, https://www.businesstoday.in/latest/policy/story/india-bans-54-chinese-apps-citing-security-threats-322489-2022-02-14; and Sandhya Sharma, 'Casualties of China's Aggression: How Galwan Clash Marked the Beginning of End for Huawei, ZTE', *Economic Times*, 3 June 2022, https://economictimes.indiatimes.com/prime/economy-and-policy/casualties-of-chinas-aggression-how-galwan-clash-marked-the-beginning-of-end-for-huawei-zte/primearticleshow/91970620.cms.

25 Pankhuri Gaur, 'India's Withdrawal from RCEP: Neutralising National Trade Concerns', *Journal of the Asia Pacific Economy*, vol. 27, no. 2, 3 April 2022, pp. 270–88, https://doi.org/10.1080/13547860.2020.1809772.

26 'State of Border Will Determine State of India–China Relationship: Jaishankar', *Indian Express*, 30 August 2022, https://indianexpress.com/article/india/india-china-ties-border-jaishankar-8120295/.

27 'India, China 18th Corps Commanders Meet to Ease Out Tension in Eastern Ladakh', *New Indian Express*, 23 April 2023, https://www.newindianexpress.com/nation/2023/apr/23/india-china-18th-corps-commanders-meet-to-ease-out-tension-in-eastern-ladakh-2568659.html.

28 V.P. Malik, 'Lessons from Tawang: The Five Changes India Needs to Make in Dealing with China', *Indian Express*, 31 December 2022, https://indianexpress.com/article/opinion/columns/lessons-from-tawang-five-changes-india-needs-dealing-with-china-8354107/.

29 Tanvi Madan, 'The Rise, Fall, and Rebirth of the "Quad"', *War on the Rocks*, 16 November 2017, https://warontherocks.com/2017/11/rise-fall-rebirth-quad/.

30 White House, 'Fact Sheet: Quad Leaders' Summit', 25 September 2021, https://www.whitehouse.gov/briefing-room/statements-releases/2021/09/24/fact-sheet-quad-leaders-summit/.

31 Sachin Parashar, 'One-China? No Need to Reiterate Our Consistent Policies, Says India', *Times of India*, 13 August 2022, https://timesofindia.indiatimes.com/india/one-china-no-need-to-reiterate-our-consistent-policies-says-india/articleshow/93530107.

cms; and Dipanjan Roy Chaudhary, 'India's One China Policy May Not Be Permanent Feature amid Beijing's Aggression', *Economic Times*, 13 June 2020, https://economictimes.indiatimes.com/news/defence/indias-one-china-policy-may-not-be-permanent-feature-amid-beijings-aggression/articleshow/76351486.cms/.

32 Rajeswari Pillai Rajagopalan, 'Is India Ready to Play the "Tibet Card" in Its Battle with China?', Observer Research Foundation, 18 November 2020, https://www.orfonline.org/research/is-india-ready-to-play-the-tibet-card-in-its-battle-with-china/.

33 Rahul Bedi, 'Why China Is So Upset About India's Predominantly Tibetan Special Frontier Force', *Wire*, 10 September 2020, https://thewire.in/security/india-china-tibetan-special-frontier-force.

34 Sana Hashmi, 'India–Taiwan Ties: A Case for Stronger Partnership', *Asie.Visions*, no. 125, November 2021, Institut Français des Relations Internationales, https://www.ifri.org/sites/default/files/atoms/files/india-taiwan_ties_since_the_1920s_a_classic_case_of_friendliness_mutual_neglect_and_redefining_ties.pdf.

35 John W. Garver, *Protracted Contest: Sino-Indian Rivalry in the Twentieth Century* (Seattle, WA: University of Washington Press, 2001).

36 Christian Wagner, 'The Role of India and China in South Asia', *Strategic Analysis*, vol. 40, no. 4, 3 July 2016, pp. 307–20, https://doi.org/10.1080/09700161.2016.1184790.

37 Hoo Tiang Boon and Glenn K.H. Ong, 'Military Dominance in Pakistan and China–Pakistan Relations', *Australian Journal of International Affairs*, vol. 75, no. 1, 2 January 2021, pp. 80–102, https://doi.org/10.1080/10357718.2020.1844142.

38 Manjari C. Miller, 'How China and Pakistan Forged Close Ties', Council on Foreign Relations, 3 October 2022, https://www.cfr.org/article/how-china-and-pakistan-forged-close-ties.

39 John Dori and Richard Fisher, 'The Strategic Implications of China's Nuclear Aid to Pakistan', Heritage Foundation, 16 June 1998, https://www.heritage.org/asia/report/the-strategic-implications-chinas-nuclear-aid-pakistan; and Asma Khalid, 'China–Pakistan Nuclear Energy Cooperation: History and Key Debates', *South Asian Voices*, 12 February 2020, https://southasianvoices.org/china-pakistan-nuclear-energy-cooperation/.

40 Chok Tsering, 'Kodari Road: Implications for Nepal, China and India', *Eurasia Review*, 1 December 2011, https://www.eurasiareview.com/01122011-kodari-road-implications-for-nepal-china-and-india-analysis/; and Gurnam Singh, 'The Karakoram Highway and Its Strategic Implications for India', *Indian Journal of Political Science*, vol. 42, no. 1, 1981, pp. 18–26, http://www.jstor.org/stable/41855073.

41 See John W. Garver, 'Development of China's Overland Transportation Links with Central, South-West and South Asia', *China Quarterly*, vol. 185, March 2006, pp. 1–22, https://doi.org/10.1017/S0305741006000026.

42 For a useful discussion, see Deep Pal, *China's Influence in South Asia: Vulnerabilities and Resilience in Four Countries* (Washington DC: Carnegie Endowment for International Peace, 13 October 2021), https://carnegieendowment.org/2021/10/13/china-s-influence-in-south-asia-vulnerabilities-and-resilience-in-four-countries-pub-85552.

43 K. Alan Kronstadt, *Pakistan–US Relations*, Congressional Research Service, 8 July 2021, https://crsreports.congress.gov/product/pdf/IF/IF11270.

44 Syed Fazal-e-Haider, 'China–Pakistan Relations: The "All-Weather" Partnership Navigates Stormy

Times', *China Brief*, vol. 22, no. 24, 30 December 2022, pp. 21–4; Sameer P. Lalwani, 'A Threshold Alliance: The China–Pakistan Military Relationship', United States Institute of Peace, 22 March 2023, https://www.usip.org/publications/2023/03/threshold-alliance-china-pakistan-military-relationship; and Madiha Faizal, '"At All Costs": How Pakistan and China Control the Narrative on the China–Pakistan Economic Corridor', Global China Project, Brookings, June 2020, https://www.brookings.edu/articles/at-all-costs-how-pakistan-and-china-control-the-narrative-on-the-china-pakistan-economic-corridor/.

45 For a discussion on China's debate on this issue, see Chen Zheng, 'China Debates the Non-interference Principle', *Chinese Journal of International Politics*, vol. 9, no. 3, September 2016, pp. 349–74, https://doi.org/10.1093/cjip/pow010.

46 Meera Srinivasan, 'China Pledges Support to Sri Lanka at UNHRC Session', *Hindu*, 26 August 2022, https://www.thehindu.com/news/international/china-pledges-support-to-sri-lanka-at-unhrc-session-in-september/article65814884.ece.

47 'India, Bangladesh to Deepen Trade and Economic Ties as Partners: Piyush Goyal', *Hindu*, 28 November 2021, https://www.thehindu.com/news/national/india-bangladesh-to-deepen-trade-and-economic-ties-as-partners-piyush-goyal/article37741784.ece.

48 Constantino Xavier, 'Sambandh as Strategy: India's New Approach to Regional Connectivity', Brookings India, January 2020, https://www.brookings.edu/wp-content/uploads/2020/01/India%E2%80%99s-New-Approach-to-Regional-Connectivity-V3_M.pdf.

49 Rathindra Kuruwita, 'Sri Lanka Continues to Back India's Adani Group', *Diplomat*, 10 March 2023, https://thediplomat.com/2023/03/sri-lanka-continues-to-back-indias-adani-group/; 'The Adani Group Crisis and the Projects in South Asian Nations', *Wire*, 7 February 2023, https://thewire.in/business/adani-group-projects-south-asian-nations; and 'Adani Meets Bangladesh PM; Fully Commissions 1,600 MW Project', *Indian Express*, 16 July 2023, https://indianexpress.com/article/cities/ahmedabad/adani-meets-bangladesh-pm-fully-commissions-1600-mw-project-8840427/.

50 John Reed and Benjamin Parkin, 'Gautam Adani's Ties with India's Narendra Modi Spur Scrutiny of Overseas Deals', *Financial Times*, 23 February 2023, https://www.ft.com/content/38ff5ff6-aebe-46ae-bb97-c8071818b55d.

51 Meera Srinivasan, 'Adani Green Withdraws from Controversial Renewable Energy Project in Sri Lanka', *Hindu*, 13 February 2025, https://www.thehindu.com/business/adani-withdraws-from-controversial-renewable-energy-project-in-sri-lanka/article69214069.ece; Ayaskant Das and Paranjoy Guha Thakuta, 'Bangladesh Top Court Orders Review of Adani Power Deal', Adani Watch, 12 December 2024, https://www.adaniwatch.org/bangladesh_s_top_court_orders_review_of_adani_power_deal; and P. Manoj, 'Adani Ports Sells $150 Million Myanmar Terminal for $30 Mn', *Economic Times*, 4 May 2023, https://infra.economictimes.indiatimes.com/news/ports-shipping/adani-ports-sells-150-million-myanmar-terminal-for-30-million/99982320.

52 Masahiro Kurita, 'Japan's "India-plus" Strategic Engagement with South Asia', *South Asian Voices*, 14 May 2020, https://southasianvoices.org/japans-india-plus-strategic-engagement-with-south-asia/.

53 See Nikhil Sahu, 'The See-saw of MCC Projects in Nepal', Vivekananda International Foundation, 10 November 2023, https://www.vifindia.org/print/12156.

54 Christian Wagner, *India as a Regional Security Provider in South Asia*, South Asia Scan, no. 8 (Singapore: Institute of South Asian Studies, June 2020).

55 Vijay Sakhuja and Sangeeta Sakhuja, 'Rajendra Chola's Naval Expedition to Southeast Asia: A Nautical Perspective', in Hermann Kulke (ed.), *Nagapattinam to Suvarnadwipa: Reflections on the Chola Naval Expeditions to Southeast Asia* (Singapore: ISEAS–Yusof Ishak Institute, 2009), pp. 76–90, https://www.cambridge.org/core/books/nagapattinam-to-suvarnadwipa/rajendra-chola-is-naval-expedition-to-southeast-asia-a-nautical-perspective/46DC50B07DC8D66753E23EC7AB37B0E7.

56 Bertil Lintner, *The Costliest Pearl: China's Struggle for India's Ocean* (London: Hurst & Company, 2019).

57 US Office of Naval Intelligence, 'The PLA Navy: New Capabilities and Missions for the 21st Century', 9 September 2015, https://www.andrewerickson.com/2015/09/u-s-office-of-naval-intelligence-2015-report-the-pla-navy-new-capabilities-and-missions-for-the-21st-century-complete-links-to-report-videos-graphics/; and Congressional Research Service, 'China Naval Modernization: Implications for US Navy Capabilities – Background and Issues for Congress', Congressional Research Service Report, 3 December 2020, https://crsreports.congress.gov/product/pdf/RL/RL33153/245.

58 Yves-Heng Lim, 'China's Rising Naval Ambitions in the Indian Ocean: Aligning Ends, Ways and Means', *Asian Security*, vol. 16, no. 3, 26 January 2020, pp. 396–412, https://doi.org/10.1080/14799855.2020.1721469.

59 David Dollar, 'Understanding China's Belt and Road Infrastructure Projects in Africa', Brookings, 30 September 2019, https://www.brookings.edu/research/understanding-chinas-belt-and-road-infrastructure-projects-in-africa/.

60 C. Raja Mohan, 'China's Two-ocean Strategy Puts India in a Pincer', *Foreign Policy*, 4 January 2022, https://foreignpolicy.com/2022/01/04/india-china-ocean-geopolitics-sri-lanka-maldives-comoros/.

61 Michael Beckley, 'The Emerging Military Balance in East Asia: How China's Neighbors Can Check Chinese Naval Expansion', *International Security*, vol. 42, no. 2, November 2017, pp. 78–119, https://doi.org/10.1162/ISEC_a_00294.

62 Lintner, *The Costliest Pearl: China's Struggle for India's Ocean*.

63 Jonathan E. Hillman, *The Emperor's New Road: China and the Project of the Century* (New Haven, CT: Yale University Press, 2020).

64 Pradumna B. Rana and Xianbai Ji, 'BRI and South Asia', in Pradumna B. Rana (ed.), *China's Belt and Road Initiative: Impacts on Asia and Policy Agenda* (Singapore: Springer, 2020), pp. 113–34, https://doi.org/10.1007/978-981-15-5171-0_6.

65 Syed Sabreena Bukhari, 'Decoding China's Ambitions in the Indian Ocean: Analysis and Implications for India', *Australian Journal of Maritime & Ocean Affairs*, vol. 14, no. 2, 3 April 2022, pp. 136–47, https://doi.org/10.1080/18366503.2021.1959737.

66 Olivia Gippner, 'Antipiracy and Unusual Coalitions in the Indian Ocean Region: China's Changing Role and Confidence Building with India', *Journal of Current Chinese Affairs*, vol. 45, no. 3, 30 May 2016, pp. 107–37, https://doi.org/10.1177/186810261604500304.

67 Shaurya Karanbir Gurung, '14 Chinese Navy Ships Spotted

68 in Indian Ocean, Indian Navy Monitoring Locations', *Economic Times*, 12 July 2018, https://economictimes.indiatimes.com/articleshow/61882634.cms?utm_source=contentofinterest%26utm_medium=text%26utm_campaign=cppst.

68 Gurmeet Kanwal, 'Pakistan's Gwadar Port: A New Naval Base in China's String of Pearls in the Indo-Pacific', Center for Strategic and International Studies, March 2018, https://csis-website-prod.s3.amazonaws.com/s3fs-public/publication/180717_Kanwal_PakistansGwadarPort.pdf.

69 *Ibid.*

70 US Department of Defense, 'Military and Security Developments Involving the People's Republic of China', 29 November 2022, https://media.defense.gov/2022/Nov/29/2003122279/-1/-1/1/2022-MILITARY-AND-SECURITY-DEVELOPMENTS-INVOLVING-THE-PEOPLES-REPUBLIC-OF-CHINA.PDF.

71 Tuneer Mukherjee, 'Sino-Indian Maritime Competition: Shadow Fighting in the Indian Ocean', *South Asian Voices*, 7 June 2020, https://southasianvoices.org/sino-indian-maritime-competition-shadow-fighting-in-the-indian-ocean/; and Darshana M. Baruah, 'Maritime Competition in the Indian Ocean', Carnegie Endowment for International Peace, 12 May 2022, https://carnegieendowment.org/2022/05/12/maritime-competition-in-indian-ocean-pub-87093.

72 'Anti-India Campaign in the Maldives Possibly Sponsored by China: Report', *Print*, 11 March 2022, https://theprint.in/world/anti-india-campaign-in-the-maldives-possibly-sponsored-by-china-report/868984/.

73 'Key Note Address by External Minister', speech delivered by Dr S. Jaishankar, Minister of External Affairs of India, New Delhi, 28 January 2021, https://mea.gov.in/Speeches-Statements.htm?dtl/33419/.

74 Press Trust of India, 'China-backed Attempt by Pak to Raise Kashmir Issue at UNSC Fails Again: Indian Diplomat', *Hindu*, 6 August 2020, https://www.thehindu.com/news/national/china-backed-attempt-by-pak-to-raise-kashmir-issue-at-unsc-fails-yet-again-indian-diplomat/article32282021.ece.

75 Anton Harder, 'Not at the Cost of China: New Evidence Regarding US Proposals to Nehru for Joining the United Nations Security Council', Cold War History Project, Working paper 76, Woodrow Wilson International Center for Scholars, https://www.wilsoncenter.org/publication/not-the-cost-china-india-and-the-united-nations-security-council-1950.

76 Atlantic Council, 'China's Shift Toward Discourse Power', in *Chinese Discourse Power: China's Use of Information Manipulation in Regional and Global Competition*, 1 December 2020, pp. 6–14, http://www.jstor.org/stable/resrep27615.5.

77 Dipanjan Roy Chaudhury, 'India Blocks China, Pakistan Move to Have BRI in NAM Papers', *Economic Times*, 17 July 2023, https://economictimes.indiatimes.com/news/india/india-blocks-china-pakistan-move-to-have-bri-in-nam-papers/articleshow/101805998.cms; and Manash Pratim Bhuyan, 'At SCO Summit, India Opposes China's Belt and Road Initiative', *Wire*, 10 June 2018, https://thewire.in/diplomacy/at-sco-summit-india-opposes-chinas-belt-and-road-initiative.

Chapter Three

1. Francine R. Frankel, *When Nehru Looked East: Origins of India–US Suspicion and India–China Rivalry* (Oxford: Oxford University Press, 2020).
2. Dennis Kux, *Estranged Democracies: India and the United States, 1941–1991* (Thousand Oaks, CA: Sage Publications, 1994).
3. Condoleezza Rice, 'Campaign 2000: Promoting the National Interest', *Foreign Affairs*, 1 January 2000, https://www.foreignaffairs.com/united-states/campaign-2000-promoting-national-interest; and Lisa Curtis, 'US–India Relations: The China Factor', The Heritage Foundation, 25 November 2008, https://www.heritage.org/asia/report/us-india-relations-the-china-factor.
4. Kux, *Estranged Democracies: India and the United States, 1941–1991*.
5. Sumit Ganguly, Andrew Scobell and Brian Shoup (eds), *US–Indian Strategic Cooperation into the 21st Century: More than Words* (London: Routledge, 2006), https://doi.org/10.4324/9780203946749.
6. See Ashley J. Tellis, 'The Merits of Dehyphenation: Explaining US Success in Engaging India and Pakistan', *Washington Quarterly*, vol. 31, no. 4, September 2008, pp. 21–42, https://doi.org/10.1162/wash.2008.31.4.21.
7. Prime Minister Atal Bihari Vajpayee was the first to describe the US as a 'natural ally' of India. See 'India–US Relations in the Emerging Global Environment', speech delivered by Atal Bihari Vajpayee, Prime Minister of India, New York, 23 September 2003, https://archive.pib.gov.in/archive/releases98/lyr2003/rsep2003/23092003/r230920035.html.
8. Ganguly, Scobell and Shoup (eds), *US–Indian Strategic Cooperation into the 21st Century: More than Words*.
9. Devirupa Mitra, 'How India Nearly Gave In to US Pressure to Enter the Iraqi Killing Zone', *Wire*, 19 March 2023, https://thewire.in/external-affairs/india-nearly-gave-us-pressure-join-iraq-war.
10. Tanvi Madan, 'The Rise, Fall, and Rebirth of the "Quad"', *War on the Rocks*, 16 November 2017, https://warontherocks.com/2017/11/rise-fall-rebirth-quad/.
11. 'Condoleezza Rice Played Key Role in Bringing India and the US Together: John Kerry', *Economic Times*, 19 June 2014, https://economictimes.indiatimes.com/news/politics-and-nation/condoleezza-rice-played-key-role-in-bringing-india-and-the-us-together-john-kerry/articleshow/36811542.cms.
12. Ashley J. Tellis, 'India as a New Global Power: An Action Agenda for the United States', Carnegie Endowment for International Peace, 15 July 2005, https://carnegieendowment.org/2005/07/14/india-as-new-global-power-action-agenda-for-united-states-pub-17079; and 'Remarks by Condoleezza Rice at Sophia University', speech delivered by Condoleezza Rice, US Secretary of State, Tokyo, 19 March 2005, https://2001-2009.state.gov/secretary/rm/2005/43655.htm.
13. 'New Framework for the India–US Defence Relationship', Manohar Parrikar Institute for Defence Studies and Analyses, 28 June 2005, https://idsa.in/resources/documents/Ind-US-Def-Rel-28.06.05; and Ministry of External Affairs, Government of India, 'Joint Statement, India–US', 18 July 2005, https://www.mea.gov.in/bilateral-documents.htm?dtl/6772/Joint_Statement_IndiaUS.
14. C. Raja Mohan, *Impossible Allies: Nuclear India, United States, and*

the Global Order (New Delhi: India Research Press, 2006); and Dinshaw Mistry, *The US–India Nuclear Agreement: Diplomacy and Domestic Politics* (Cambridge: Cambridge University Press, 2014), https://doi.org/10.1017/CBO9781139683487.

15 Seema Sirohi, *Friends with Benefits: The India–US Story* (New Delhi: HarperCollins, 2023). In addition to India and the US, the exercises included Australia, Japan and Singapore.

16 Sanjaya Baru, *The Accidental Prime Minister: The Making and Unmaking of Manmohan Singh* (Gurgaon: Penguin Books India/Viking, 2014).

17 Bibek Debroy et al. (eds), *Making of New India: Transformation Under Modi Government* (New Delhi: Wisdom Tree, in association with Dr. Syama Prasad Mookerjee Research Foundation, 2019); and Office of Press Secretary, 'US–India Joint Strategic Vision for the Asia-Pacific and Indian Ocean Region', 25 January 2015, https://obamawhitehouse.archives.gov/the-press-office/2015/01/25/us-india-joint-strategic-vision-asia-pacific-and-indian-ocean-region.

18 Joshua T. White, 'After the Foundational Agreements: An Agenda for US–India Defense and Security Cooperation', Brookings, 11 January 2021, https://www.brookings.edu/research/after-the-foundational-agreements-an-agenda-for-us-india-defense-and-security-cooperation/; see also Amrita Nayak Dutta, 'Explained: The Two New US–India Agreements, Signed as Part of Growing Defence Ties', *Indian Express*, 27 August 2024, https://indianexpress.com/article/explained/explained-global/two-new-us-india-agreements-a-short-history-of-growing-defence-ties-9534765/. LEMOA facilitates the exchange of supplies and allows the two armed forces access to each other's facilities. COMCASA enables secure communications between the two militaries. BECA allows for the sharing of geospatial intelligence and information between the partnering countries. SOSA allows the US and its partners to give priority to each other's goods and services for national defence, thereby ensuring supply-chain resilience during emergencies.

19 Alan K. Kronstadt, 'India–US: Major Arms Transfers and Military Exercises', Congressional Research Service, 5 December 2024, https://www.congress.gov/crs-product/IF12438.

20 *Ibid.*; see also Sameer P. Lalwani and Vikram J. Singh, 'A Big Step Forward in US–India Defense Ties', United States Institute of Peace, 6 June 2023, https://www.usip.org/publications/2023/06/big-step-forward-us-india-defense-ties.

21 'India Defence Exports at Record ₹13,000 Crore, US Biggest Importer', *Mint*, 9 July 2022, https://www.livemint.com/news/india-defence-exports-at-record-rs-13-000-crore-us-biggest-importer-11657369829286.html.

22 White House, 'Joint Statement from the United States and India', 22 June 2023, https://bidenwhitehouse.archives.gov/briefing-room/statements-releases/2023/06/22/joint-statement-from-the-united-states-and-india/.

23 *Ibid.*

24 White House, 'A National Security Strategy of Engagement and Enlargement', 1994, https://history.defense.gov/Portals/70/Documents/nss/nss1994.pdf.

25 Rajeswari Pillai Rajagopalan, 'Indo-US Relations in the Bush White House', *Strategic Analysis*, vol. 25, no. 4, 1 July 2001, pp. 545–56, https://doi.org/10.1080/09700160108458977.

26 Srinath Raghavan, *1971: A Global History of the Creation of Bangladesh* (Cambridge, MA: Harvard University Press, 2013).

27 Satinder Lambah, *In Pursuit of Peace: India Pakistan Relations Under Six Prime Ministers* (New Delhi: Penguin, 2023).

28 Jason A. Kirk, 'India's Season of Discontent: US–India Relations Through the Prism of Obama's "Af-Pak" Policy, Year One', *Asian Affairs: An American Review*, vol. 37, no. 3, 31 August 2010, pp. 147–66, https://doi.org/10.1080/00927678.2010.503922.

29 Some of the related arguments can be found in Nicholas Howenstein and Sumit Ganguly, 'India–Pakistan Rivalry in Afghanistan', SIPA Journal of International Affairs, 25 March 2010, https://jia.sipa.columbia.edu/india-pakistan-rivalry-afghanistan.

30 Interview with senior Indian officials in the Indian Embassy, Washington, September 2009.

31 'Full Texts of Donald Trump's Speech on South Asia Policy', *Hindu*, 22 August 2017, https://www.thehindu.com/news/international/full-texts-of-donald-trumps-speech-on-south-asia-policy/article19538424.ece.

32 Bharath Gopalaswamy and James B. Cunningham, 'Review of President Trump's South Asia Strategy', Atlantic Council, 11 December 2018, https://www.atlanticcouncil.org/in-depth-research-reports/report/review-of-president-trump-s-south-asia-strategy/.

33 'We Support India's Right to Self-defense: US to Ajit Doval on Pulwama Terror Attack', *India Today*, 16 February 2019, https://www.indiatoday.in/india/story/pulwama-terror-attack-latest-us-nasa-john-bolton-ajit-doval-phone-call-1457454-2019-02-16.

34 Pranab Dhal Samanta, 'US Played Key Role in Release of Wing Commander Abhinandan Varthaman', *Economic Times*, 13 March 2019, https://economictimes.indiatimes.com/news/defence/us-played-key-role-in-release-of-wing-commander-abhinandan-varthaman/articleshow/68367092.cms.

35 Suhashini Haider, 'India's Move on Article 370 Is "Illegal and Invalid", Says China', *Hindu*, 5 August 2020, https://www.thehindu.com/news/national/indias-article-370-abrogation-illegal-says-china/article32275663.ece.

36 John Cherian, 'International Reaction to Abrogation of Article 370: Muted Response', *Frontline*, 13 September 2019, https://frontline.thehindu.com/cover-story/article29382230.ece.

37 Sumit Kumar, 'Indo-US Counter-terrorism Cooperation Foundations, Dimensions and Limitations', South Asia Terrorism Portal, 23 October 2018, https://www.satp.org/faultline-chapter-details/volume-23/indo-us-counter-terrorism-cooperation-foundations-dimensions-and-limitations.

38 Carina Van de Wetering, *India as a Strategic Partner: The Bush Administration* (New York: Palgrave Macmillan, 2016), https://doi.org/10.1057/978-1-137-54862-7_5.

39 Interview with senior officials in India's Ministry of External Affairs and Prime Minister's Office, New Delhi, April 2005.

40 White House, 'National Security Strategy', 12 October 2022, https://bidenwhitehouse.archives.gov/briefing-roomstatementsreleases/2022/10/12/fact-sheetthe-biden-harris-administrationsnational-security-strategy/.

41 'Confluence of the Two Seas', speech delivered by Abe Shinzo, Prime Minister of Japan, New Delhi, 22 August 2007, https://www.mofa.go.jp/region/asia-paci/pmv0708/speech-2.html.

42 Aditi Malhotra, 'Engagement, Not Entanglement: India's Relationship with the Quad', *Georgetown Journal of International Affairs*, 1 May

2023, https://gjia.georgetown.edu/2023/05/01/engagement-not-entanglement-indias-relationship-with-the-quad/.

43 'The Future of the Indo-Pacific – Japan's New Plan for a "Free and Open Indo-Pacific" – "Together with India, as an Indispensable Partner"', speech delivered by Kishida Fumio, Prime Minister of Japan, New Delhi, 20 March 2023, https://www.mofa.go.jp/policy/page25e_000278.html.

44 Australia Government Defence, 'Defence White Paper 2013', https://www.defence.gov.au/about/strategic-planning/defence-white-paper.

45 'PM's Keynote Address at Shangri-La Dialogue', speech delivered by Narendra Modi, Prime Minister of India, Singapore, 1 June 2018, https://www.pmindia.gov.in/en/news_updates/pms-keynote-address-at-shangri-la-dialogue/.

46 C. Raja Mohan, 'Donald Trump's "Indo-Pacific" and America's India Conundrum', ISAS Insights no. 476, Institute of South Asian Studies, 13 November 2017, https://www.isas.nus.edu.sg/wp-content/uploads/media/isas_papers/ISAS%20Insights%20No.%20476-%20Donald%20Trump's%20'Indo-Pacific'%20and%20America's%20India%20Conundrum.pdf.

47 National Security Strategy Archive, 'National Security Strategy 2017', p. 16.

48 The declassified version of Trump's Indo-Pacific strategy was released in 2020. See 'US Strategic Framework for the Indo-Pacific', USNI News, 15 January 2021, https://news.usni.org/2021/01/15/u-s-strategic-framework-for-the-indo-pacific.

49 Ibid.; and National Security Strategy Archive, 'National Security Strategy 2017'.

50 For the origins of the Indo-Pacific as a term, see Hansong Li, 'The "Indo-Pacific": Intellectual Origins and International Visions in Global Contexts', Modern Intellectual History, vol. 19, no. 3, September 2022, pp. 807–33, https://doi.org/10.1017/S1479244321000214.

51 'Keynote Address', speech delivered by Narendra Modi, Prime Minister of India, at the 17th Asia Security Summit, IISS Shangri-La Dialogue, Singapore, 1 June 2018, https://www.iiss.org/globalassets/media-library---content--migration/images-delta/dialogues/sld/sld-2018/documents/narendra-modi-sld18.pdf.

52 'Arc of Freedom and Prosperity: Japan's Expanding Diplomatic Horizons', speech delivered by Aso Taro, Minister for Foreign Affairs of Japan, Tokyo, 30 November 2006, https://www.mofa.go.jp/announce/fm/aso/speech0611.html.

53 'Confluence of the Two Seas', speech delivered by Abe Shinzo.

54 Kevin Rudd, 'Former Australian PM Kevin Rudd Writes to TSG, Says He Didn't Torpedo the Quad', Sunday Guardian Live, 7 August 2021.

55 'India G20 Presidency LIVE: EAM Dr S. Jaishankar Addresses Forum for Nationalist Thinkers', speech delivered by Dr S. Jaishankar, Hyderabad, 2023, https://www.youtube.com/watch?v=eqTJI8txIII.

56 Madan, 'The Rise, Fall, and Rebirth of the "Quad"'.

57 Suhashini Haidar and Kallol Bhattacherjee, 'First Quad Summit | Quad Leaders for "Open, Free" Indo-Pacific', Hindu, 12 March 2021, https://www.thehindu.com/news/national/first-quad-summit-meeting/article60690519.ece.

58 White House, 'Fact Sheet: Quad Leaders' Summit', 25 September 2021, https://www.whitehouse.gov/briefing-room/statements-releases/2021/09/24/fact-sheet-quad-leaders-summit/; and White House, 'FACT SHEET: Quad Leaders' Tokyo Summit 2022', 24 May 2022, https://www.whitehouse.gov/briefing-room/

59 statements-releases/2022/05/23/fact-sheet-quad-leaders-tokyo-summit-2022/.
59 White House, 'Indo-Pacific Strategy of the United States', 11 February 2022, https://bidenwhitehouse.archives.gov/wp-content/uploads/2022/02/U.S.-Indo-Pacific-Strategy.pdf.
60 *Ibid.*, p. 16.
61 Emma Chanlett-Avery, K. Alan Kronstadt and Bruce Vaughn, 'The "Quad": Cooperation Among the United States, Japan, India, and Australia', Congressional Research Service, 30 January 2023, https://crsreports.congress.gov/product/pdf/IF/IF11678.
62 Sumitha Narayanan Kutty and Rajesh Basrur, 'The Quad: What It Is – and What It Is Not', *Diplomat*, 24 March 2021, https://thediplomat.com/2021/03/the-quad-what-it-is-and-what-it-is-not/.
63 Patrick Gerard Buchan and Benjamin Rimland, 'Defining the Diamond: The Past, Present, and Future of the Quadrilateral Security Dialogue', Center for Strategic and International Studies, 16 March 2020, https://www.csis.org/analysis/defining-diamond-past-present-and-future-quadrilateral-security-dialogue.
64 Jonathan Stromseth, 'ASEAN and the Quad: Strategic Impasse or Avenue for Cooperation?', Brookings, 23 September 2021, https://www.brookings.edu/blog/order-from-chaos/2021/09/23/asean-and-the-quad-strategic-impasse-or-avenue-for-cooperation/.
65 Matt Little, 'Jewel of the Indo-Pacific: The Quad as a Maritime Security Diamond', Center for International Maritime Security, 10 November 2021, https://cimsec.org/jewel-of-the-indo-pacific-the-quad-as-a-maritime-security-diamond/; and US Department of State, 'Guidelines for Quad Partnership on Humanitarian Assistance and Disaster Relief (HADR) in the Indo-Pacific', 23 September 2022, https://www.state.gov/guidelines-for-quad-partnership-on-humanitarian-assistance-and-disaster-relief-hadr-in-the-indo-pacific/.
66 Rajeswari Pillai Rajagopalan, 'At IAEA, India Supports AUKUS', *Diplomat*, 3 October 2022, https://thediplomat.com/2022/10/at-iaea-india-supports-aukus/.
67 Shashank Mattoo, 'India, AUKUS Explore Tech Cooperation Possibilities', *Mint*, 16 March 2023, https://www.livemint.com/news/world/india-aukus-explore-tech-cooperation-possibilities-11678899129642.html.
68 Patrick Kingsley, 'What Is the I2U2?', *New York Times*, 14 July 2022, https://www.nytimes.com/2022/07/14/world/middleeast/i2u2-india-israel-uae-us.html.
69 See Giorgio Cafiero, 'The Geopolitics of the India–Middle East–Europe Economic Corridor', Arab Center Washington, 10 October 2023, https://arabcenterdc.org/resource/the-geopolitics-of-the-india-middle-east-europe-economic-corridor/.
70 See US Department of State, 'Joint Statement by the Quad Foreign Ministers', 21 January 2025, https://www.state.gov/joint-statement-by-the-quad-foreign-ministers/.
71 See US Department of Defense, 'Readout of Secretary of Defense Pete Hegseth's Meeting with Australia's Deputy Prime Minister and Minister for Defence, Richard Marles', 7 February 2025, https://www.defense.gov/News/Releases/Release/Article/4060748/readout-of-secretary-of-defense-pete-hegseths-meeting-with-australias-deputy-pr/; and US Department of State, 'Joint Statement on the Trilateral United States–Japan–Republic of Korea Meeting in Munich', 15 February 2025,

https://www.state.gov/joint-statement-on-the-trilateral-united-states-japan-republic-of-korea-meeting-in-munich/.
72 See White House, 'United States–India Joint Leaders' Statement', 13 February 2025, https://www.whitehouse.gov/briefings-statements/2025/02/united-states-india-joint-leaders-statement/.
73 Sanjib Kr Baruah, 'Donald Trump's Comment on India–Pakistan Does Not Reflect US Policy: Michael Kugelman', *Week*, 1 June 2005, https://www.theweek.in/theweek/current/2025/05/24/expert-on-us-relations-with-india-pakistan-and-afghanistan-michael-kugelman-interview.html.
74 See Edward Wong, 'Trump's Vision: One World, Three Powers?', *New York Times*, 26 May 2025, https://www.nytimes.com/2025/05/26/us/politics/trump-russia-china.html.

Chapter Four

1 J.D. Miller, *India, Japan and Australia: Partners in Asia* (Canberra: Australian National University Press, 1968); and Ian Hall, 'Building an Indo-Pacific Security Partnership', in David Lowe and Eric Meadows (eds), *Rising Power and Changing People: The Australian High Commission in India* (Canberra: Australian National University Press, 2022), pp. 183–99, https://doi.org/10.22459/RPCP.2022.10.
2 'Australia–Japan–India Trilateral Dialogue 2019: Leadership, Partnership and ASEAN Centrality in the Emerging Indo-Pacific', Griffith Asia Institute, 2020, https://www.griffith.edu.au/__data/assets/pdf_file/0025/1007728/AJI-trilateral-dialogue.pdf.
3 Premesha Saha, 'The 1998 Pokhran Nuclear Tests: Reactions and Responses from the Indo-Pacific', Observer Research Foundation, 11 May 2023, https://www.orfonline.org/expert-speak/the-1998-pokhran-nuclear-tests/; and Purnendra Jain, 'From Condemnation to Strategic Partnership: Japan's Changing View of India (1998–2007)', Institute of South Asian Studies, 10 March 2008, https://www.isas.nus.edu.sg/wp-content/uploads/media/isas_papers/41_WP.pdf.
4 Strobe Talbott, *Engaging India: Diplomacy, Democracy, and the Bomb* (Washington DC: Brookings Institution Press, 2004).
5 Rajesh Basrur and Sumitha Narayanan Kutty, 'Modi's India and Japan: Nested Strategic Partnerships', *Internation l Politics*, vol. 59, no. 1, February 2022, pp. 67–89, https://doi.org/10.1057/s41311-021-00288-2; Australian Government Department of Foreign Affairs and Trade, 'Joint Statement on a Comprehensive Strategic Partnership Between Republic of India and Australia', https://www.dfat.gov.au/geo/india/joint-statement-comprehensive-strategic-partnership-between-republic-india-and-australia; and Dhruva Jaishankar, 'The Australia–India Strategic Partnership: Accelerating Security Cooperation in the Indo-Pacific', Lowy Institute, 16 September 2020, https://www.lowyinstitute.org/publications/australia-india-strategic-partnership-accelerating-security-cooperation-indo-pacific.
6 'Confluence of the Two Seas', speech delivered by Abe Shinzo, Prime Minister of Japan, New Delhi, 22 August 2007, https://www.mofa.go.jp/region/asia-paci/pmv0708/speech-2.html.

7   Kevin Rudd, 'Why the Quad Alarms China', *Foreign Affairs*, 6 August 2021, https://www.foreignaffairs.com/articles/united-states/2021-08-06/why-quad-alarms-china.

8   Australian Government, 'Australia in the Asian Century White Paper', October 2012, available at East Asia Forum, https://www.eastasiaforum.org/wp-content/uploads/2014/04/australia-in-the-asian-century-white-paper.pdf.

9   Australian Government Department of Foreign Affairs and Trade, '2017 Foreign Policy White Paper', 23 November 2017, https://www.dfat.gov.au/publications/minisite/2017-foreign-policy-white-paper.

10 Ryan Ashley, 'Japan's New National Security Strategy Is Making Waves', Foreign Policy Research Institute, 4 January 2023, https://www.fpri.org/article/2023/01/japans-new-national-security-strategy-is-making-waves/; Ministry of Defense of Japan, 'National Security Strategy of Japan', December 2022, https://www.mod.go.jp/j/policy/agenda/guideline/pdf/security_strategy_en.pdf; Ministry of Defense of Japan, 'National Defense Strategy', 16 December 2022, https://www.mod.go.jp/j/policy/agenda/guideline/strategy/pdf/strategy_en.pdf; and Ministry of Defense of Japan, 'Defense Buildup Program', 16 December 2022, https://www.mod.go.jp/j/policy/agenda/guideline/plan/pdf/program_en.pdf.

11 See 'Remarks by EAM, Dr. S. Jaishankar at Asia Society Policy Institute in New York', speech delivered by Dr S. Jaishankar, Minister of External Affairs of India, New York, 25 September 2024, https://www.mea.gov.in/Speeches-Statements.htm?dtl/38341/Remarks_by_EAM_Dr_S_Jaishankar_at_Asia_Society_Policy_Institute_in_New_York.

12 See Jyotsna Bakshi, *Russia and India: From Ideology to Geopolitics 1947–1998* (New Delhi: Dev Publications,1999).

13 See Sergey Radchenko, *Unwanted Visionaries: The Soviet Failure in Asia at the End of the Cold War* (New York: Oxford University Press, 2014); Rakesh Krishnan Simha, 'Primakov: The Man Who Created Multipolarity', Russia Beyond, 27 June 2015, https://www.rbth.com/blogs/2015/06/27/primakov_the_man_who_created_multipolarity_43919; and Eugene Rumer, 'The Primakov (Not Gerasimov) Doctrine in Action', Carnegie Endowment for International Peace, 5 June 2019, https://carnegieendowment.org/2019/06/05/primakov-not-gerasimov-doctrine-in-action-pub-79254.

14 International Monetary Fund, 'World Economic Outlook Database', April 2025, https://www.imf.org/en/Publications/WEO/Issues/2025/04/22/world-economic-outlook-april-2025.

15 Embassy of India, Moscow, Russia, 'India–Russia Bilateral Relations', June 2024, https://indianembassy-moscow.gov.in/bilateral-relations-india-russia.php.

16 'Remarks by EAM, Dr. S. Jaishankar at Asia Society Policy Institute in New York'.

17 Pieter D. Wezeman et al., 'Trends in International Arms Transfers, 2023', Stockholm International Peace Research Institute, March 2024, https://www.sipri.org/sites/default/files/2024-03/fs_2403_at_2023.pdf.

18 IISS Military Balance+; Sameer Lalwani and Tyler Sagerstrom, 'What the India–Russia Defence Partnership Means for US Policy', *Survival*, vol. 63, no. 4, 2021, pp. 149–82.

19 Ashok Sharma, 'India Ramps Up Domestic Defense Production', *Diplomat*, 7 April 2022, https://thediplomat.com/2022/04/india-ramps-up-domestic-defense-

production/; and India Brand Equity Foundation, 'Defence Manufacturing Industry in India', April 2023, https://www.ibef.org/industry/defence-manufacturing.

[20] Sudhi Ranjan Sen and Peter Martin, 'US Seeks to Wean India from Russia Weapons with Arms-aid Package', Bloomberg, 17 May 2022, https://www.bloomberg.com/news/articles/2022-05-17/us-seeks-to-wean-india-from-russia-weapons-with-arms-aid-package.

[21] Ministry of Foreign Affairs of the Russian Federation, 'Foreign Minister Sergey Lavrov's Answers to Questions During the Raisina Dialogue Conference, New Delhi, March 3, 2023', 3 March 2023, https://mid.ru/en/foreign_policy/news/1856843/; and Dinakar Peri, 'Raisina Dialogue | Indo-Pacific a Divisive Concept: Sergey Lavrov', *Hindu*, 15 January 2020, https://www.thehindu.com/news/national/indo-pacific-a-divisive-concept-sergey-lavrov/article30572634.ece.

[22] 'Raisina Dialogue 2024: "Makes Sense to Give Russia Multiple Options", FM Jaishankar on Russia–China Ties', *Mint*, 23 February 2024, https://www.livemint.com/news/world/raisina-dialogue-2024-makes-sense-to-give-russia-multiple-options-jaishankar-on-russia-china-ties-11708667256163.html.

[23] See, for instance, Rajan Menon and Eugene Rumer, 'Russia and India: A New Chapter', Carnegie Endowment for International Peace, 20 September 2022, https://carnegieendowment.org/2022/09/20/russia-and-india-new-chapter-pub-87958; see also Shyam Saran, 'Former Foreign Secretary Shyam Saran Writes: China Is Firmly in Russia's Corner – India Needs to Take Note', *Indian Express*, 6 April 2023, https://indianexpress.com/article/opinion/columns/former-foreign-secretary-shyam-saran-writes-china-is-firmly-in-russias-corner-india-needs-to-take-note-8540982/.

[24] 'Address by External Affairs Minister, Dr. S. Jaishankar at the India–Russia Business Forum, Mumbai', speech delivered by Dr S. Jaishankar, Minister of External Affairs of India, Mumbai, 11 November 2024, https://www.mea.gov.in/Speeches-Statements.htm?dtl/38502/Address_by_External_Affairs_Minister_Dr_S_Jaishankar_at_the_IndiaRussia_Business_Forum_Mumbai.

[25] Louisa Brooke-Holland, 'Integrated Review 2021: The Defence Tilt to the Indo-Pacific', House of Commons Library, 11 October 2021, https://commonslibrary.parliament.uk/research-briefings/cbp-9217/; 'Indo-Pacific Tilt: Foreign Secretary's Speech', speech delivered by James Cleverly, UK Foreign Secretary, Singapore, 29 September 2022, https://www.gov.uk/government/speeches/foreign-secretary-james-cleverlys-speech-on-the-indo-pacific-tilt-september-2022; Ministère de l'Europe et des Affaires étrangères, 'The Indo-Pacific: A Priority for France', https://www.diplomatie.gouv.fr/en/country-files/regional-strategies/indo-pacific/the-indo-pacific-a-priority-for-france/; Government of the Netherlands, 'Indo-Pacific: Guidelines for Strengthening Dutch and EU Cooperation with Partners in Asia', 13 November 2020, https://www.government.nl/documents/publications/2020/11/13/indo-pacific-guidelines; and European Council, Council of the European Union, 'Indo-Pacific: Council Adopts Conclusions on EU Strategy for Cooperation', 19 April 2021, https://www.consilium.europa.eu/en/press/press-releases/2021/04/19/indo-pacific-council-adopts-conclusions-on-eu-strategy-for-cooperation/.

26 David Hutt, 'The "Indo-Pacific" Vision: Room for Britain and France?', *Forbes*, 14 November 2017, https://www.forbes.com/sites/davidhutt/2017/11/14/the-indo-pacific-vision-room-for-britain-and-france/.

27 Garima Mohan, 'A European Strategy for the Indo-Pacific', *Washington Quarterly*, vol. 43, no. 4, 1 October 2020, pp. 171–85, https://doi.org/10.1080/0163660X.2020.1850447; and Giulio Pugliese, 'The European Union's Security Intervention in the Indo-Pacific: Between Multilateralism and Mercantile Interests', *Journal of Intervention and Statebuilding*, vol. 17, no. 1, 1 January 2023, pp. 76–98, https://doi.org/10.1080/17502977.2022.2118425.

28 White House, 'National Security Strategy', October 2022, https://bidenwhitehouse.archives.gov/wp-content/uploads/2022/10/Biden-Harris-Administrations-National-Security-Strategy-10.2022.pdf.

29 NATO, 'Relations with Partners in the Indo-Pacific Region', 11 April 2023, https://www.nato.int/cps/en/natohq/topics_183254.htm.

30 Roger Cohen, 'From Red Carpet to Doghouse: Macron Returns from China to Allied Dismay', *New York Times*, 11 April 2023, https://www.nytimes.com/2023/04/11/world/europe/macron-china-allies.html.

31 'Speech by President von der Leyen on EU–China Relations to the Mercator Institute for China Studies and the European Policy Centre', speech delivered by Ursula von der Leyen, President of the European Commission, Brussels, 30 March 2023, https://www.eeas.europa.eu/delegations/japan/speech-president-von-der-leyen-eu-china-relations-mercator-institute-china_en?s=169.

32 Rajeswari Pillai Rajagopalan, 'Strengthening the France–India Partnership', *Diplomat*, 16 May 2022, https://thediplomat.com/2022/05/strengthening-the-france-india-partnership/.

33 Foreign, Commonwealth & Development Office and Prime Minister's Office, '2030 Roadmap for India–UK Future Relations', 4 May 2021, https://www.gov.uk/government/publications/india-uk-virtual-summit-may-2021-roadmap-2030-for-a-comprehensive-strategic-partnership/2030-roadmap-for-india-uk-future-relations.

34 'India, EU Hold First-ever Security, Defence Consultations', *Economic Times*, 12 June 2022, https://economictimes.indiatimes.com/news/defence/india-eu-hold-first-ever-security-defence-consultations/articleshow/92165767.cms.

35 Sachin Parashar, 'Nato's Door Open for More Engagement with India: US', *Times of India*, 1 April 2023, https://timesofindia.indiatimes.com/india/natos-door-open-for-more-engagement-with-india-us/articleshow/99159078.cms; and C. Raja Mohan, 'India's NATO Engagement: Old Inhibitions and New Imperatives', Institute of South Asian Studies, 12 July 2022, https://www.isas.nus.edu.sg/papers/indias-nato-engagement-old-inhibitions-and-new-imperatives/.

36 See C. Raja Mohan and Hernaikh Singh (eds), *Coping with China–India Rivalry: South Asian Dilemmas* (Singapore: World Scientific, 2023); and C. Raja Mohan and Hernaikh Singh (eds), *Biden and Beyond: US Rethinks South Asia* (Singapore: World Scientific, 2024).

37 Touqir Hussain, 'US–China Rivalry', *DAWN*, 17 May 2023, https://www.dawn.com/news/1753753; and 'Pakistan Minister Warned Against Sacrificing Partnership with China for US', *Hindustan Times*, 1 May 2023, https://www.hindustantimes.com/world-news/pakistan-minister-warned-against-sacrificing-partnership-with-china-for-us-report-101682904202707.html.

38 Indo-Asian News Service, 'India and Nepal Ink Pacts to Enhance Physical Connectivity, Tourism & Other Sectors', *Economic Times*, 2 June 2023, https://travel.economictimes.indiatimes.com/news/destination/international/india-and-nepal-ink-pacts-to-enhance-physical-connectivity-tourism-other-sectors/100692024.

39 Gaurav Raja Dahal, 'The Nepal Factor in the Indo-Pacific Strategy', *Kathmandu Post*, 19 October 2021, http://kathmandupost.com/columns/2021/10/19/the-nepal-factor-in-the-indo-pacific-strategy.

40 Rishi Gupta, 'Millennium Challenge Corporation (MCC) in Nepal: Facts, Disputes and the US–China Contest', Vivekananda International Foundation, April 2022, https://www.vifindia.org/sites/default/files/Millennium-Challenge-Corporation-in-Nepal.pdf; Santosh Sharma Poudel, 'Nepal's MCC Debate Reflects Flaws in Its Decision-Making', *Diplomat*, 18 February 2022, https://thediplomat.com/2022/02/nepals-mcc-debate-reflects-flaws-in-its-decision-making/; and Kamal Dev Bhattarai, 'The Indo-Pacific vs. the Belt and Road: Nepal's Great MCC Debate', *Diplomat*, 30 January 2020, https://thediplomat.com/2020/01/the-indo-pacific-vs-the-belt-and-road-nepals-great-mcc-debate/.

41 Nitasha Kaul, 'Beyond India and China: Bhutan as a Small State in International Relations', *International Relations of the Asia-Pacific*, vol. 22, no. 2, May 2022, pp. 297–337.

42 Foundation for Non-Violent Alternatives, 'Resetting India's Tibet Policy 2022', 6 February 2023, https://fnvaworld.org/resetting-indias-tibet-policy-2022/.

43 Lucas Myers, 'How the US Could Counter China in Myanmar', *Asia Times*, 28 January 2022, https://asiatimes.com/2022/01/how-the-us-could-counter-china-in-myanmar/; and Anu Anwar and Geoffrey Macdonald, 'Bangladesh's Balancing Act amid the US Indo-Pacific Strategy', United States Institute of Peace, 1 April 2020, https://www.usip.org/publications/2022/04/bangladeshs-balancing-act-amid-us-indo-pacific-strategy.

44 Soumyodeep Deb and Tual Sawn Khai, 'The Changing Dynamics of China–Myanmar Relations Post the Military Coup – From Hedging to Bandwagoning?', APSA Preprints, 20 January 2023, https://doi.org/10.33774/apsa-2023-h9gjt; and Zo Tum Hmung and John Indergaard, 'Time Is Running Out for India's Balancing Act on the Myanmar Border', United States Institute of Peace, 15 June 2023, https://www.usip.org/publications/2023/06/time-running-out-indias-balancing-act-myanmar-border.

45 Snm Abdi, 'Bangladesh: Why Is "Ally" US Undermining India in Its Backyard?', Moneycontrol, 21 July 2023, https://www.moneycontrol.com/news/opinion/bangladesh-why-is-ally-us-undermining-india-in-its-backyard-10999291.html.

46 Ajeyo Basu, 'China's "Look South Policy" Aims to Dominate Bay of Bengal, Isolate India in Backyard', Firstpost, 13 May 2023, https://www.firstpost.com/world/chinas-look-south-policy-aims-to-dominate-bay-of-bengal-isolate-india-in-backyard-12591822.html.

47 Suhashini Haider, 'India Welcomes US–Maldives Defence Agreement', *Hindu*, 14 September 2020, https://www.thehindu.com/news/national/india-welcomes-us-maldives-defence-agreement/article32601889.ece.

48 Interview with Indian and US officials, December 2020.

49 C. Raja Mohan, 'India's Geopolitics and Southeast Asian Security', *Southeast Asian Affairs*, 2008, pp. 43–60.

50 Lee Hsien Loong, 'The Endangered Asian Century', *Foreign Affairs*, 4 June 2020, https://www.foreignaffairs.com/articles/asia/2020-06-04/lee-hsien-loong-endangered-asian-century.

51 'PM's Keynote Address at Shangri La Dialogue (June 01, 2018)', speech delivered by Narendra Modi, Prime Minister of India, Singapore, 1 June 2018, https://www.mea.gov.in/Speeches-Statements.htm?dtl/29943/Prime+Ministers+Keynote+Address+at+Shangri+La+Dialogue+June+01+2018.

52 Association of Southeast Asian Nations, 'ASEAN Outlook on the Indo-Pacific', 23 June 2019, https://asean.org/asean-outlook-on-the-indo-pacific/.

53 Evan A. Laksmana, 'Whose Centrality? ASEAN and the Quad in the Indo-Pacific', *Journal of Indo-Pacific Affairs*, vol. 3, no. 5, 22 December 2020, pp. 106–17.

54 Sharon Seah and Kei Koga, 'ASEAN and the Quad Inch Closer Together', *Foreign Policy*, 24 May 2023, https://foreignpolicy.com/2023/05/24/quad-asean-southeast-asia-china-geopolitics-indo-pacific/.

55 William Choong, 'The Quad and the Indo-Pacific: Going Slow to Go Further', *Perspective*, ISEAS–Yusof Ishak Institute, 23 September 2021, https://www.iseas.edu.sg/wp-content/uploads/2021/09/ISEAS_Perspective_2021_125.pdf.

56 White House, 'Quad Leaders' Joint Statement', 20 May 2023, https://bidenwhitehouse.archives.gov/briefing-room/statements-releases/2023/05/20/quad-leaders-joint-statement/.

57 'Jokowi: Aim Is to Make Asean Region Stable', *New Straits Times*, 8 May 2023, https://www.nst.com.my/news/nation/2023/05/906846/exclusive-jokowi-aim-make-asean-region-stable-nsttv.

58 'The State of Southeast Asia: 2023 Survey Report', ISEAS–Yusof Ishak Institute, 9 February 2023, https://www.iseas.edu.sg/articles-commentaries/state-of-southeast-asia-survey/the-state-of-southeast-asia-2023-survey-report-2/.

59 Veerle Nouwens, 'US Allies in the Indo-Pacific Align on China', International Institute for Strategic Studies, 1 June 2023, https://www.iiss.org/online-analysis/online-analysis/2023/05/us-allies-in-the-indo-pacific-align-on-china/.

60 Bilahari Kausikan, 'Navigating the New Age of Great-power Competition', *Foreign Affairs*, 11 April 2023, https://www.foreignaffairs.com/united-states/china-great-power-competition-russia-guide.

Chapter Five

1 Priya Chacko, *Indian Foreign Policy: The Politics of Postcolonial Identity from 1947 to 2004* (New York: Routledge, 2012).

2 Satu P. Limaye, *US–Indian Relations: The Pursuit of Accommodation* (Boulder, CO: Westview Press, 1993).

3 See the history of relations in the Cold War captured by Dennis Kux, *Estranged Democracies: India and the United States, 1941–1991* (Thousand Oaks, CA: Sage Publications, 1994).

4 Parama Sinha Palit, 'The Kashmir Policy of the United States: A Study of the Perceptions, Conflicts and Dilemmas', *Strategic Analysis*, vol. 25, no. 6, September 2001, pp. 781–803, https://doi.org/10.1080/09700160108458997.

5 Vivek Chadha, 'Indian Army's Approach to Counter Insurgency Operations: A Perspective on Human Rights', Manohar Parrikar Institute

for Defence Studies and Analyses, 2016, https://idsa.in/occasionalpapers/indian-army-counter-insurgency_vchadha_110216.
6. Richard C. Bush, '30 Years After Tiananmen Square, a Look Back on Congress' Forceful Response', Brookings, 29 May 2019, https://www.brookings.edu/blog/order-from-chaos/2019/05/29/30-years-after-tiananmen-square-a-look-back-on-congress-forceful-response/.
7. Josef Joffe, 'Clinton's World: Purpose, Policy, and Weltanschauung', *Washington Quarterly*, vol. 24, no. 1, 1 March 2001, pp. 139–54, https://doi.org/10.1162/016366001561410.
8. Robert Hathaway, 'The US–India Courtship: From Clinton to Bush', *Journal of Strategic Studies*, vol. 25, no. 4, December 2002, pp. 6–31, https://doi.org/10.1080/01402390412 31302855.
9. 'A Balance of Power that Favors Freedom', speech delivered by Condoleezza Rice, US National Security Advisor, New York City, 1 October 2002, https://awpc.cattcenter.iastate.edu/2017/03/21/a-balance-of-power-that-favors-freedom-oct-1-2002/.
10. Anand Giridharadas, 'India Has a Soft Spot for Bush', *New York Times*, 10 January 2009, https://www.nytimes.com/2009/01/11/weekinreview/11giridharadas.html.
11. 'The US, India and Nuclear Technology', speech delivered by George W. Bush, US President, New Delhi, 3 March 2006, http://www.presidentialrhetoric.com/speeches/03.03.06.html.
12. 'Remarks by President Obama in Address to the People of India', speech delivered by Barack Obama, US President, New Delhi, 27 January 2015, https://obamawhitehouse.archives.gov/the-press-office/2015/01/27/remarks-president-obama-address-people-india.
13. Vibhav M. and Irfan Nooruddin, 'Trump, Modi, and the Illiberal Consensus', *India Review*, vol. 22, no. 2, 15 March 2023, pp. 118–27, https://doi.org/10.1080/14736489.2023.2180915.
14. Michael Kugelman, 'India's Illiberal Turn Won't Shake Its Relationship with the United States', *Foreign Policy*, 28 February 2020, https://foreignpolicy.com/2020/02/28/riots-hindu-modi-trump-delhi-brutal-violence-us-india-relationship/.
15. Robert A. Manning, 'Does Biden's "Democracy v. Autocracy" Framework Make Sense?', *Hill*, 13 June 2022, https://thehill.com/opinion/national-security/3521187-does-bidens-democracy-v-autocracy-framework-make-sense/.
16. White House, 'US–India Joint Leaders' Statement: A Partnership for Global Good', 25 September 2021, https://www.whitehouse.gov/briefing-room/statements-releases/2021/09/24/u-s-india-joint-leaders-statement-a-partnership-for-global-good/.
17. See, for example, the *New York Times* editorial on Modi's visit to Washington in June 2023: The Editorial Board, 'The India Quandary', *New York Times*, 22 June 2023, https://www.nytimes.com/2023/06/22/opinion/biden-modi-meeting.html.
18. Milan Vaishnav, 'The Challenge of India's Democratic Backsliding', *Democracy: A Journal of Ideas*, 24 September 2021, https://democracyjournal.org/magazine/62-special-issue/the-challenge-of-indias-democratic-backsliding/.
19. Nahal Toosi et al., 'On India, Say Nothing', *Politico*, 3 February 2023, https://www.politico.com/newsletters/national-security-daily/2023/03/02/on-india-say-nothing-00085164.
20. Chietiigj Bajpaee, 'Why India's Souring Relations with Canada

Could Have Wider Implications for the West', *Guardian*, 20 September 2023, https://www.theguardian.com/commentisfree/2023/sep/20/india-souring-relations-canada-assassination-foreign-policy; John Reed, John Paul Rathbone and Demetri Sevastopulo, 'Alleged Plot to Assassinate Sikh Separatist Complicates US–India Ties', *Financial Times*, 23 November 2023, https://www.ft.com/content/66809c9a-1a0d-4e88-adbf-5b2baece6aac; and Kapil Komireddi, 'Biden's Friendship with Modi Is Already Under Threat', *New York Times*, 12 December 2023, https://www.nytimes.com/2023/12/12/opinion/india-us-sikh-assassination.html.

21 Alisha Rahaman Sarkar, 'India Says Murdering Separatists Abroad Is "Not Our Policy"', *Independent*, 27 September 2023, https://www.independent.co.uk/asia/india/jaishankar-canada-nijjar-murder-india-b2419350.html.

22 See Reuters, 'Ex-RAW Agent with Shocking Charges of Pannun Murder Plot Was Arrested by Delhi Police', *Economic Times*, 21 October 2024, https://economictimes.indiatimes.com/news/india/ex-raw-agent-with-shocking-us-charges-of-pannun-murder-plot-was-arrested-by-delhi-police/articleshow/114374654.cms.

23 C. Raja Mohan, 'Beyond Trudeau: Connected Politics of India and the Anglosphere', *ISAS Brief*, Institute of South Asian Studies, 5 October 2023, https://www.isas.nus.edu.sg/papers/beyond-trudeau-connected-politics-of-india-and-the-anglosphere/.

24 Ajay Bisaria and Nadir Patel, 'Carney's Burden: Trump, Trade, and a New World Order', *Hindustan Times*, 1 May 2025, https://www.hindustantimes.com/opinion/carneys-burden-trump-trade-a-new-world-order-101746022854746.html.

25 White House, 'National Security Strategy', 12 October 2022, https://bidenwhitehouse.archives.gov/wp-content/uploads/2022/10/Biden-Harris-Administrations-National-Security-Strategy-10.2022.pdf.

26 Michael Beckley and Hal Brands, 'China's Threat to Global Democracy', *Journal of Democracy*, vol. 34, no. 1, January 2023, pp. 65–79.

27 Charles Edel and David O. Shullman, 'China's Authoritarianism: How Beijing Is Fueling Repression Worldwide', *Foreign Affairs*, 16 September 2021, https://www.foreignaffairs.com/articles/china/2021-09-16/how-china-exports-authoritarianism.

28 White House, 'United States–India Joint Leaders' Statement', 13 February 2025, https://www.whitehouse.gov/briefings-statements/2025/02/united-states-india-joint-leaders-statement/#:~:text=The%20leaders%20hailed%202025%20as,systematically%20map%20changes%20to%20the.

29 David M. Malone, C. Raja Mohan and Srinath Raghavan (eds), *The Oxford Handbook of Indian Foreign Policy* (Oxford: Oxford University Press, 2015), https://doi.org/10.1093/oxfordhb/9780198743538.001.0001.

30 Vivek Kaul, 'The Tale of Two Economies: What Changed in 30 Years', *Mint*, 23 June 2020, https://www.livemint.com/news/india/the-tale-of-two-economies-what-changed-in-30-years-11592930762996.html.

31 Jonathan D. James, 'The Prospect of "Chindia" as a World Power', *E-International Relations*, 6 December 2019, https://www.e-ir.info/2019/12/06/the-prospect-of-chindia-as-a-world-power/.

32 Harsh V. Pant and Anant Singh Mann, 'India's Challenge to the BRI: Shaping the Global Normative Consensus', in Paulo Afonso B. Duarte (ed.), *The Palgrave Handbook of Globalization with Chinese Characteristics: The Case of the Belt and Road Initiative* (Singapore: Springer

Nature, 2023), pp. 459–73, https://doi.org/10.1007/978-981-19-6700-9_27; and Pankhuri Gaur, 'India's Withdrawal from RCEP: Neutralising National Trade Concerns', *Journal of the Asia Pacific Economy*, vol. 27, no. 2, 3 April 2022, pp. 270–88, https://doi.org/10.1080/13547860.2020.1809772.

[33] 'Crisis and Cooperation: Imperatives in Times of the Pandemic', speech delivered by Dr S. Jaishankar, Minister of External Affairs of India, Hyderabad, 16 November 2020, https://www.youtube.com/watch?v=ZMjIFp2r-sY&pp=ygVOUyBKYWlzaGFua2FyIHZpcnR1YWwgYWRkcmVzcyBhdCBJU0lsIEh5ZGVyYWJhZCwgRGVjJY2FuIERpYWxvZ3VlLCBOb3ZlbWJlcjciAyMDIw.

[34] Robert E. Lighthizer, 'Trump's Trade Policy Is Making America Stronger', *Foreign Affairs*, 20 July 2020, https://www.foreignaffairs.com/articles/china/2020-07-20/trumps-trade-policy-making-america-stronger; see also Matthew C. Klein and Michael Pettis, *Trade Wars Are Class Wars: How Rising Inequality Distorts the Global Economy and Threatens International Peace: With a New Preface* (New Haven, CT: Yale University Press, 2021).

[35] 'Remarks by National Security Advisor on Renewing American Economic Leadership', speech delivered by Jake Sullivan, US National Security Advisor, Washington DC, 27 April 2023, https://www.whitehouse.gov/briefing-room/speeches-remarks/2023/04/27/remarks-by-national-security-advisor-jake-sullivan-on-renewing-american-economic-leadership-at-the-brookings-institution/.

[36] White House, 'FACT SHEET: The United States and India – Global Leadership in Action', 24 September 2021, https://www.whitehouse.gov/briefing-room/statements-releases/2021/09/24/fact-sheet-the-united-states-and-india-global-leadership-in-action/.

[37] 'The Top 10 Economies of the World in 2024', *Forbes India*, 10 April 2024, https://www.forbesindia.com/article/explainers/top-10-largest-economies-in-the-world/86159/1.

[38] Alexandre Tanzi, "IMF Now Sees Global Growth More Reliant on China and India', Bloomberg, 22 April 2025, https://www.bloomberg.com/news/articles/2025-04-22/imf-now-sees-global-growth-more-reliant-on-china-and-india.

[39] Megha Mandavia, 'Apple's Big Bet on India Gets Bigger Still', *Wall Street Journal*, 11 April 2022, https://www.wsj.com/articles/apples-big-bet-on-india-gets-bigger-still-11649682365.

[40] The four pillars of IPEF are trade, supply chains, a clean economy and a fair economy. In May 2022, the United States launched the Indo-Pacific Economic Framework for Prosperity, or IPEF, with a dozen initial Partners across the Indo-Pacific. US Department of Commerce, 'Indo-Pacific Economic Framework for Prosperity', https://www.commerce.gov/ipef.

[41] Jordan Fabian and Sankalp Phartiyal, 'Trump Asks Apple to Stop Moving iPhone Production to India', Bloomberg, 15 May 2025, https://www.bloomberg.com/news/articles/2025-05-15/trump-wants-apple-to-stop-moving-iphone-production-to-india.

[42] Press Trust of India, '"India Would Be One of the First Trade Deals We Sign": US Treasury Secretary', *Hindu*, 29 April 2025, https://www.thehindu.com/news/national/india-would-be-one-of-first-trade-deals-we-sign-us-treasury-secretary/article69504705.ece.

[43] S&P Global, 'China Slows, India Grows', 28 November 2023, https://www.spglobal.com/_assets/documents/ratings/research/101590079.pdf.

44. Indira Chowdhury, 'Internationalism and Indian Science: A Historical Reflection', Center for the Advanced Study of India, 27 August 2013, https://casi.sas.upenn.edu/iit/chowdhury; see also Robert S. Anderson, *Nucleus and Nation: Scientists, International Networks, and Power in India* (Chicago, IL: University of Chicago Press, 2010).

45. 'Had Nehru Accepted US Offer, India Will Not Have to Try for NSG Membership: Rasgotra', *Hindu*, 13 June 2016, https://www.thehindu.com/news/national/Had-Nehru-accepted-U.S.-offer-India-will-not-have-to-try-for-NSG-membership-Rasgotra/article14420389.ece; see also Maharaja Krishna Rasgotra, *A Life in Diplomacy* (New Delhi: Penguin, 2019).

46. George Perkovich, *India's Nuclear Bomb: The Impact on Global Proliferation* (Berkeley, CA: University of California Press, 2001).

47. For a history of the space programme, see Amrita Shah, *Vikram Sarabhai, a Life* (New Delhi: Penguin, 2007); see also U.R. Rao, *India's Rise as a Space Power* (Delhi: Foundation Books, 2014).

48. Perkovich, *India's Nuclear Bomb: The Impact on Global Proliferation*; and Limaye, *US–Indian Relations: The Pursuit of Accommodation*.

49. Francine R. Frankel (ed.), *Bridging the Non-Proliferation Divide: The United States and India* (Delhi: Konark Publication, 1995).

50. Raja Mohan, *Impossible Allies: Nuclear India, United States, and the Global Order* (New Delhi: India Research Press, 2006).

51. Anant Krishnan, 'China Says "No Change" on India's Entry as NSG Meets in Bern', *India Today*, 23 June 2017, https://www.indiatoday.in/world/story/china-india-nuclear-suppliers-group-bern-switzerland-984337-2017-06-23.

52. Mohan, *Impossible Allies: Nuclear India, United States, and the Global Order*.

53. Abhishek Chakraborty, 'India and US to Jointly Design, Manufacture Nuclear Reactors in India', NDTV.com, 31 March 2025, https://www.ndtv.com/world-news/india-us-to-jointly-design-manufacture-nuclear-reactors-in-india-8054762.

54. Seema Sirohi, *Friends with Benefits: The India–US Story* (New Delhi: HarperCollins, 2023).

55. Rakesh Sood, 'India and Non-Proliferation Export Control Regimes', Occasional Paper no. 150, Observer Research Foundation, April 2018, https://orfonline.org/wp-content/uploads/2018/04/ORF_OccasionalPaper_150_NonProliferation_FinalForUpload.pdf.

56. White House, 'FACT SHEET: United States and India Elevate Strategic Partnership with the Initiative on Critical and Emerging Technology (ICET)', 31 January 2023, https://www.whitehouse.gov/briefing-room/statements-releases/2023/01/31/fact-sheet-united-states-and-india-elevate-strategic-partnership-with-the-initiative-on-critical-and-emerging-technology-icet/.

57. White House, 'Joint Statement from the United States and India', 22 June 2023, https://bidenwhitehouse.archives.gov/briefing-room/statements-releases/2023/06/22/joint-statement-from-the-united-states-and-india/.

58. Vivek Mishra, 'India and the U.S. Make a Strategic Case for Health Cooperation', Observer Research Foundation, 20 December 2022, https://www.orfonline.org/research/india-and-the-u-s-make-a-strategic-case-for-health-cooperation/; and 'Vaccines: India, US Discuss Cooperation in Pharma Sector, Health News', *Economic Times*, 11 May 2021, https://health.economictimes.indiatimes.com/news/pharma/india-us-discuss-cooperation-in-pharma-sector/82541673.

59 'Huawei and ZTE Left Out of India's 5G Trials', BBC News, 5 May 2021, https://www.bbc.com/news/business-56990236; and 'US Lawmakers Applaud India's Decision to Not Allow Chinese Companies to Conduct 5G Trials', *Times of India*, 6 May 2021, https://timesofindia.indiatimes.com/business/india-business/us-lawmakers-applaud-indias-decision-to-not-allow-chinese-companies-to-conduct-5g-trials/articleshow/82423678.cms.

60 White House, 'Quad Principles on Technology Design, Development, Governance, and Use', 25 September 2021, https://www.whitehouse.gov/briefing-room/statements-releases/2021/09/24/quad-principles-on-technology-design-development-governance-and-use/.

61 Press Trust of India, 'India, US, South Korea Explore Cooperation in Tech Sector', *Economic Times*, 15 March 2024, https://cio.economictimes.indiatimes.com/news/next-gen-technologies/india-us-south-korea-explore-cooperation-in-tech-sector/108512540.

62 Jawaharlal Nehru, *The Discovery of India* (Delhi: Oxford University Press, 1985).

63 Vineet Thakur, 'India's Diplomatic Entrepreneurism: Revisiting India's Role in the Korean Crisis, 1950–52', *China Report*, vol. 49, no. 3, August 2013, pp. 273–98, https://doi.org/10.1177/0009445513502266.

64 Steven Wilkinson, *Army and Nation: The Military and Indian Democracy Since Independence* (Cambridge, MA: Harvard University Press, 2015).

65 C. Raja Mohan, 'India's Regional Security Cooperation: The Nehru Raj Legacy', Institute of South Asian Studies, 7 March 2013, https://www.isas.nus.edu.sg/papers/168-indiaocos-regional-security-cooperation-the-nehru-raj-legacy/.

66 Dinakar Peri, 'India, Egypt Ties: From Fighter Jet Development in the 1960s to Collaborating on Defence Industry Today', *Hindu*, 24 January 2023, https://www.thehindu.com/news/national/india-egypt-ties-from-fighter-jet-development-in-the-1960s-to-collaborating-on-defence-industry-today/article66428318.ece.

67 A.G. Noorani, *Brezhnev's Plan for Asian Security: Russia in Asia* (Bombay: Jaico, 1975); and Parliament of India Digital Library, 'Extract from the Debate During Question Hour on Starred Question No. 465 in Lok Sabha on July 14, 1977 on Asian Collective Security', *Lok Sabha Debates*, vol. 4, no. 29, https://eparlib.nic.in/bitstream/123456789/1862/1/lsd_06_02_14-07-1977.pdf.

68 C. Raja Mohan, 'India's Military Diplomacy: Legacy of International Peacekeeping', Institute of South Asian Studies, 13 June 2014, https://www.isas.nus.edu.sg/papers/190-indiaocos-military-diplomacy-legacy-of-international-peacekeeping/; and Dhruva Jaishankar, 'India's Military Diplomacy: Taking the Leap', Brookings, 12 January 2017, https://www.brookings.edu/opinions/indias-military-diplomacy-taking-the-leap/.

69 Interviews with senior officials of the Government of India, December 2018.

70 Constantino Xavier, 'India's Expatriate Evacuation Operations: Bringing the Diaspora Home', Carnegie India, 4 January 2017, https://carnegieindia.org/2017/01/04/india-s-expatriate-evacuation-operations-bringing-diaspora-home-pub-66573.

71 Saneet Chakradeo, 'Neighbourhood First Responder: India's Humanitarian Aid and Relief', Centre for Social and Economic Progress, 18 August 2020, https://csep.org/policy-brief/neighbourhood-first-responder-indias-humanitarian-assistance-and-disaster-relief/; and Abhishek Mishra, 'India's Vision of SAGAR: Humanitarian Assistance

72 and Disaster Relief Operations in the Indian Ocean Region', Observer Research Foundation, 3 February 2020, https://www.orfonline.org/expert-speak/indias-vision-of-sagar-humanitarian-assistance-and-disaster-relief-operations-in-the-indian-ocean-region-61000/.

72 Andrew Greene, 'India Building Island Base in Mauritius as It Strengthens Military Ties with Australia', ABC News, 4 August 2021, https://www.abc.net.au/news/2021-08-04/india-building-secret-mauritius-military-base-defence-australia/100348254; Dennis Hardy, 'Will India Try Again for a Military Base in Seychelles?', *Diplomat*, 26 July 2022, https://thediplomat.com/2022/07/will-india-try-again-for-a-military-base-in-seychelles/; and Shubhajit Roy, 'Explained: India, Oman Ties and Why Its Top Defence Official's Delhi Visit Important', *Indian Express*, 30 January 2022, https://indianexpress.com/article/explained/explained-india-oman-ties-defence-officials-mohammed-nasser-al-zaabi-delhi-visit-7748422/.

73 Sushim Mukul, 'Why Maldives President Muizzu Wants Indian Troops Out', *India Today*, 5 March 2024, https://www.indiatoday.in/world/story/maldives-indian-military-personnel-navy-army-air-force-indian-muizzu-ocean-china-jaishankar-china-agreement-2510713-2024-03-05; see also Rajat Pandit, 'In Reset of Ties, Male Agrees to Steps on Defence Cooperation', *Times of India*, 9 January 2025, https://timesofindia.indiatimes.com/india/in-reset-of-ties-male-agrees-to-steps-on-defence-cooperation/articleshow/117064403.cms.

74 Laxman Kumar Behera, 'Made in India: An Aspiring Brand in Global Arms Bazaar', *Defense & Security Analysis*, vol. 38, no. 3, 3 July 2022, pp. 336–48, https://doi.org/10.1080/14751798.2022.2084815; and Arpan A. Chakraborty and Gitanjali Sinha, 'From Imports to Exports: Analysing India's Defence Sector Evolution and Atmanirbharata', ACS Publishers, 2024, https://pure.jgu.edu.in/id/eprint/9164/.

75 Ministry of Defence, Government of India, 'Defence Exports Surge to a Record High of Rs 23,622 Crore in Financial Year 2024–25, a Growth of 12.04% over 2023–24', Press release, 1 April 2025, https://pib.gov.in/PressReleasePage.aspx?PRID=2117348.

76 See Anit Mukherjee, 'India as a Net Security Provider: Concept and Impediments', S Rajaratnam School of International Studies, August 2014.

77 Edward Luce, 'India Will Never Be America's Ally', *Financial Times*, 5 May 2023, https://www.ft.com/content/d842b152-86d4-4dde-ad14-17bfb2993859.

78 Ashley J. Tellis, 'America's Bad Bet on India', *Foreign Affairs*, 1 May 2023, https://www.foreignaffairs.com/india/americas-bad-bet-india-modi.

79 'Fireside Chat with Kurt Campbell', Aspen Institute, 8 December 2022, https://youtu.be/dzp3_UmZIKY.

80 'Asian Allies Fear Being Dumped by China', *The Economist*, 6 March 2025, https://www.economist.com/asia/2025/03/06/asian-allies-fear-being-dumped-by-trump; see also David Santoro, 'The End of Extended Deterrence in Asia', *Foreign Affairs*, 22 May 2025, https://www.foreignaffairs.com/china/end-extended-deterrence-asia.

81 Vijay Gokhale, 'What Should India Do Before the Next Taiwan Strait Crisis?', Carnegie India, 17 April 2023, https://carnegieendowment.org/research/2023/04/what-should-india-do-before-the-next-taiwan-strait-crisis?lang=en.

82 See Aaron-Mathew Lariosa, 'India to Take on Future US Navy Ship Maintenance per Agreement', USNI

83 News, 14 September 2023, https://news.usni.org/2023/09/14/india-to-take-on-future-u-s-navy-ship-maintenance-per-agreement.

83 Mehul Srivastava, Charles Clover and Humza Jilani, 'China's J-10 "Dragon" Shows Teeth in India–Pakistan Combat Debut', *Financial Times*, 9 May 2025, https://www.ft.com/content/ff46ca13-a64d-4ba1-833e-1bb348880aec.

84 See, for example, Fatima Idrees, 'Pakistan–Afghanistan Relations', 31 May 2024, https://papers.ssrn.com/sol3/papers.cfm?abstract_id=4807211; see also Amira Jadoon, 'Decoding Pakistan's 2024 Airstrikes in Afghanistan', *War on the Rocks*, 7 March 2025, https://warontherocks.com/2025/03/decoding-pakistans-2024-airstrikes-in-afghanistan/.

85 'The Tit-for-tat Conflict Between Iran and Pakistan', IISS *Strategic Comments*, vol. 30, no. 4, March 2024.

86 Admiral Raja Menon, 'How India's New Naval Base at Andamans Will Force Beijing to Reassess Its Strategy', *Indian Express*, 21 March 2023.

87 IISS, '*Military Balance 2025*: Defence Spending and Procurement Trends', 12 February 2025, https://www.iiss.org/publications/the-military-balance/2025/defence-spending-and-procurement-trends/.

88 Karl Dewey, Fenella McGerty and Viraj Solanki, 'Personnel vs Capital: The Indian Defence Budget', IISS Military Balance blog, 14 April 2023, https://www.iiss.org/online-analysis/military-balance/2023/04/indian-defence-budget/#:~:text=India's%202023%20INR5.,for%20defence%20procurement%20and%20modernisation.

89 Global Firepower Ranks (2005–Present), https://www.globalfirepower.com/global-ranks-previous.php.

90 For the history of the Indian nuclear-weapons programme up to the late 1990s, see Perkovich, *India's Nuclear Bomb: The Impact on Global Proliferation*.

91 Federation of American Scientists, 'Status of World Nuclear Forces', 26 March 2025, https://fas.org/initiative/status-world-nuclear-forces/.

92 Hans M. Kristensen et al., 'Chinese Nuclear Weapons, 2025', Bulletin of the Atomic Scientists, 12 March 2025, https://thebulletin.org/premium/2025-03/chinese-nuclear-weapons-2025/.

93 Lyle Morris and Rakesh Sood, 'Appendix: Recent China–India Border Conflicts and the Role of Nuclear Weapons', in *Understanding China's Perceptions and Strategy Toward Nuclear Weapons: A Case Study Approach*, Defense Threat Reduction Agency, September 2024, https://asiasociety.org/sites/default/files/2024-09/23P0033_TECREP_FL%20082624%20FINAL.pdf.

Conclusion

1 See, for example, Scott Kennedy, 'The United States' Illiberal Turn Recasts a Potential Deal with China', Center for Strategic and International Studies, March 2025, https://www.csis.org/analysis/united-states-illiberal-turn-recasts-potential-deal-china.

2 Alexander B. Gray, 'Trump Will End US Passivity in the Western Hemisphere', *Foreign Policy*, 13 January 2025; for a longer view of the concept, see Andrew F. Krepinevich and Eric Lindsey, *Hemispheric Defense in the 21st Century* (Washington DC: Center for Strategic and Budgetary Assessments, 2013), https://csbaonline.org/uploads/documents/Hemispheric-Defense-in-the-21st-Century.pdf.

3 See, for example, two essays by Michael Beckley: 'The Strange Triumph of a Broken America', *Foreign Affairs*, January/February 2025, https://www.foreignaffairs.com/united-states/strange-triumph-broken-america-michael-beckley?check_logged_in=1; and 'The Age of American Unilateralism', Foreign Affairs, 16 April 2025, https://www.foreignaffairs.com/united-states/age-american-unilateralism.

4 See Kurt Campbell and Rush Doshi, 'Underestimating China: Why America Needs a New Strategy of Allied Scale to Offset Beijing's Enduring Advantages', *Foreign Affairs*, May/June 2025, https://www.foreignaffairs.com/china/underestimating-china.

5 'Secretary of Defense Lloyd J. Austin III Participates in Fullerton Lecture Series in Singapore', speech delivered by Lloyd J. Austin III, US Secretary of Defense, Singapore, 27 July 2021, https://www.defense.gov/News/Transcripts/Transcript/Article/2711025/secretary-of-defense-lloyd-j-austin-iii-participates-in-fullerton-lecture-serie/.

6 White House, 'National Security Strategy 2022', 12 October 2022, p. 22, https://bidenwhitehouse.archives.gov/briefing-room/statements-releases/2022/10/12/fact-sheet-the-biden-harris-administrations-national-security-strategy/.

7 Stephen Biddle and Eric Labs, 'Does America Face a "Ship Gap" with China?', *Foreign Affairs*, 19 March 2025, https://www.foreignaffairs.com/united-states/does-america-face-ship-gap-china; see also Miyeon Oh and Michael Cecire, 'Why the United States, South Korea, and Japan Must Cooperate in Shipbuilding', RAND, 6 May 2025, https://www.rand.org/pubs/commentary/2025/05/why-the-united-states-south-korea-and-japan-must-cooperate.html.

8 Government of Japan, 'A Kishida Perspective on the Future of Asia', Nikkei Asia, 26 May 2022, https://ps.nikkei.com/kishidafoa2022/.

9 Gabriele Steinhauser, Jayu Wang and Timothy Martin, 'Trump's Ukraine Shift Unsettles US Allies in Asia', *Wall Street Journal*, 23 February 2025, https://www.wsj.com/world/asia/trumps-ukraine-shift-unsettles-u-s-allies-in-asia-ecb97120; see also Jude Blanchette and Gerard DiPippo, 'From Strategic Ambiguity to Strategic Anxiety: Taiwan's Trump Challenge', RAND, 26 March 2025, https://www.rand.org/pubs/commentary/2025/03/from-strategic-ambiguity-to-strategic-anxiety-taiwans.html.

10 Bec Strating, 'Understanding Doubts over US Extended Deterrence over Asia', Lowy Institute, 15 April 2025, https://www.lowyinstitute.org/the-interpreter/understanding-doubts-over-us-extended-nuclear-

deterrence-asia; see also Tayheun Kim, 'North Korea's Efforts to Attain De Facto Nuclear Weapon State Status and ROK–US Response Strategy', *38 North*, 14 March 2025, https://www.38north.org/2025/03/north-koreas-efforts-to-attain-de-facto-nuclear-weapon-state-status-and-rok-us-response-strategy/.

[11] Press Information Bureau, Government of India, '6th Meeting of ASEAN–India Trade in Goods Agreement Joint Committee Held in New Delhi', 23 November 2024, https://www.pib.gov.in/PressReleaseIframePage.aspx?PRID=2076227.

[12] Xinhua, 'China–ASEAN Cooperation Yields Fruitful, Win–Win Results: Report', 11 April 2025, http://english.news.cn/20250411/2004e3c2733740c2bfd81ce6bc487a48/c.html.

[13] Rajat Kahthuria, 'Free Trade Agreement with UK Opens a Path to Deals with US, EU', *Indian Express*, 8 May 2025, https://indianexpress.com/article/opinion/columns/free-trade-agreement-with-uk-opens-a-path-to-deals-with-us-eu-9989186/.

[14] C. Raja Mohan, 'India and Asean in a Changing World', Institute of South Asian Studies, 14 October 2024, https://www.isas.nus.edu.sg/papers/india-and-asean-in-a-changing-world/.

[15] Joyeeta Bhattacharjee, 'SAARC vs BIMSTEC: The Search for the Ideal Platform for Regional Cooperation', Observer Research Foundation, 17 August 2023, https://www.orfonline.org/research/saarc-vs-bimstec-the-search-for-the-ideal-platform-for-regional-cooperation.

[16] Antara Chakraborthy, 'Hindu Nationalism: Impact on Multicultural Societies', Rajaratnam School of International Studies, 7 March 2023, https://rsis.edu.sg/rsis-publication/rsis/hindu-nationalism-impact-on-multicultural-societies/; see also Sarita Dash, 'Hindu Nationalism and Its Ramifications', in Sarita Dash, *Cultural Dimensions of India's Look-Act East Policy* (Singapore: Palgrave Macmillan, 2023), pp. 405–35.

INDEX

9/11 76, 82, 84, 86

A

Abe Shinzo 86, 87, 89, 90, 103, 104
Adani Group 63, 64
Afghanistan 82, 83, 85, 86, 158
anti-imperialism 47, 49
Arunachal Pradesh 52
Asia
  economy 12, 13
Asia-Pacific 15, 79, 87
Association of Southeast Asian Nations (ASEAN) 20, 43, 57, 89, 93, 118, 119, 120, 121, 122, 124, 138, 150, 177
AUKUS 12, 93, 97, 120, 122, 178
Australia 76, 86–91, 96, 112, *181*
  and China 104
  and India 101, 102, 103, 104, 124, 138
  and Indo-Pacific 87, 104

B

Bay of Bengal 67, 78, 117, 152, 179
Bengal 34
Bharatiya Janata Party (BJP) 75
Biden, Joe 12, 15, 41, 58, 81, 86, 89, 92, 95, 97, 112, 116, 119, 122, 133, 135, 140, 142
Boxer Rebellion 46
BRICS 38, 43, 48, 57, 71, 106
British Crown 24, 30
British East India Company 24, 27, 30
British India 14, 24, 26, 27, 28, 32
Buddhism 46, 65

Bush, George W. 12, 15, 75–78, 82–86, 103, 130, 131, 132, 144

C

Canada
  and India 134, 135
Central Treaty Organization (CENTO) 35
Chiang Kai-shek 47
China
  and Asia 12, 86, 87, 88, 92, 95, 102, 103, 104, 121, 123, 128, 129, 137
  and US 11, 13, 19, 66, 73, 86, 88, 89, 96, 108, 110, 114–119, 122, 127, 129, 130, 133, 146, 154, 155
  Belt and Road Initiative 67, 71, 138
  defence 13, 19, 114, 153, 159, *181*
  economy 11, 12, 13, 19, 50, 54, 55, 60, 65, 137
  People's Liberation Army (PLA) 18, 53, 56
  People's Liberation Army Navy (PLAN) 65, 66, 67, 68
  string of pearls strategy 67
  two-ocean strategy 66
China–Myanmar Economic Corridor (CMEC) 67
China–Nepal Economic Corridor (CNEC) 61
China–Pakistan Economic Corridor (CPEC) 61
Chinese Communist Party (CCP) 51, 130
Clinton, Bill 82, 84, 103, 129, 130, 131, 139, 144
Cold War 11, 14, 16, 20, 23, 33, 35, 37, 38, 42, 73, 82, 87, 102, 105, 106, 113, 114, 116, 122, 127, 129, 130, 144, 149, 152
communism 16, 35, 36, 46, 48, 49, 59, 70, 73, 76,

Note: Page numbers are italicised where terms appear in figures or maps.

115, 127, 129, 136, 142, 143, 148
Congress Party. See Indian National Congress (INC)
COVID-19 53, 92
Curzon, Lord 29, 32

D

Dalai Lama 51, 58, 116
decolonisation 16, 23, 32, 33, 47, 50, 110, 111, 124, 129
democracy 179
   and India 16, 19, 129, 131–136, 143
   and US 129, 131, 133, 135
   Summit for Democracy 133
Deng Xiaoping 37
Dixit, J.N. 32
Doklam plateau 53, 87, 91

E

East Asia 15, 94, 97
East Asia Summit 87, 118, 150, 177
Europe 24, 32, 46, 94, 96, 114, 122
   and Asia 110, 111, 112, 122
   and British India 27, 29
   and China 112

G

G4 43
G7 43, 120
G20 43
Galwan valley 53, 57, 58, 89
Gandhi, Indira 74, 76
Gandhi, Rajiv 75
Gandhi, Sonia 78
Ganges 34
Global South 43, 136
Gorbachev, Mikhail 75
Great Game 27
Great Sepoy Revolt 24
Gujarat 55
Gulf Cooperation Council (GCC) 43

H

Hasina, Sheikh 63, 64, 117
Himalayas 18, 46, 50, 52, 53, 65, 87, 116, 153, 156, 158

I

India
   borders 34, 38, 69, 72, 87, 91, 102, 127, 138, 156, 158
   defence 42, 56, 57, 64, 121, 124, 130, 146, 148–152, 157, 159, 175, *181*
   economy 16, 41, 43, 54, 56, 59, 62, 63, 64, 70, 71, 72, 88, 106, 107, 115, 118, 136, 137, 140, 141, 176, 177
   grand strategy 32
   multilateralism 150, 153
   nationalism 33, 34
   non-alignment 17, 20, 23, 33, 35, 55, 76, 78, 91, 95, 111, 121, 151, 154
   non-proliferation 128, 144, 145, 146
   political class 37, 49, 75, 90, 95
   technology 142, 146, 148
   trade 37, 38, 39, 41, 42, 46, 56, 59, 62, 97, 99, 107, 109, 141, 152, 176
   viceroy 29, 32
India and Africa 26, 28, 30, 31
India and Asia 14, 15, 19, 20, 31, 33, 35, 43, 48, 108, 121, 123, 125, 128, 137, 174
India and Bangladesh 34, 36, 39, 63, 64, 82, 91, 115, 116, 117, 154, 178
India and China 13, 14, 17, 19, 20, 30, 34, 37, 38, 39, 44, 51, 63, 87, 108, 115, 116, 119, 121, 123, 127, 128, 137, 146, 153, 154, 156
   borders 50, 52–58, 64, 69, 70
   colonisation 46, 47
   military crises 13, 18, 36, 37, 38, 42, 45, 48, 51, 52, 53, 55, 56, 57, 58, 65, 70, 73, 91, 102, 109, 161
   miscalculations 45, 48, 49
   partnership attempts 46, 47, 48, 49, 51, 52, 55, 56, 69, 70, 72, 73, 123, 127, 138
   power gap 50, 54, 55, 59
India and Europe 110, 111, 124, 128, 137, 143, 148, 150
   and China 113
   defence 113
India and Indo-Pacific *8*, 87, 98, 108, 119, 123, 124, 128, 151
India and Japan 30, 31, 64
India and Pakistan 34, 36, 39, 48, 56, 63, 82, 83, 98, 114, 130, 157, 158, 160, 178
India and Russia 17, 27, 29, 38, 41, 42, 48, 51, 81, 105, 106, 108, 109, 124, 127, 150
   and China 106, 109
   defence 106, 107, 109, 123, 124
India and South Asia 17, 50, 60, 72, 117, 178, 179
India and Soviet Union 33, 36, 37, 41
India and United Kingdom 111, 113, 150
India and US 14, 16, 17, 20, 35, 40, 41, 44, 46, 48, 51, 55, 58, 64, 65, 72, 75, 76, 79, 82, 84, 108, 109, 119, 121, 123, 124, 128, 129, 131, 132, 134, 135, 137, 140, 143, 153, 154, 156
   and China 14, 15, 17, 18, 19, 36, 40, 41, 73, 74, 80, 86, 88, 95, 115, 116, 120, 127, 129, 133, 135, 144, 154, 155
   civil-nuclear initiative 77, 78, 85, 90, 98, 145, 146, 160
   defence 75–81, 85, 88, 89, 94, 97, 98, 123
   distrust of US 75, 82, 83, 95
India Centre 33
Indian Army 29, 34, 35, 46, 58, 107, 148
   expeditionary operations 30, 31
Indian National Congress (INC) 47, 55, 76, 78
Indian Navy 67, 76, 151, 152
Indian Ocean 14, 15, 16, 17, 24, 30, 32, 41, 46, 76, 79, 86, 88, 89, 94, 98, 113, 117, 152, 153, 161
   and China 65, 66, 67, 68

and India 50, 65, 72
Indochina 31
Indo-Pacific 86, 87, 89, 93, 96, 103, 104, 117
Indo-Pacific strategy 15, 41
　Asia 14
　India 15, 18
　Japan 14
　US 12, 14, 15, 16
Indus 34
Ishiba Shigeru 97

J

Jaishankar, Subrahmanyam 43, 50, 70, 90, 107
Japan 76, 86, 87, 88, 89, 97, 112, *181*
　and India 101, 102, 103, 104, 124, 138
　and Indo-Pacific 87, 90, 111
　Imperial Japanese Army 14, 47

K

Karakoram Highway 60
Kargil conflict 56
Kashmir 34, 36, 39, 48, 60, 63, 70, 71, 73, 82, 83, 84, 106, 127, 128, 130, 131, 132, 157
Kennedy, John F. 36, 73

L

Ladakh 52, 53, 55, 57, 89, 109
line of actual control (LAC) 52, 54

M

Malabar exercises 58, 75, 91
Malacca Dilemma 66
Malacca Strait 66, 67
Malaya 31
Malay States Guides 31
Mao Zedong 37, 46, 66, 69, 73, 102, 136, 160
Modi, Narendra 39, 40, 41, 43, 55, 56, 64, 87, 89, 97, 98, 107, 108, 119, 133, 152, 159
　and US 79, 80, 81, 91, 95, 97, 98, 118, 123, 132, 134, 136
Mughals 24
Myanmar 64, 67, 68, 116

N

National Democratic Alliance (NDA) 55, 56, 79, 89
nationalism
　anti-India nationalism 59, 63
　Chinese 46, 47, 49, 50
　Indian 46, 47, 49, 50, 56, 180
NATO 112, 113, 122
Nehru, Jawaharlal 16, 24, 33, 34, 35, 37, 76, 111, 118, 127, 136, 143, 148, 149
　and China 16, 47, 48, 51
Nepal 115
Nixon, Richard 36
Non-Aligned Movement (NAM) 33, 42, 43, 71
Nuclear Non-Proliferation Treaty (NPT) 77, 102, 143
nuclear weapons 34, 48, 60, 61, 70, 71, 75, 77, 78, 82, 102, 106, 127, 128, 131, 143, 144, 161

O

Obama, Barack 12, 15, 79, 83, 86, 87, 116, 132, 139
One China policy 58, 70

P

Pacific Island states 92
Pacific Ocean 14, 15, 68, 86
　and China 65, 66
Pakistan 84, 149, 158, 161, *181*
　and China 51, 60, 61, 67, 68, 70, 114, 115, 160
　and United Kingdom 113
　and US 36, 41, 60, 61, 63, 75, 81–86, 115, 130, 131, 144, 145, 157
　Pakistan Army 34, 85
　Pakistan First policy 114
Pannun, Gurpatwant Singh 134
Partition 33, 34, 39, 59, 62
Patel, Vallabhbhai 48
petroleum 42, 107, 109, 124
Pulwama terror attack 84
Punjab 34
Putin, Vladimir 106, 110

Q

Quadrilateral Security Dialogue (Quad) 12, 14, 15, 18, 40, 43, 58, 74, 86, 89, 90, 91, 92, 93, 95, 96, 101, 103, 104, 108, 117, 119, 120, 122, 124, 133, 140, 141, 146, 147, 148, 158, 178
　and China 90, 93, 118
　military aspects 93, 94, 119

R

Raj 24, *25*, 26, 44, 51, 59, 60, 62, 148
　borders 24, 27, 28, 29, 30, 51
　defence 24, 27, 28
　grand strategy 27
　policies 26, 27
Reagan, Ronald 75, 129, 144
Regional Comprehensive Economic Partnership (RCEP) 56, 138
Russia 159
　and China 108, 109, 133
　and Europe 105, 107, 109, 110
　economy 106, 107
Russia–India–China (RIC) 38, 48, 57, 106
Russia–Ukraine war 11, 41, 42, 107, 108, 109, 111, 112, 133

S

Second World War 31, 34, 47, 48, 102, 105, 110, 129
security politics 23, 26, 27, 32–38, 40, 44
Sikkim 53
Siliguri Corridor 53
Singh, Manmohan 55, 78, 85
South Asia 34, 62, 88, 92, 113
　and China 50, 59, 60, 61, 114
　and Russia 114

South China Sea 30, 54, 117
Southeast Asia 14, 29, 30, 31, 73, 88, 92, 121
Southeast Asia Treaty Organisation (SEATO) 35
Soviet Union 16, 20, 50, 73, 74, 76, 91, 102, 105, 106, 107, 108, 110, 114, 122, 127, 129, 159, 160
Special Frontier Force 58
Sri Lanka 62, 64, 66, 67, 68, 150, 153
   Colombo West International Terminal 63

T

Tagore, Rabindranath 46
Taiwan 58, 66, 155
terrorism 77, 84, 98, 130
Tibet 48, 50, 51, 52, 58, 60, 116
Trans-Pacific Partnership (TPP) 139
Trump, Donald 12, 15, 41, 58, 79, 84, 88, 89, 91, 92, 95, 96, 97, 98, 132, 133, 136, 139, 142, 145, 155
   and Asia 86, 87, 96, 97
   and China 91, 96, 97, 118
   and Indo-Pacific 104, 116, 119, 120, 121, 122, 133
   and Pakistan 83
   and Russia 109, 112, 125
tsunami 89

U

United Kingdom 47, 82, 114, 135, 159
   and Indo-Pacific 110, 111, 113
   British special forces 31
United Nations 17, 35, 43, 49, 62, 70, 71, 84, 91, 114
United Progressive Alliance (UPA) 55, 56, 78, 79, 89, 90, 104
United States 64, 76, 86, 89, 96, 159, *181*
   and Afghanistan 86, 114, 115, 131, 158
   and Asia 12, 13, 19
   and Asia-Pacific 79
   and China 12, 13, 16, 18
   and Europe 110, 111, 129
   and Indo-Pacific 86, 87, 88, 89, 92, 95, 98, 110, 112, 114, 155
   and Kashmir 84
   and Russia 88, 89, 108, 114, 133
   and South Asia 84, 85, 106, 114, 130
   military 58, 66
   National Security Strategy (NSS) 86, 87, 88, 89, 111, 135
   war on terror 82, 84, 86

V

Varthaman, Abhinandan 84

W

Washington Consensus 62
Western Hemisphere 70
   and Asia 13, 16
   and China 11, 12, 48, 54, 112, 133, 136, 137
   and India 16, 17, 33, 40, 41, 43, 48, 49, 94, 95, 106, 109, 111, 124, 127, 130, 132, 134, 135, 136, 142, 148, 149, 159
   and Pakistan 61
   and Russia 108, 133
   and Soviet Union 110
   and Sri Lanka 62

X

Xi Jinping 55, 56, 96

Z

Zheng He 65

THE ADELPHI SERIES

Marcus Willett

CYBER OPERATIONS AND THEIR RESPONSIBLE USE

Adelphi 511–513
published November 2024;
234x156; 360pp;
Paperback: 978-1-032-98909-9
eBook: 978-1-003-60133-3

available at
amazon

OR

Routledge
Taylor & Francis Group

Adelphi 514–515
published January 2025;
234x156; 200pp;
Paperback: 978-1-041-02004-2
eBook: 978-1-003-61730-3

Joshua Rovner

STRATEGY AND GRAND STRATEGY

IISS
THE INTERNATIONAL INSTITUTE
FOR STRATEGIC STUDIES

www.iiss.org/publications/adelphi

THE ADELPHI SERIES

EVALUATING JAPAN'S NEW GRAND STRATEGY

'Robert Ward shines a brilliant light on the transformation seen in Japan's grand strategy during the past 15 years, placing it in its historical context but crucially also illuminating how Japanese society has come to understand the threat to the country's security posed by North Korea, Russia and above all China. Delivering the new grand strategy will not be easy, but this book shows that it can be done and that it has strong winds behind it.'

BILL EMMOTT, Chairman of the Trustees, IISS, and author of *Deterrence, Diplomacy and the Risk of Conflict Over Taiwan*

Robert Ward

available at
amazon

OR

Routledge
Taylor & Francis Group

Adelphi 516; published May 2025; 234x156; 156pp;
Paperback: 978-1-041-10132-1
eBook: 978-1-003-65351-6

Geopolitical stresses in the Indo-Pacific are increasing and intensifying. These stresses derive from China's more assertive regional behaviour; growing alignments between China and Russia on the one hand and Russia and North Korea on the other; and most recently from the apparent recalibration of United States foreign policy under the second Trump administration. They have magnified Japan's significance as a strategic actor both in the Indo-Pacific and beyond.

As such, it is of global importance whether Japan can meet the grand-strategic goals that it established in its 2022 National Security Strategy, National Defense Strategy and Defense Buildup Program. This *Adelphi* book evaluates Japan's new grand strategy, considering whether it and associated reforms are sufficiently robust to fulfil Japan's goal of ensuring its security even in the scenario of a Chinese attack on Taiwan.

IISS
THE INTERNATIONAL INSTITUTE
FOR STRATEGIC STUDIES

www.iiss.org/publications/adelphi

JOURNAL SUBSCRIPTION INFORMATION

Six issues per year of the *Adelphi* Series (Print ISSN 1944-5571, Online ISSN 1944-558X) are published by Taylor & Francis Group, 4 Park Square, Milton Park, Abingdon, Oxon, OX14 4RN, UK.

Send address changes to Taylor & Francis Customer Services, Informa UK Ltd., Sheepen Place, Colchester, Essex CO3 3LP, UK.

Subscription records are maintained at Taylor & Francis Group, 4 Park Square, Milton Park, Abingdon, OX14 4RN, UK.

Subscription information:
For more information and subscription rates, please see tandfonline.com/pricing/journal/tadl). Taylor & Francis journals are available in a range of different packages, designed to suit every library's needs and budget. This journal is available for institutional subscriptions with online only or print & online options. This journal may also be available as part of our libraries, subject collections, or archives. For more information on our sales packages, please visit: librarianresources.taylorandfrancis.com.

For support with any institutional subscription, please visit help.tandfonline.com or email our dedicated team at subscriptions@tandf.co.uk.

Subscriptions purchased at the personal rate are strictly for personal, non-commercial use only. The reselling of personal subscriptions is prohibited. Personal subscriptions must be purchased with a personal check, credit card, or BAC/wire transfer. Proof of personal status may be requested.

Back issues:
Please visit https://taylorandfrancis.com/journals/customer-services/ for more information on how to purchase back issues.

Ordering information:
To subscribe to the Journal, please contact: T&F Customer Services, Informa UK Ltd, Sheepen Place, Colchester, Essex, CO3 3LP, United Kingdom. Tel: +44 (0) 20 8052 2030; email: subscriptions@tandf.co.uk.

Taylor & Francis journals are priced in USD, GBP and EUR (as well as AUD and CAD for a limited number of journals). All subscriptions are charged depending on where the end customer is based. If you are unsure which rate applies to you, please contact Customer Services. All subscriptions are payable in advance and all rates include postage. We are required to charge applicable VAT/GST on all print and online combination subscriptions, in addition to our online only journals. Subscriptions are entered on an annual basis, i.e., January to December. Payment may be made by sterling check, dollar check, euro check, international money order, National Giro or credit cards (Amex, Visa and Mastercard).

Disclaimer: The International Institute for Strategic Studies and our publisher Taylor & Francis make every effort to ensure the accuracy of all the information (the "Content") contained in our publications. However, The International Institute for Strategic Studies and our publisher Taylor & Francis, our agents (including the editor, any member of the editorial team or editorial board, and any guest editors), and our licensors make no representations or warranties whatsoever as to the accuracy, completeness, or suitability for any purpose of the Content. Any opinions and views expressed in this publication are the opinions and views of the authors, and are not the views of or endorsed by The International Institute for Strategic Studies and our publisher Taylor & Francis. The accuracy of the Content should not be relied upon and should be independently verified with primary sources of information. The International Institute for Strategic Studies and our publisher Taylor & Francis shall not be liable for any losses, actions, claims, proceedings, demands, costs, expenses, damages, and other liabilities whatsoever or howsoever caused arising directly or indirectly in connection with, in relation to, or arising out of the use of the Content. Terms & Conditions of access and use can be found at http://www.tandfonline.com/page/terms-and-conditions.

All Taylor & Francis Group journals are printed on paper from renewable sources by accredited partners.